HIGHER GOALS FOR AMERICA:

DOING BETTER THAN THE BEST

HIGHER GOALS FOR AMERICA:

DOING BETTER THAN THE BEST

Stuart S. Nagel, University of Illinois

UNITED
PRESS OF
AMERICA

LANHAM • NEW YORK • LONDON

Copyright © 1989 by

University Press of America,® Inc.

4720 Boston Way
Lanham, MD 20706

3 Henrietta Street
London WC2E 8LU England

British Cataloging in Publication Information Available

Library of Congress Cataloging-in-Publication Data

Nagel, Stuart S., 1934–
Higher goals for America : doing better than the best / Stuart S. Nagel.
p.   cm.
Bibliography: p.
Includes indexes.
1. Political planning– –United States. 2. United States– –Politics and
government– –1981– 3. Policy sciences. I. Title.
JK271.N34   1989   88–31498 CIP
320.973– –dc19
ISBN 0–8191–7306–1 (alk. paper).
ISBN 0–8191–7307–X (pbk. : alk. paper)

All University Press of America books are produced on acid-free paper.
The paper used in this publication meets the minimum requirements of American
National Standard for Information Sciences—Permanence of Paper for Printed Library
Materials, ANSI Z39.48–1984.   ∞

To Michael Dukakis,

George Bush,

and Future Presidential Candidates

SUMMARY TABLE OF CONTENTS

Page

Introduction

INTRODUCTION:

GOALS, INCENTIVES, LAW, AND POLICY

The purpose of this book is to bring together a number of ideas that relate to the analysis of public policy issues for the presidential campaigns of 1988. The material should also be applicable in part to 1992 and thereafter since the emphasis is on long-term concerns.

The book is organized in terms of (1) the need for higher goals for America, (2) incentives for achieving higher goals, (3) improving American constitutional effectiveness, and (4) public policy substance and methods. That is a logical order to start with goals to be achieved on a high level of generality or applicability. We then deal with middle-range means for achieving them, with an emphasis on economic incentives, political structures, and legal rules. We then proceed to the nitty gritty of specific policy problems and systematic methods for analyzing them.

On the matter of higher goals, we are concerned with (1) economic goals like unemployment, inflation, and consumer standards, (2) political goals like world peace, free speech, and government efficiency, (3) social goals like reduction of crime, poverty, and discrimination while increasing educational levels, and (4) science policy goals like better health and environmental conditions. These goals are expressed in ways that go beyond the traditional definitions, which may be lacking in sufficient ambition. What has traditionally been considered the best achievable may involve setting our sights unduly low. This may be especially so regarding national productivity. It can be defined in terms of maximizing societal benefits minus societal costs, including nonmonetary benefits and costs. Our business firms may often be maximizing their income minus expenses, but our society may not be adequately maximizing its benefits minus costs, even for widely agreed upon benefits and costs.

On the matter of incentives, all policy problems can be improved by encouraging socially desired behavior through a variety of subsidies, tax breaks, and other incentives. The intermediate object in each field is to increase the benefits of doing right, decrease the costs of doing right, decrease the benefits of doing wrong, increase the costs of doing wrong, and increase the probability that the benefits and costs will occur. One can also encourage socially desired behavior by physically limiting one's options such as not having non-biodegradable containers available for littering, or by mentally limiting one's options such as seeking to socialize people so that it is unthinkable to resort to gunplay when one is insulted. Those kinds of perspectives can be helpful for encouraging socially desired behavior relevant to unemployment-inflation, economic regulation, crime reduction, equitable racial treatment, housing, environmental protection, energy conservation, technological innovation, and compliance with legality by public officials.

On the matter of constitutional effectiveness, one can think in terms of restricting governmental abuses and having effective and efficient implementation of governmental policy. Governmental abuses are potentially most serious in the areas of freedom of communication, separating the innocent from the guilty, and providing equal treatment under law. Of those abuses, interfering with freedom of speech may be the most detrimental to having a creative problem-solving society. Non-interference may also need to be supplemented with affirmative encouragement of innovative ideas. The most important government structures may be how the legislative, executive, and judicial branches relate to each other, and how the national government relates to the states and cities. There is a need for multiple sources of ideas which is provided for by separation of governmental powers and federalism. Closely related is the need for diversity or pluralism among political parties, interest groups, and public opinion.

On the matter of public policy substance and methods, there is a need to apply the more general ideas to specific policy problems in the political, economic, social, and science policy areas. One important cross-cutting set of ideas relates to how to process a set of goals to be achieved, alternative policies available for achieving them, and relations between goals and alternatives in order to choose or explain the best policy, combination, allocation, or predictive decision rule. A good evaluation system should be capable of dealing with a multiple dimensions on multiple goals, missing information, numerous alternatives, conflicting constraints, and the need for simplicity in drawing and presenting conclusions.

One important feature of this book is that it is concerned with issues relevant to the presidential campaigns of Democrats and Republicans, or liberals and conservatives within the political parties. The goals are the type that can be endorsed by diverse ideological viewpoints, and yet they are not clichés. The use of incentives can also receive widespread endorsement as can basic human rights and effective-efficient government structures. Systematic methods for analyzing policy problems tend to appeal to conservatives as involving a transfer of business analysis methods to government projects. They tend to appeal to liberals as involving an attempt at systematic socio-economic planning. Most important, the ideas in this book are based on the basic idea that the total society will be better off through higher goals, productivity growth, incentives, civil liberties and rights, constitutional effectiveness, and systematic policy analysis. Through such means, everyone can be better off including rich and poor, blacks and whites, men and women, old and young, North and South, rural and urban, and other social divisions. This is contrasted to the idea that for one group to be better off, another group has to be worse off.

Thanks are owed to many persons who helped in the development of this book. They include members of the Policy Studies Organization who have authored or edited relevant articles, book chapters, and books. The Policy Studies Organization is an association of political and social scientists who are interested in the application of social science to important policy problems. Thanks are owed to publishers of the author's previous work which provide a source of further details such as *Public Policy: Goals, Means, and Methods* (St. Martin's Press, 1984) and *Policy Studies: Integration and Evaluation* (Greenwood-Praeger, 1988). Thanks are also owed to specific individuals who participated in the drafting and development of these ideas over the years such as Marian Neef, Miriam Mills, and especially Joyce Nagel. Madelle Becker was responsible for creatively designing the typesetting for this book using the latest computerized technology. It is hoped that this book will help America in doing better than the best in the formation and implementation of more effective, efficient, and equitable public policy programs.

DETAILED TABLE OF CONTENTS

Contents

Contents

LIST OF TABLES

PART ONE:

THE NEED FOR HIGHER GOALS

FOR AMERICA

1

DOING BETTER THAN THE BEST

One of President Carter's mottos was, "Why not the best?" President Kennedy used to say when people would question his high goals that it was better to aim higher and only get half-way there than to aim not so high and get all the way there. Achieving the optimum is considered to be a high goal, although that partly depends on how the optimum is defined. The optimum may, however, not be high enough, or at least what is customarily considered to be the optimum.

The purpose of this chapter is to pursue that thought in the context of public policy problems, especially policy problems that are as fundamental as unemployment and inflation. If unemployment and inflation can both be reduced to close to 0%, then the economy almost by definition is in a state of high prosperity. Such prosperity leads to improvements in all other problems such as reduced poverty, discrimination, crime, and health problems. It can also have positive effects on conditions of consumers, farmers, labor, the environment, housing, and education, as well as civil liberties and international peace.

In addition to talking about doing better than the optimum on unemployment and inflation, the chapter also discusses doing better than the optimum on crime reduction and other social indicators. This chapter is also concerned with general means for achieving the goals, including an incentives-growth perspective. It also addresses the question of whether it is better to set one's goals not so high and fully achieve them, or to seek to

23

achieve more than the optimum and not get all the way there.[1]

DOING BETTER THAN THE OPTIMUM ON UNEMPLOYMENT

Optimum unemployment can be defined as having no more than 3% of the labor force out of work. If the figure goes below 3% there may be insufficient movement upward from less to more appropriate jobs. The Humphrey-Hawkins legislation specifies 4% as the target figure. One could, however, talk about unemployment that is below 0%, or better than 0%.

For example, suppose there are 25 people in a society and 10 are in the labor force. Of the 10 in the labor force, 2 are unemployed for a 20% unemployment figure. If a job is found for 1 of the 2 unemployed workers, then we have 10% unemployment. If both formerly unemployed workers are employed and there is no new unemployment, then we have 0% unemployment.

GETTING CREDIT FOR ADDING TO THE LABOR FORCE

If we expand the labor force, the unemployment figure is recalculated using a new base or denominator. Thus, if we improve the real or perceived job opportunities so that 4 of the 15 people who were not in the labor force now become job seekers, then unemployment will go up to 4/14 or 29%. In other words, the unemployment figure as a social indicator in effect penalizes expanding the labor force. This may be an important defect in so important a social indicator.

Perhaps it might make more sense to say that putting to work someone who is formerly outside the labor force should be counted as partly offsetting one person who is already in the labor force but unemployed. Suppose we find jobs for all 4 of those new additions to the labor force. One could then say that unemployment has now dropped to 2/14 or 14% from the figure of 20%. Thus adding people to the labor force and finding jobs for them does reduce the unemployment figure even if the previously unemployed people are not found jobs.

One could say that 0/14 in this context is better than 0/10 even if they

---

[1] On goal setting and measurement in policy analysis, see David Alberts, *A Plan for Measuring the Performance of Social Programs* (New York: Praeger, 1970); Robert Dorfman, *Measuring Benefits in Government Investments* (Washington, D.C.: Brookings, 1964); Thomas Cook (ed.), "Performance Measurement in Public Agencies," *Policy Studies Review*, symposium issue (1986); and S. Nagel, *Public Policy: Goals, Means, and Methods* (New York: St. Martin's, 1984) pp. 33-138. On national social indicators, see Duncan MacRae, *Policy Indicators: Links Between Social Science and Public Debate* (Chapel Hill, N.C.: Duke University, 1986); Michael Carley, *Social Measurement and Social Indicators: Issues of Policy and Theory* (Boston: Allen and Unwin, 1981); and K. Gilmartin et al., *Social Indicators: An Annotated Bibliography of Current Literature* (New York: Garland, 1979).

both represent 0% unemployment. Is 2/14 worse than, equal to, or better than 0/10? The answer is "equal to" if finding jobs for 4 people formerly outside the labor force is worth as much to society as finding jobs for 2 unemployed people who were already in the labor force. In other words, the answer to the question depends on the trade-off between employing unemployed people "out of" versus "in" the labor force. A 2 to 1 trade-off seems reasonable.

A well-employed society should have a combination of a low percentage of unemployed people (as determined by the quantity of unemployed divided by the total labor force) and a high percentage of the total adult population in the labor force. Thus a society of 25 people is not doing so well on employment opportunities if it has 18 adults and only 10 are in the labor force, whereas another society of 25 people with 18 adults has 14 in the labor force. In other words, we need to place more emphasis on bringing more people into the labor force who are willing and capable of working. That includes older people, disabled people, and single parents receiving public aid. Older people often have skills that could still be applied, especially in a white collar society. Disabled people and public aid parents can often be trained to qualify for profitable and satisfying jobs. The public aid parents may also need day-care services. Training and day care involves tax expenditures, but the investment may be worthwhile if public aid expenses are reduced even more than the tax expenditure.

In the unemployment context, doing better than the optimum means seeking not only to get unemployment down close to about 3% or 4%, but also seeking to get the percentage of the labor force up close to maybe 80% or 90% of the adult population. In an optimizing society, virtually every adult should be provided with sufficient job opportunities, job training, and related services so that virtually every adult will be constructively employed.

GETTING CREDIT FOR LESSENING UNDEREMPLOYMENT

Doing better than the optimum in the employment context should also include having an expanding economy such that anyone who wants to take on a second job can do so. Thus we need to emphasize a third measure which gets at the extent to which employed people are fully employed. These are really two sub-measures.

One relates to the percent of employed people who work full-time. If only 6 of the 10 people in the labor force have at least full-time employment, then we have a less well-employed society than if the figure were 9 out of 10. Full-time employment can be defined as working 40 hours a week, although the standard as to what constitutes full-time employment has over the years involved a reduction in the number of hours. It is appropriate to reduce the number of hours as society becomes more productive and people can produce more output in fewer hours and thus receive more salary or wages for fewer hours of work.

The other measure of full employment could relate to the percentage of people who would like to have a second job who do have a second job. Suppose all 10 people are employed 40 hours a week, but 4 of them would like to work more, but there is no more work available for them. That is a less satisfactory situation than all 4 being able to obtain extra work or only 3 seeking extra employment.

It is more important to employ unemployed people in the labor force than to provide more employment to those who already have a part time, seasonal, or full time job. If the desirability tradeoff is 2 to 1 for unemployed in the labor force versus unemployed out of the labor force, then the desirability trade-off is probably about 3 to 1 for finding jobs for the unemployed in the labor force versus the under-employed. A more precise measure might consider the degree of underemployment for each worker.

A SUMMARY INDEX

Thus we now have an expanded concept of doing better than the optimum of 3% or 4% unemployment. The expanded concept includes:

1. Providing jobs for older people.
2. Providing jobs for disabled people.
3. Providing jobs for single parent public aid recipients.
4. Providing jobs for others outside the labor force, including those who might otherwise be discouraged or depressed about finding jobs.
5. Providing full-time jobs for those who are only working part-time or on seasonal jobs.
6. Providing second jobs for those who want them.
7. Providing jobs for those who are already part of the labor force but are totally unemployed.

Category 7 has traditionally been the only category of jobless people counted as unemployed. By obtaining jobs for the other six categories as well as category 7, we are doing better than the traditional optimum.

All these ideas can be incorporated into a new index of employment in accordance with the formula

$$E = (F + P/3)/(L + A/2),$$

where

E =   Employment Index.
F =   Number of fully employed people in the economy. That is 6 people in our hypothetical economy.
P =   Number of people partly employed. That is 2 people in the economy.
L =   Number of people in the labor force. That is 10 people.
A =   Number of able-bodied people who are not in the labor force, i.e., who are not actively seeking jobs. That is 8 additional people.

That means the denominator of the index is 10 + 8/2, or 14. The numerator is 6 + 2/3, or 6.67. Thus, the Employment Index is 6.67/14, or 48%. This is in contrast to the traditional unemployment percentage which would be 2/10, or 20%, with a complement of 100% - 20%, or 80%.

The above formula has the following advantages over the traditional unemployment percentage:

1. It emphasizes the more positive goal of seeking high employment, rather than the more negative goal of seeking low unemployment.
2. The denominator considers both people in the labor force and also able-bodied people outside the labor force at the 2 to 1 tradeoff mentioned above.
3. The numerator considers both people partly employed and also those fully employed at the 3 to 1 tradeoff mentioned above. Partly employed could include those who are fully employed, but who are seeking additional work.
4. This index enables a society to in effect do better than 0% unemployment or 100% employment by fully employing people and by finding jobs for able-bodied people not counted in the labor force.

Both the Employment Index and the traditional unemployment percentage are incapable of going below 0% or above 100%. This is so under the Employment Index because one cannot employ more than all the people in the labor force plus all the able-bodied people not in the labor force. We could redefine the Index in order to allow for improvements in the employment picture that would exceed 100%. Doing so would mean using last year's labor-force base or denominator, but this year's employed people or numerator. Thus suppose last year, or in the last time period, the denominator was 14 people and the numerator was 6.67. Suppose further that 10 more people were added to the labor force for whom jobs were found. That would cause the numerator to go up to 16.67, and the Employment Index to go up to 16.67/14, or 119%. This is in contrast to adding the 10 newly employed people to both the numerator and the denominator. That would give an Employment Index of 16.67/24, or 70%, which seems more meaningful.

Along related lines, one could subtract one unemployed person from the traditional unemployment percentage for every newly employed person who is brought into the labor force. With enough subtractions one could go below 0% unemployment. That, however, would undesirably hide the fact that there are still some unemployed people in the labor force. One can, however, recognize that 0% unemployment with more people brought into the labor force and less underemployed people is better than 0% unemployment with lots of discouraged people outside the active labor force and lots of underemployed people within it. Thus it is possible to do better than 0% unemployment without getting into the conceptual problems of a negative percentage.[2]

DOING BETTER THAN THE OPTIMUM ON INFLATION

Doing the optimum with regard to inflation can be defined as staying below double-digit inflation for many countries. In the United States, 3% inflation might be considered optimum. Getting below 3% could be considered undesirable from the point of view of the long-term desirability of improved wages, products, and national income. One could, however, talk about inflation that is below 0% or better than 0% while still having improved real wages, products, and national income.

For example, suppose last year a type of worker cost $10 an hour and this year the cost is $15 an hour. That sounds like 50% inflation, as determined by calculating ($15 - $10)/$10. In order for wages (as the price of labor) to go up only 3%, those workers would have to receive a wage increase (in light of these calculations) of only $.30. To have negative inflation, the workers would have to take a reduction in their $10 wage to something less than $10. This is the traditional way of calculating inflation. It can be applied to any specific price, average price, or set of prices.

GETTING CREDIT FOR INCREASED QUANTITATIVE BENEFITS

Suppose, however, those same workers become more productive so that

---

[2]On measuring and reducing unemployment, see Stephen Bailey, *Congress Makes a Law: The Story Behind the Employment Act of 1946* (New York: Columbia University Press, 1950); Paula Duggan, The *New American Unemployment* (Washington, D.C.: Center for Regional Policy, 1985); Eli Ginzberg, *The Unemployed* (New York: Harper, 1963); and D. Baumer and Carl Van Horn, *The Politics of Unemployment* (Washington, D.C.: Congressional Quarterly, 1985). An even more ambitious notion of being fully employed might take into consideration job satisfaction. This would mean that if two societies are fully employed in the full sense of the summary index, then the society in which 80% of the people report being pleased with their jobs is a better employed society than a second society with a lower than 80% job-satisfaction rate. One could thus discount or multiple the employment figure by the job satisfaction percentage in each society. An ideal society might be defined partly as one in which the people so enjoy their work that they would continue doing it even if they were to become independently wealthy as a result of receiving a large inheritance or winning a lottery.

they are producing $30 worth of goods in the second year, whereas they were only producing $12 worth of goods in the first year. That means the benefit/cost ratio for the first year was $12/$10, or 120%. The benefit/cost ratio for the second year was $30/$15 or 200%. Thus, the benefit/cost ratio rose 80 percentage points from last year to this year. That is a more meaningful figure than just noting that the cost rose 50% from $10 to $15 from last year to this year. It is unbalanced to look only at costs without looking at benefits, or to look only at benefits without looking at costs.

In light of those considerations, we can have a form of negative inflation or disinflation if benefit/cost ratios go up even if costs do not go down. Calculating benefit/cost ratios are more difficult than simply calculating costs. In this context, however, we are not necessarily talking about subjective benefits, but instead mainly about units of production. That is not such a difficult indicator to measure. It is relatively easy to measure bushels per acre, automobiles produced, or gallons of milk manufactured by cows or bottling plants. To determine the benefit/cost ratio for various products or industries, one divides the total production by the total cost bill for the year. Estimates may be necessary where different products are attributable to the same costs. It is, however, better to use imperfect estimates of a correct measure like benefit/cost ratios than perfect estimates of a wrong measure (like price increases which ignore increases or decreases in benefits).

GETTING CREDIT FOR INCREASED QUALITATIVE BENEFITS

One could extend this analysis still further by talking about benefits in a qualitative as well as a quantitative sense. For example, suppose a milk-producing firm produced 50 gallons of milk last year at a wage bill or total cost of $100. That is a benefit/cost ratio of 50/$100, or 1/2, or .50. Suppose this year it produces 80 gallons of milk through new technology at a cost of $120. That is a benefit/ cost ratio of 80/$120 or .67. Suppose further that this year's milk has a new quality that enables it to last twice as long without getting sour. There should be some way of considering that improved benefit in the numerator of the benefit/cost ratio.

The best way might be to talk not in terms of 80 gallons of milk but in terms of the new market price. That price should be higher if people are willing to spend more for longer-lasting milk. Maybe the old price was $2 a gallon, and the new price is $2.50 a gallon. That means the old benefit/cost ratio expressed in dollars was (50x2)/$100, or $100/$100, or 1.0. The new benefit/cost ratio is (80x$2.50)/$120, or $200/$120, or 1.67. That further means the benefit/cost ratio rose from 1.00 to 1.67, which is a 67% rise even though the cost of producing milk went up.

To be more precise, one would have to adjust the price increase of $2.00

to $2.50 for inflation. Thus if prices in general are up 10%, then only 90% of that incremental $.50, or $.45 can be, attributed to improved quality. Some of the $.50 increment might also be due to favorable changes in consumer tastes, reduction in the supply of the product, or manipulated prices. Those factors though tend to explain price changes over a longer time period, rather than just one year to the next. There is no question that measuring improvements in qualitative benefits is more difficult than quantitative benefits. Again, however, it is better to try to estimate the increase in qualitative benefits than to ignore them completely.

A SUMMARY INDEX

How might one pull these ideas together to create a new summary index of benefits received per dollar spent. The new index could be called the National B/C Index analogous to the National Employment Index discussed above. The index would divide benefits by costs so as to emphasize the more positive goal of seeking higher benefits relative to costs, rather than the more negative goal of seeking lower costs relative to benefits.

The total national cost is approximately the same as the total national income plus what is spent outside the United States. The quantitative benefits in the numerator could not meaningfully lump together a variety of products like automobiles, nine staplers, oranges, etc. Instead we could use a basket of products the way the Department of Labor determines the Consumer Price Index. Suppose the basket consists of automobiles, staplers, and oranges. To calculate the benefit/cost ratio from one year to the next would involve determining the average car price for cars in general or for a specific type of car for last year and this year. Doing so would also involve determining such things as (1) improved mileage in the average car from last year to this year, (2) improved or worsened durability, and (3) improved safety. Each of those criteria could be roughly measured in percentage terms such that we might obtain three percentages like +10%, +6%, and +2%. If we treat each criterion equally, then the average improvement in benefits is 6%. If the average cost goes up 3%, then the benefits have improved twice as much as costs have worsened. That gives us a 2.00 score on the B/C Index, although it could be called an index of change in benefits/change in costs.

Some benefits are more important than others. Consumer surveys could be made to determine relative weights. Consumers, for example, might consider improved mileage to be twice as important as improved durability or safety, especially when gasoline prices are high. If mileage receives a relative weight of 2 and durability and safety a relative weight of 1 apiece, then the components of the B/C Index would be 10% + 10% + 6% + 2% divided by 4, instead of 10% + 6% + 2% divided by 3. The new B/C Index would be 7%, rather than 6%. Weights could also be assigned to automobiles versus staplers versus oranges. That is no different than the present assigning of weights to the products in the shopping basket from which the Consumer Price Index is now calculated. The National B/C Index would thus be a weighted average somewhat like the Consumer Price Index.

The advantages of the B/C Index over the CPI include the following:

1. People prefer scoring in which a high score is desirable to scoring in which a low score is desirable, although one could work with the complement of the traditional inflation index.
2. The B/C% Index considers improvements or worsening in benefits not just changes in costs.
3. The B/C Index can be treated as a measure of national productivity, and thereby encourage more sensitivity to national productivity.
4. A special B/C Index could be developed just for the cost of labor. It would involve dividing the changes in the current labor productivity index by changes in wage costs.
5. The B/C Index is capable of going over 100% if the percent change in benefits is greater than the percent change in cost.

The fact that the B/C Index can go over 100% is analogous to having negative inflation. A decrease in costs from $4 to $2 with benefits remaining constant at $12 is the equivalent of an increase in benefits from $12 to $24 with costs remaining constant at $4 or rising slightly. Thus we obtain the equivalent of negative inflation or disinflation, not by concentrating on trying to get prices down, but rather by concentrating more meaningfully on trying to get benefits up.[3]

DOING BETTER THAN THE OPTIMUM ON CRIME REDUCTION

Presidential administrations seem to think they are doing well on crime if the crime rate does not increase. That is a rather unambitious standard. It means that if crime is rampant at 90 crimes per 100 people per year, then that standard has been met so long as crime does not move up to 91 crimes per 100 people. Even asking for a 10% reduction seems unambitious since that would only mean going down from 90 crimes to 9 crimes less, or 81 crimes.

---

[3]On measuring and reducing inflation, see Paula Prentice, *Inflation* (Washington, D.C.: U.S.D.A. Economics and Statistics Section, 1981); Otto Eckstein, *Inflation: Prospects and Remedies* (Washington, D.C.: Center for National Policy, 1983); David Slawson, *The New Inflation* (Princeton, N.J.: Princeton University Press, 1981); and Paul Peretz, *The Political Economy of Inflation in the United States* (Chicago: University of Chicago Press, 1983).

An ambitious goal analogous to getting unemployment and inflation below 0% would involve getting crime below 0 crimes per 100 people. That raises two questions. One is how is it conceptually possible? The other is how is it empirically possible?

On the matter of being conceptually possible, suppose we have a society with 100 people. Last year, 20 of them were victims of crime. For the sake of simplicity, let us assume the crimes were all equally severe, although a more sophisticated method would weight the crimes in terms of the maximum or average sentence given to those who are convicted of each type of crime. Suppose further that another society or year also had 100 people and 20 crimes, but an additional 15 people were victims of negligence or other forms of civil wrongdoing. Suppose also that the second society had another 10 people who were fired from their jobs or lost their licenses for job wrongdoing. Clearly the first society would be the most desirable society to live in. Likewise if both societies had zero crime, but the second society had a number of instances of civil wrongdoing and bad job performance, then the first society would in effect be doing better than zero crime on a broadened wrongdoing index.

CONSIDERING CIVIL WRONGDOING

We need an index broader than a crime index or crime indexes to measure wrongdoing in the United States and elsewhere. There has possibly been too much emphasis on crime as a form of wrongdoing and too little emphasis on other important forms of wrongdoing. Crime indexes can be broadened by including white collar crimes as well as street crimes. White collar crimes include violations of the laws that relate to embezzlement, consumer fraud, anti-trust, safe work places, environmental protection, discrimination, housing codes, and fair labor standards, provided that the law allows for fines and/or jail sentences. If the law only allows for injunctions or damages paid to victims, then it is a matter of civil wrongdoing.

One could measure civil wrongdoing by gathering data on all court and administrative proceedings in which a defendant has been found liable or a defendant has agreed to pay damages or cease and desist without being found liable. Our society has collectively decided that criminal wrongdoing is more serious than civil wrongdoing. Therefore, each crime committed should receive about two or three times as much weight as each civil wrong, other things held constant. A more sophisticated measure would talk in terms of degrees of civil wrongs, as measured by the average amount of damages awarded.

CONSIDERING JOB WRONGDOING

If we are going to have a comprehensive Wrongdoing Index (WDI), it should also include job wrongdoing as an important form of wrongdoing in a society that is seeking to be productive and efficient. Job wrongdoing does not simply mean working slowly or inaccurately within a permissible range. It means performing poorly enough to be fired if one is an employee, or to have one's license suspended or removed if one is a professional person or in a licensed business. Being laid off because business is bad is not the same as being fired due to bad individual behavior. A more precise index would consider the relative severity of different kinds of firings. Employer wrongdoing is a form of civil wrongdoing if it is subject to damages or an injunction.

If the Department of Labor can gather information on employment on a city-by-city basis every month, then it should be able to gather information on firings on at least a national basis, although preferably on a state-by-state basis. That kind of information is relevant to paying unemployment compensation since fired employees are not entitled to compensation. Gathering statistics on firings and license suspensions-removals could be useful to studies designed to determine how to increase the competency of employees, professionals, and business firms. One could study variations across time periods, places, types of occupations, individuals, and other units of analysis to obtain useful insights.

A SUMMARY INDEX

Thus we have now converted the concept of getting crime down into the concept of getting wrongdoing down, where wrongdoing is substantially broader than just criminal wrongdoing. Those ideas can be summarized in the following Wrongdoing Index

$$WD1 = 3(CRW/POP) + 2(CVW/POP) + (FLW/L),$$

where

$WD1$ = Wrongdoing Index
CRW = Criminal Wrongdoing (from FBI crime reports).
POP = National population (from census data).
CVW = Civil wrongdoing (from statistics of courts and administrative agencies).
FLW = Firings and license withdrawals (to be gathered by the Department of Labor).
L = Total labor force (also a Department of Labor figure).

To partially take into consideration the relative severity of criminal wrongdoing, civil wrongdoing, and firings, we give each of those measures weights of 3, 2, and 1, respectively. Sometimes the same act like stealing from a client may be a crime, a cause for civil action, and grounds for suspension of one's license. That is a form of triple counting which may or may not be justified by the severity of the act. The best way to calculate relative severity would be to talk in terms of types of crimes with each type having a different severity depending on the average sentence. Likewise one could measure degrees of severity among civil wrongs, depending on the average damages awarded. Firings and license withdrawals could be measured for each type of occupation in terms of how many dollars the average occupation holder is likely to be losing. One could then talk in terms of three separate wrongdoing indexes. They could be combined together rather grossly with the 3-2-1 weighing, or by using more sophisticated methods for putting all the subtypes of wrongdoing on a commensurate monetary or non-monetary scale.

We divide criminal and civil wrongdoing by the national population in order to talk in terms of wrongdoing per capita. We divide instances of firings and license withdrawals by the size of the labor force in order to obtain an analogous ratio. If we subtract the number of firings and license withdrawals from the size of the labor force, then we obtain a measure of the number of people in the labor force who are doing reasonably right or well on their jobs. There is, however, no figure from which we can subtract the number of crimes in order to determine the number of compliances. We have no way of knowing how many opportunities people had to commit crimes in which they refrained from doing so. The same is true of civil wrongdoing. We could determine the percent of people who have been convicted of a crime over the past year and likewise the percent of people who have not been convicted of a crime. The latter percent would be a rough measure of rightdoing, although it refers to people rather than to acts.

The best way to convert the Wrongdoing Index (WDI) into a Rightdoing Index (RDI) is to calculate the complement the way 7% unemployment can be expressed as 93% employment. More specifically, if crimes per capita is 2%, civil wrong per capita is 4%, and firings-license withdrawals is 5%, then the sum of those three percentages is 11% and the complement or Rightdoing Index is 89%. To calculate a weighted Rightdoing Index using the 3-2-1 weighing system the three products would be 3 times 2%, plus 2 times 4%, and plus 1 times 5%, for a total of 19%. We would then divide the 19% by the sum of the weights to get a weighted average percent. That means 19% divided by 6 which is 3.17%. Subtracting that figure from 100% gives a Rightdoing Index of about 97%. A Rightdoing Index emphasizes the positive, but the Wrongdoing Index may be easier to grasp. The important point is that both broadly include civil and job wrongdoing, as well as criminal wrongdoing.

We could then subtract the number of crimes or the CRW figure from the number of crimes solved. The subtraction would yield the number of unsolved crimes. Doing so would in effect be saying that only unsolved crimes are a form of wrongdoing. That would not be true. The victim of a solved crime is just as much a victim as the victim of an unsolved crime, although the victim of a solved crime might feel better later. Solved crimes are better than unsolved crimes for obtaining some (1) victim compensation and maybe consolation, (2) deterrence of the individual defendant from committing other crimes, and (3) deterrence of other potential wrongdoers from committing similar crimes. Nevertheless, the distinction between solved and unsolved crimes seems best left to indexes designed to judge the efficiency of the police or the criminal justice system, rather than the desirability of the society.

There is no analogous way of talking about civil wrongs reported versus civil wrongs solved. The way we know about civil wrongs is through the records of civil courts and administrative agencies. We would, however, only want to use records showing injunctions issued and damages awarded, not merely complaints filed. The filing of a civil complaint is roughly the equivalent of the reporting of a crime. Merely filing a civil complaint though does not indicate that a civil wrong has been committed. Likewise the firings and dismissals tend to be confirmations of wrongdoing, in contrast to allegations of misbehavior.[4]

OTHER FIELDS OF PUBLIC POLICY

Every field of public policy lends itself to thinking along the lines just presented. All policy problems are thus capable of being conceived as having a level of achievement that would traditionally be considered optimum. They also have a level of achievement that can be considered as doing better than the optimum. Table 1-1 summarizes some of the possibilities.

The arrangement is roughly random order. It is difficult and unnecessary to try to arrange major policy problems in order of importance. One could offer something in favor of every problem being the most important problem. They are all essential to the smooth functioning of a society and to general societal happiness.

---

[4]On measuring and reducing crime, see Samuel Walker, *Sense and Nonsense About Crime: A Policy Guide* (Monterrey, Calif.: Brooks/Cole, 1985); Joseph Sheley, *America's Crime Problem: An Introduction to Criminology* (Belmont, Calif.: Wadsworth, 1985); and the President's Commission on Law Enforcement and Administration of Criminal Justice, *The Challenge of Crime in a Free Society* (Washington, D.C.: U.S. Government Printing Office, 1967).

TABLE 1-1. DOING BETTER THAN THE BEST

Policy Problem	An Optimum Society	A Better than Optimum Society
A. *Economic problems*		
Unemployment	Zero unemployment	That plus a higher percent of adults in the labor force and fully employed
Inflation	Zero inflation	That plus increased benefits for prices paid
Consumer	Zero fraud	That plus giving useful information
B. *Political problems*		
Word peace	Zero casualties	That plus world cooperation
Free speech	Zero interference	That plus providing a supportive atmosphere for innovative ideas
Government	Zero waste and corruption	That plus creativity, popular participation, equity, and due process
C. *Social problems*		
Crime	Zero crime	That plus zero civil wrongdoing and job wrongdoing
Poverty and discrimination	Zero poverty and discrimination	That plus productive job satisfaction
Education	Zero functional illiteracy	That plus rising to one's maximum, with broadness and inquisitiveness in education
D. *Science problems*		
Health	Zero non-aging diseases	That plus health robustness and greater longevity
Environment	Zero pollution	That plus reclamation and renewal

ECONOMIC PROBLEMS

Inflation and unemployment policy have already been discussed. Consumer policy is closely related to inflation policy, just as labor policy is closely related to unemployment, poverty, and discrimination. Consumer policy though also illustrates well the distinction between traditional optimums which emphasize removing obvious wrongs, while neglecting the less obvious. The obvious wrongs tend to be sins of commission like consumer fraud, which involves active deception. The less obvious wrongs tend to be sins of omission or failures to take affirmative action, such as failing to supply consumers with useful information that could enable them to be more rational consumers.

POLITICAL PROBLEMS

Having world peace as measured by zero war casualties would be wonderful. That is true of the achievement level in the middle column labeled "An Optimum Society" for every policy problem in Table 1-1. If, however, there are two time periods and both have zero war casualties, the better time period would be the one that has more world cooperation. That includes cooperation regarding unemployment, inflation, crime, free speech, poverty, discrimination, health, environment, education, consumer policy, and government institutions. The specialized agencies of the United Nations strive to achieve those cooperation goals, such as the World Health Organization, the International Labor Organization, and the United Nations Economic, Social, and Cultural Organization.

The United States has a reasonably good record on not interfering with freedom of speech. The main exceptions are where another constitutional right is in conflict such as (1) due process in criminal proceedings requiring avoidance of prejudicial pretrial newspaper publicity, (2) equal treatment under the law requiring some restrictions on campaign expenditures, and (3) the right to privacy requiring restrained newspaper reporting on the private lives of non-public figures. One could measure the degree of free speech by looking to the number of people held in jail for activities that are critical of the government or other institutions. Getting a score of zero on such interference may, however, not be enough. A society deserves a higher score on free speech if in addition to non-interference, it provides a supportive atmosphere for innovative ideas. That can include (1) requiring radio, TV, and other mass media to be willing to sell time to groups critical of society's institutions, (2) requiring the mass media to give free time to all major candidates if they give free time to any one candidate for office, and (3) making inexpensive cable TV time available to fringe groups who would otherwise not be able to buy time to communicate their ideas.

An important policy problem is the problem of improvements needed in the structures and procedures for policy formation and implementation. That can be considered a meta-problem since it cuts across all the specific problems, although so does free speech, education, unemployment, poverty, and still other problems. The Reagan administration has been conducting a strong campaign against waste and corruption in government. It would be fine if all waste, corruption, and other forms of inefficiency were eliminated. Again, however, that ignores the sins of omission whereby the government operates wastefully and ineffectively because it is not encouraging creativity with regard to developing new ideas for dealing better with public policy problems. One could also say that if two societies are equally devoid of waste and corruption, the second society is the better one if it stimulates more popular participation in government activities, more equity/fairness in the distribution of benefits and costs, and more due process in enabling those who have been wrongly denied benefits or subjected to costs to be able to defend themselves with witnesses, cross-examination, and counsel.

SOCIAL PROBLEMS

In the 1960s, there was talk about eliminating the poverty gap by spending 15 billion dollars to bring every poor family up to the line separating being poor from not being poor. That line was roughly figured at $4,000 a year for a family of four as of 1965. The price now is much higher. The important point though is that poverty means more than just being below an annual income level. If poor families were brought up to that level, they would be better off. If, however, they still have high unemployment, low education, and dead-end jobs, they are not likely to have the happiness that goes with having middle-class employment opportunities. Thus going beyond the optimum of zero poverty means having an economy and education system whereby everyone can have access to a job that provides productive job satisfaction. In a super-ideal world, everyone would enjoy their productive jobs so much that they would continue at their jobs even if they were to become independently wealthy and would no longer need to work for the income.

Closely related to poverty is the policy problem of discrimination. In the 1960's, legislation was passed at the national, state, and local levels providing for fair employment, open housing, public accommodations, and other rights against discriminatory treatment. If there were 100% compliance, we would then have a form of zero discrimination. The absence of such racial and related discrimination in the housing field, for example, does not sufficiently help blacks if their incomes are so low that they cannot afford decent non-discriminatory housing. What is needed to make non-discrimination more meaningful is the economic ability and education to be able to take advantage of fair opportunities in employment, consumer rights, and other activities.

On the matter of goals for educational policy, the United States and most countries would be pleased to achieve 100% functional literacy or zero functional illiteracy. Literacy means being able to read and write at a bare minimum level. Functional literacy means being able to read and write sufficiently to be able to complete job applications and to carry on the reading and writing aspects of a normal job. A goal that is better than that optimum would be to have zero functional illiteracy and have every one rise to their maximum educational achievement level. One could also seek to achieve higher quality standards in education. The standards might include the kind of broadness which is tested for in the National Educational Assessment Program. Educational quality could also include stimulating a high level of inquisitiveness, as contrasted to rote learning of facts and doctrines.

SCIENCE POLICY PROBLEMS

On the matter of health policy, a society might be considered operating at the optimum if governmental programs have succeeded in stimulating the development and distribution of cures and vaccines for all non-aging or non-degenerative diseases. Merely not having diseases is an excellent societal condition. It is even better though to have a society without diseases plus a high degree of robust health or wellness. That manifests itself in people being energetic and mentally healthy which may also involve productive job satisfaction. Also on the matter of health we may be reaching the point where there will be no need to tolerate even aging diseases like cancer, heart disease, and diabetes. The time may come when modern genetics will make it possible to change the genes of people not yet conceived so as to adjust their biological clocks. Doing so will mean growing to adulthood, but not into old age. People would still die as a result of accidents, although a super-optimum society would have a minimum of accidents as a form of civil wrongdoing. Many people now say they would not want to live indefinitely, but that is probably a sour-grapes attitude since living indefinitely is not currently available. People are probably no more likely to commit suicide at age 300 than they would be now at age 30.

As for environmental protection, one might consider conditions as being optimum if there were no pollution regarding air, water, solid waste, noise, radiation, or other forms of pollution. That would be fine. The absence of air pollution, however, might make urban and rural slums more visible. What is also needed is more reclamation and conservation of land that has been ruined or damaged from strip mining, erosion, overgrazing, and other forms of bad land use. What is also needed is more urban and rural renewal of buildings and other man-made structures, but in such a way as to minimize the disruption to the present occupants.[5]

GENERAL MEANS FOR ACHIEVING THE GOALS

The purpose of this section is not to discuss in detail how to achieve low unemployment, low inflation, or low crime rates, or how to get below zero percent or above 100 percent on any specific social indicator. Rather the purpose is to talk on a relatively high level of generality as to how such high goals can be achieved.

AN INCENTIVES PERSPECTIVE

All policy problems can be viewed as problems that involve encouraging socially desired behavior. A good check list for generating ideas on how public policy can encourage socially desired behavior is to think in terms of:

1. Increasing the benefits of doing right.
2. Decreasing the costs of doing right.
3. Increasing the costs of doing wrong.
4. Decreasing the benefits of doing wrong.
5. Increasing the probability that the benefits and costs will occur.

Each specific problem involves different doers, benefits, and costs. For example, an incentives approach to the problems of unemployment and inflation might involve the following five-pronged approach in accordance with the above framework:

1. Tax incentives to business firms and labor unions for keeping prices and wages down. Also monetary incentives to employers to hire the unemployed and monetary incentives to the unemployed to accept training and jobs.
2. Decreasing the costs of finding jobs and workers through better information systems.
3. Increasing the costs of violating price-wage guidelines and work incentives by withdrawing benefits and (in rare cases) by fines and other negative

---

[5]On an incentive-growth perspective, see Ira Magaziner and Robert Reich, *Minding America's Business: The Decline and Rise of the American Economy* (New York: Harcourt, Brace, 1982); Amitai Etzioni, *An Immodest Agenda: Rebuilding America Before the Twenty-First Century* (New York: McGraw Hill, 1983); Paul Roberts, *The Supply Side Revolution* (Cambridge, Mass.: Harvard University Press, 1984); and Victor Canto et al., *Foundations of Supply-Side Economics* (New York: Academic Press, 1983).

penalties.
4. Confiscating the benefits of price-wage violations by special taxes on the gains.
5. More accurate information on prices, wages, and unemployment in order to allocate the benefits and costs more effectively.

As a second example of this kind of perspective, we might look at crime reduction. The following five-pronged approach would be especially appropriate there:

1. The main benefit of complying with the law should be that doing so gives one access to opportunities that are cut off to law violators. That means legitimate career opportunities must be provided to those who would otherwise turn to crime.
2. One cost of doing right may be a loss of prestige among youthful gang members who consider criminal behavior an indicator of toughness. There is a need for working to redirect such peer group values so that toughness can be displayed in more constructive ways.
3. The costs of doing wrong can include negative incentives of long prison sentences, but it may be more meaningful to emphasize the withdrawal of career opportunities which would otherwise be present.
4. Provisions should be made for facilitating the confiscation of the property gains of criminal wrongdoing and decreasing the vulnerability of the targets of crime to lessen the benefits obtained.
5. The probability of arrest and conviction can be increased partly through more professionalism among law enforcement personnel.

One could apply that kind of analysis to all 11 policy problems in Table 1-1, as well as other more specific policy problems. One might consider such an approach to be an optimum set of procedures for optimizing societal goals. One can, however, do better than the optimum with regard to procedure as well as substance. Doing better in this context means not having situations occur where people need to be stimulated to do the right thing or deterred from doing the wrong thing. There are two ways to arrange for such situations to never occur, either by making them physically or mentally impossible.

An example of making wrongdoing physically impossible is not allowing cars to be sold that can go faster than a certain speed limit, such as 55 miles per hour except in short spurts. Then there is much less need to have a system of punishments for doing wrong or a system designed to determine who the wrongdoers are. Another example would be prohibiting the manufacture of certain kinds of aerosol cans that do great harm to the ozone in the environment. Still another example would be prohibiting the existence of nuclear breeder reactors to supply energy in view of their likelihood of leading to the production of bomb-grade plutonium.

An example of making certain kinds of wrongdoing mentally impossible or close to it is murder, robbery, burglary, and other street crimes among most middle-class people. When affronted in a store, on a bus, or elsewhere, the average person never thinks of the possibility of pulling a gun or going home and getting one in order to kill the person who has insulted him. It is an unthinkable thought. Likewise, when driving late at night and observing a convenience store or a gas station that is open with no customers around, the average person never thinks of robbing the place. It is a thought as unthinkable as flapping one's arms to fly to an appointment when one is late. The reason murder and robbery are unthinkable is not that they are physically impossible or because of a fear of the penalties, but because for most people their socialization has been such that those thoughts are not within the realm of one's normal thinking.

A society operating at the optimum or above it on various policy problems can thus be defined as a society which distributes benefits and costs in such a way as to encourage socially desired behavior with regard to unemployment, inflation, crime, and other social problems, but which also does as much as possible to make undesirable behavior impossible and/or unthinkable.

A GROWTH PERSPECTIVE

In discussing the general means for achieving the super-optimum goals, one must recognize that those means are going to cost large amounts of money for appropriate subsidies, tax breaks, and some forms of regulation. A super-optimum perspective tends to be optimistic in setting goals and in believing that the means can be found for achieving them. This is not, however, a naive optimism, but rather one that is based on what is realistically possible, especially if one proceeds with a positive orientation.

A growth perspective implies that the funding to support the achievement of the super-optimum goals will come mainly from growth of the economy, rather than from a redistribution of wealth. In fact, a redistribution from the rich to the poor may interfere with economic growth by unduly reducing incentives to save, invest, and even work as hard or as well as one otherwise would, regardless whether one is rich or poor. Likewise, a distribution from the poor to the rich through regressive taxes and investment incentives could also similarly interfere with economic growth and public morale.

A growth perspective tends to be endorsed by both conservatives (who favor supply-side economics and Reaganomics) and by liberals (who favor industrial policy and economic planning). They even tend to agree that the main means to economic growth is tax breaks and subsidies, although they may disagree as to exactly what form they should take. President Reagan originally put considerable faith in the idea of a 30% across-the-board tax-cut to stimulate the economy. The economy was not very well stimulated, partly because of conflicting tight-money policies to reduce inflation, but also because tax cuts with no strings attached may tend to wind up disproportionately in real estate, luxury goods, and higher executive salaries. Gary Hart had indicated a willingness to provide tax breaks to business much higher than 30% provided that the tax breaks are only given if the money is used for modernizing industrial practices, giving on-the-job training, or other productivity-improving activities.

Some of the costs could be covered by improving the U.S. defense capability at a lower cost by concentrating more on weapons systems which are more effective and efficient. That may mean more emphasis on Trident submarines and low-flying cruise missiles, and less emphasis on easily destroyed B-1 bombers, aircraft carriers, and MX missile silos. It may also mean more realistic defensive systems, such as a radar and laser-firing system for destroying enemy nuclear submarines, rather than a star wars system for supposedly destroying all incoming enemy missiles. Making defense expenditures more effective and efficient and thereby reducing them makes more sense, in contrast to increasing questionable defense expenditures by taking from on-the-job training programs and subsidies for technological innovation and implementation. It is no coincidence that the United States and the Soviet Union have been ranking lowest among the industrial nations on productivity growth as of about 1980, and highest among the industrial nations on defense expenditures.

On the matter of bi-partisan growth, both conservatives and liberals also tend to endorse the idea of more systematic governmental decision-making in order to achieve economic growth. Conservatives consider such decision-making to be a form of bringing good business-practice to government. Liberals consider it to be a form of economic planning. Systematic governmental decision-making manifests itself in using contemporary methods of benefit-cost analysis to (1) choose among discrete alternatives, (2) choose under conditions of risk, (3) choose where doing too much or too little is undesirable, and (4) to allocate scarce resources in light of given goals and relations.

HIGH SOCIETAL GOALS AND SOCIETAL HAPPINESS

One might question whether it is socially desirable to set societal goals substantially higher than one is likely to achieve. The same question might be raised concerning individual goals. Some people say that it is better to set one's goals low and achieve them than it is to set one's goals high and not achieve them. They further argue that happiness is not measured by achievement, but by the size of the gap between goals and achievement.[6]

That philosophy of minimizing the gap has many defects. Carried to its logical extreme, we should all have as our goals in life to be no more than winos, and other forms of derelicts. Then it would be difficult to fail if we set our sights so low. This is sometimes referred to as happiness by "downward comparisons." It is epitomized in the idea of telling people who have no shoes that they should be glad to have feet. People who are severely disabled or economically destitute would thus be told how happy or satisfied they should be just to be alive.

Actually it would be quite difficult for most people to achieve the goal of being a derelict. Most people have been socialized into having much higher goals. It might thus be impossible for them to bring their goals drastically down without becoming very unhappy. Doing so would result in a gap between expectations and achievement. Those who do not like a downward comparisons approach to obtaining happiness sometimes reject it on the grounds that it is morally undesirable. A firmer basis would be to show through logical reasoning and empirical data that downward comparisons do not bring as much happiness as upward achievement.

One might be happy with low goals if everyone else also had low goals. If, however, an individual or a country is highly unusual in having low goals, the individual or country is going to be unhappy unless it can isolate itself from being aware of how well others are doing. This is consistent with the findings reported by Michalos about the importance of deprivation relative to one's reference group.

In feudalistic times, people may have been happy to get through the day without bubonic plague, starvation, or being caught in the middle of a feudalistic war. In modern times, people expect a lot more regarding public policy toward health, poverty, and violent death than people in the dark ages. This is consistent with the idea that one's goals become higher as one's capabilities become greater.

Suppose one person has a goal of earning $100,000 a year, or of producing $100,000 worth of useful goods a year, whichever sounds better. Suppose that person, however, is capable of achieving only $50,000 a year. Suppose further that another person only has in mind to achieve $10,000 a year in the same

---

[6]For a discussion of the extensive literature on the relation between happiness and the gap between goals and achievement, see Alex Michalos, "Multiple Discrepancies Theory," 16 *Social Indicators Research* 347-414 (1985) and "What Makes People Happy?" Unpublished paper presented at the Conference on Quality of Life in Oslo, Norway (1986). The emphasis in most of that literature is on individual happiness based on comparing individuals, rather than on comparing societal happiness across nations.

society and fully succeeds. Not many people would rather be the "successful" $10,000 a year person over the "unsuccessful" $50,000 a year person. In other words, people judge others and themselves in terms of what they achieve more than or as well as the gap between goals and achievement. The gap between goals and achievement may also be quite important to happiness, as Michalos indicates.

The person who has a $100,000 goal is more likely to achieve at the $50,000 level than a person who has only a $50,000 level. There seems to be a natural tendency not to achieve goals fully. This is so because goals are like incentives that stimulate further effort, especially when they are just out of reach like the carrot that hangs in front of the donkey to make the donkey move forward. This point is in effect saying that high goals are desirable because they stimulate greater productivity and creativity and thereby benefit society, even if individuals with high goals are not happy. Thus high societal goals can be justified pragmatically.

Contrary to the position which recommends setting one's goals low or "realistically" to achieve happiness, there are numerous examples of people who are saddened by having achieved their goals and having lost the excitement of the pursuit. One does not have to be Alexander the Great to want new things to conquer. Business people and others sometimes say that getting an uncontrollable flood of mail is bad, but much worse is getting no mail at all. In other words, people like to have something in their boxes to be done. They do not like having nothing to do as a result of having achieved their goals. What this point is in effect saying is that there is a hill-shaped relation between happiness as an effect and the goals-achievement gap as a cause. That means happiness is low if the gap is either very small or very large. The gap-theory people tend to overemphasize the right side of the hill-shaped curve where happiness goes down as the gap becomes bigger, rather than the left side of the hill-shaped curve where happiness goes down as the gap becomes smaller. The optimum gap is somewhere in the middle.

In management by objectives, it is considered much better to have 50% achievement on a big objective than 100% achievement on a small objective. For example, on a 0 to 100 scale, if a big objective is scored 90, then 50% achievement would be worth 45 points. A specific small objective might be scored 5, and 100% success would receive the full 5 points. Thus in this example, 50% success on a 90-point objective would be nine times as worthy as 100% success on a 5-point objective. One might object to this on the grounds that saying a 45-point achievement is better or more worthy than a 5-point achievement is not the same as saying that it is more happiness-producing. One might further argue there is an implied assumption that achievement is good or worthy for society regardless of the personal happiness of the achiever. That assumption may be true, but what is really being argued is that achievement brings both personal happiness and societal happiness, and that achievement is encouraged by having high but realistically attainable goals.

Applying the same kind of reasoning to societal goals as is expressed in those points, one can say that no goals are too high so long as they are physically possible. Even what is physically possible may be subject to change. It is thus socially desirable for a society to be an optimizing society, or one that is seeking to achieve the optimum or the super-optimum on various social indicators. That is true with regard to public policies concerning unemployment, inflation, crime, world peace, free speech, poverty, discrimination, health, environment, education, consumers, and government structures/procedures. It is hoped that this chapter and book will stimulate further ideas along the lines of doing better than the optimum, both with regard to what it means and how to do it.

REFERENCES

Alberts, D., *A Plan for Measuring the Performance of Social Programs* (New York: Praeger, 1970).

Bailey, S. , *Congress Makes a Law: The Story Behind the Employment Act of 1946* (New York: Columbia University Press, 1950).

Baumer, D., and C. V. Horn, *The Politics of Unemployment* (Washington, D.C.: Congressional Quarterly, 1985).

Carley, M., *Social Measurement and Social Indicators: Issues of Policy and Theory* (Boston: Allen and Unwin, 1981).

Canto, V., D. Joines, and A. Laffer, *Foundations of Supply-Side Economics* (New York: Academic Press, 1983).

Cook, T. (ed.), *Performance Measurement in Public Agencies*, (Westport, Conn.: Greenwood Press, 1986).

Dorfman, R., *Measuring Benefits in Government Investments* (Washington, D.C.: Brookings, 1964).

Duggan, P., *The New American Unemployment* (Washington, D.C.: Center for Regional Policy, 1985).

Eckstein, 0., *Inflation: Prospects and Remedies* (Washington, D.C.: Center for National Policy, 1983).

Etzioni, A., *An Immodest Agenda: Rebuilding America Before the Twenty First Century* (McGraw-Hill, New York: 1983).

Gilmartin, K. et al., *Social Indicators: An Annotated Bibliography of Current Literature* (New York: Garland, 1979).

Ginzberg, E., *The Unemployed* (New York: Harper, 1963).

MacRae, D., *Policy Indicators: Links Between Social Science and PublicDebate* (Chapel Hill, NC: Duke University, 1986).

Magaziner, I. and R. Reich, *Minding America's Business: The Decline and Rise of the American Economy* (New York: Harcourt, Brace, 1982).

Michalos, A. C., Multiple Discrepancies Theory (MDT), 16 *Social Indicators Research* 347-414 (1985).

Michalos, A. C., What Makes People Happy? (unpublished paper presented at the Conference on Quality of Life in Oslo, Norway, 1986).

Nagel, S., *Public Policy: Goals, Means, and Methods* (New York: St. Martin's, 1984) pp. 33-138.

Peretz, P., *The Political Economy of Inflation in the United States* (Chicago: University of Chicago Press, 1983).

Prentice, P., *Inflation* (Washington, D.C.: U.S.D.A. Economics and Statistics Section, 1981).

President's Commission on Law Enforcement and Administration of Justice: 1967, *The Challenge of Crime in a Free Society* (Washington, D.C.: U.S. Government Printing Office, 1967),

Roberts, P., *The Supply Side Revolution* (Cambridge, Mass.: Harvard University Press, 1984).

Sheley, J., *America's Crime Problem: An Introduction to Criminology* (Belmont, Calif: Wadsworth, 1985).

Slawson, D., *The New Inflation* (Princeton, N.J., Princeton University Press, 1981).

Walker, S., *Sense and Nonsense About Crime: Policy Guide* (Monterey, Calif.: Brooks/Cole, 1985).

2

NATIONAL PRODUCTIVITY AS A SPECIAL GOAL

Socio-economic reforms can be readily adopted when they are supported by both liberals and conservatives, although they may not do so for the same reasons. Examples include some aspects of the criminal justice system. For instance, in the last few years, there has been a substantial change across the country in decreasing criminal sentencing discretion. Liberals perceive the previous discretion as resulting in sentences that are discriminatory along class, race, sex, and other lines. Conservatives perceive the previous discretion as resulting in sentences that have been unduly lenient. As a result, one finds liberals like Senator Kennedy joining with conservatives like Senator Thurmond to support decreased sentencing discretion in the federal courts.

DEFINITIONS AND HISTORICAL CONTEXT

The field of productivity may be an even better example. Liberals and conservatives are in agreement that the nation would be better off if it were more productive. Virtually everyone would endorse the idea of being able to produce 20 units of desired output with only 5 units of effort, rather than 10 units of effort. Likewise virtually everyone would endorse the idea of being able to get as much as 30 output units rather than 20, for 10 units of effort. That may have been the main appeal of the Reagan campaign, namely, the idea of increased productivity and creativity for the United States. The Carter campaign may have made the mistake of over-emphasizing the traditional Democratic party concern for equalizing the pie when the American people were more concerned with having a bigger pie to equalize.

American history seems to involve alternating periods of growth and

49

equalization. We were in a period of industrial and geographical development from the end of the equalizing Reconstruction Era to the administrations of Theodore Roosevelt and Woodrow Wilson. Both these presidencies pushed the progressive income tax and forms of economic regulation that were consumer-oriented. The 1920's resumed business growth, and the depression and World War II also focused more on growth than equality. The 1960's was a period of equalizing with regard to poverty, civil rights, women, gays, handicapped, aged, children, and even animals, although further equality of opportunity still needs to be obtained. That period extended until about 1980. We now seem to be re-entering an era in which the emphasis will again be on bi-partisan growth and productivity. The periods of growth are not necessarily Republican periods, and the periods of equalization are not necessarily Democratic periods. The growth in the late 1800's was promoted by both Cleveland and McKinley. The equality of the early 1900's was associated with both Theodore Roosevelt and Woodrow Wilson. The renewed emphasis on growth from 1920 to 1960 involved both Republican and Democrat presidents, as did the equalization period from 1960 to 1980.

A concern for productivity may especially occur in times of inflation when prices are rising with nothing to show for the price increases in terms of a better quantity or quality of products. Wage and price increases are justifiable and acceptable if they are based on increased productivity. If a worker who was formerly being paid $3 an hour now produces twice as much in an hour, he or she should receive $6 an hour although something may have to be deducted to cover the cost of buying and maintaining the capital equipment which may have made possible that increased productivity. Likewise, if a $1 head of lettuce spoils in a week, and a new technology is developed that will enable lettuce to last for a month, the seller should be entitled to charge more especially if there are additional costs involved, but also because there will be increased demand due to the better product. A strong concern for productivity also occurs in time of recession or depression when so many potentially productive people are not producing in accordance with their skills. Keynesian fiscal policy and Friedman monetary policy may be relevant to dealing with inflation and unemployment, but such policies are too broad relative to policies that are specifically focused on improving productivity.

The forthcoming era of new productivity might also be called the era of new incentives. The concept of "incentives" however emphasizes the main means for bringing about the new productivity, rather than the goals toward which those means are directed. By incentives in this context are meant government policies designed to reward various segments of the population for doing things that are productivity-increasing, as contrasted to a regulatory approach which emphasizes controls and penalties. Tax incentives are the main incentives that government has available for stimulating the new productivity. This is especially true of the federal government, given its control over corporate and individual income taxes, but also state and local governments, given their control over property taxes. Tax foregoing is also more politically feasible than outright cash grants since taxpayers are more willing to support government policies that do not involve explicit government expenditures. Tax foregoing also enables the recipients of the incentives to preserve their self-respect more than if they were receiving an outright cash grant, just as farmers prefer indirect price supports over the direct subsidies associated with the Brannan Plan.

SPECIFIC MEANS AND GOALS

The federal government can develop a list of business activities which will increase national productivity that business firms might otherwise not engage in. Engaging in those activities can then entitle the participating business firms to various types of tax breaks including depreciation or expense allowances, tax credits, or even tax exemption under special circumstances. A good example of such an activity might be hiring willing and able people who are otherwise unemployed. This may be true of many welfare recipients including those who are receiving aid to the aged, disabled, unemployed, or those caring for dependent children. If through a tax subsidy a business firm can be encouraged to hire such a person who otherwise would be unemployed, then society is better off in two ways. First, the individual is adding to the gross national product which constitutes an increased benefit to society's benefits and costs. Second, the subsidy is probably costing society less than the former welfare payments, which means a societal cost reduction.

That example helps clarify what increased productivity means. In a general sense, it means increasing societal benefits or income while holding constant or decreasing societal costs. It can also mean holding constant societal benefits, while decreasing societal costs. In either situation, the positive difference between societal benefits and societal costs has been increased. The term productivity is also sometimes defined so as to refer just to increased benefits regardless of costs, or benefits divided by costs, but benefits minus costs is the preferred criterion when those criteria conflict. Society would prefer a situation involving $100 in benefits and $60 in costs for a net gain of $40, rather than $10 in benefits and $3 in costs for a net gain of only $7, even though the latter situation involves a 10/3 benefit/cost ratio and the former situation involves a worse 10/6 ratio. Other terms besides productivity are also used to refer to improving benefits minus costs, such as profitability, net benefits, efficiency, or effectiveness, but productivity has the semantic advantage arousing more positive connotations than the other concepts, as well as being more commonly understood.

Other business activities that seem appropriate to stimulate through tax subsidies include: (1) Developing and implementing new technologies. When a new technology is developed that enables workers to produce more with less labor, that usually means an increase in the quantity and possibly the quality of the products produced, with the cost per item produced being less than the former more labor intensive cost. (2) Locating plants and job opportunities in high unemployment areas. This is like putting welfare recipients to work. The marginal rate of return tends to be higher in moving someone from unemployment to employment, as contrasted to a move from one form of employment to another. Stimulating business firms to locate in such areas can be aided by local property-tax exemption, as well as federal income tax incentives. (3) Subsidizing business firms to engage in programs designed to upgrade the work of groups who have traditionally been discriminated against in obtaining jobs that are commensurate with their skills such as blacks, handicapped, and the aged. The subsidies would cover advertising available jobs in media likely to reach those groups. The subsidies might also be designed to facilitate transportation and housing patterns to bring discriminated, under-employed, and unemployed people closer to the job opportunities. (4) Expanding business operations as a result of technological developments that enable prices to be reduced so that larger quantities could be sold, as contrasted to seeking expansion through increased advertising. (5) Developing training programs so as to upgrade the skills of workers and thereby make them more productive, with the cost of training generally being substantially less than the increased product which the workers are able to produce.

The above business activities cluster around two kinds of activities. One relates to technological development as emphasized in points 1 and 4. The other relates to a more productive hiring and training as emphasized in points 2, 3, and 5 and the earlier point about welfare recipients. In order to make the hiring and training opportunities more meaningful, it is desirable not only to stimulate business to make them available, but also to stimulate the potential worker participants to take advantage of those opportunities. In the case of welfare recipients, this may mean offering such incentives as being able to keep the first $60 or so earned each month and about $1 out of every $2 earned until a welfare cutoff figure is reached. That kind of system clearly makes more sense than deducting from the welfare payments every dollar that a welfare recipient earns as was done prior to the late 60's, or having an exemption substantially less than about $60 or $1 out of every $2 earned (which is the current system). The Nixon-Moynihan family assistance plan originally proposed such incentives for encouraging productive work on the part of welfare recipients, but the plan never passed due partly to Watergate distractions, and it was not combined with a business incentives program to provide jobs for welfare recipients and other unemployed and underemployed people.

In order to make the technological incentives more meaningful it is desirable to stimulate basic research in the universities. Business firms do have the capability of implementing new technologies especially with tax subsidies to cover the costs. Business firms do not do so well though in running departments of physics, genetics, psychology, or other fields of knowledge which is the province of universities. American universities have been quite productive in producing basic research and teaching, as indicated by where the Nobel prize winners are and where foreign students choose to go. Unfortunately, American industry has not taken sufficient advantage of the creativity of American academic research. It is ironic that Japanese industry is more computerized than American industry in spite of the fact that much of the basic computer technology was developed in American universities. Getting American business to implement new research ideas can be done partly through tax subsidies, but there is also a need for further stimulation of basic research especially in these times of tight academic budgets.

Tax exemption for American universities though is not the answer since they are already tax exempt. What can be done, however, is to allow tax credits to people who make university contributions. Under the present system a person earning $10 who contributes $1 to his or her favorite university receives an itemized deduction bringing his net taxable income down to $9, or $10 minus $1. If the tax rate is 20 percent, the tax in this hypothetical situation is $1.80, or $9 times .20. If however the government were to provide a $1 tax credit in addition to the $1 deduction, then the tax to be paid would only be $.80, or $1.80 minus $1.00. That kind of tax credit could provide a strong incentive to contribute much needed funding from private individuals and business firms to American universities. The tax law could also specify that the contributions must be earmarked for research purposes rather than athletic, dormitory, or other university activities.

The above analysis emphasizes the role of business, welfare recipients, and universities in the new productivity. What, however, is the role of the great mass of middle class-people who are not business executives, welfare recipients, or professors? Their role is mainly to be the beneficiaries of the increased GNP at lower cost, that these incentives can bring about. That increased GNP gets widely spread, partly because middle-class people tend to work for the business firms that are in a position to benefit from these subsidies and to use the subsidies to increase their productivity and the income of their workers. That includes large and small business since both are capable of improving their hiring practices and of adopting improved technologies. The bulk of the American population could also benefit from the new productivity by virtue of having a reduced work week if the new productivity can result in producing as much or more with a 30-35 hour work week as we were formerly producing with a 40 hour work week. That would also enable more jobs to be spread around if each person is working less but is still as productive and therefore still earning the same or more income. Ordinary middle-class people can also take advantage of the tax subsidies by investing their money in activities that would entitle them to tax deductions or tax credits. At the present time, there may be an over-investment on the part of middle-class people in real estate because of the real estate tax breaks. Money tied up in real estate may represent lost opportunities to society for having those funds invested in more productive technological development.

ALTERNATIVES TO AN INCENTIVES-PRODUCTIVITY PROGRAM

It is important to distinguish the above incentives-productivity program from related programs that emphasize governmental tax cuts. The key distinction is that the tax cuts described here are made in return for the taxpayers doing things considered helpful to national productivity. The Kemp-Roth proposed legislation involves a 30 percent tax cut across the board without strings attached. Such legislation may represent a tremendous missed opportunity to be able to use a large quantity of potential rewards, if there are no productivity strings attached to the tax cut. The taxes saved may go into savings or consumption that could stimulate the economy, although possibly in an inflationary way if the increased attempt to consume is not adequately met by increased production. Much of the taxes saved may go into increased dividends, real estate purchases, and other purchases that in themselves contribute little if anything toward increased productivity. Likewise, increased property-tax reductions and restrictions like those associated with California Proposition 13 do little for increased productivity unless strings are attached whereby property holders are required to do something worthwhile in return for the tax reductions. That something might include changing the insulation or the heating system of their property so as to better conserve energy and thereby reduce society's energy costs. The property tax reductions could also be more selective so as to encourage property development in depressed areas, or residential development in areas that have job opportunities but lack adequate housing for a local labor force.

There are basically two alternatives to the above incentives program for seeking increased societal productivity. One alternative is to try to achieve it through controls and penalties for lack of productivity. That alternative does not work so well. One can generally encourage socially desired behavior better through rewards, rather than punishments. That may even be true of traditional criminal law. The main reason middle-class people do not commit robberies is not because they are so afraid of the jail penalties which they may not receive for a first offense anyhow. Instead what keeps middle-class people in line may mainly be the available career opportunities that would be lost to them if they got arrested for a robbery. On the other hand, poor teenage blacks and whites do not have those rewards for good behavior so readily available. For them committing a mugging may often be a wise entrepreneurial decision given the alternative incentives available. Regardless how meaningful penalties like jail and fines are in the traditional criminal context, they do not generally work so well in the realm of economic matters like occupational safety, environmental protection, and increased productivity. They especially lack effectiveness when they require expensive, time-consuming and difficult litigation in order to be imposed.

The second basic alternative for obtaining increased societal productivity is to leave the matter to the marketplace. That also does not work so well either with regard to improved technology or improved hiring practices. The new technologies often require massive investment which takes years to pay off. American business and possibly business in general does not want to wait that long for a large capital investment to become profitable, and even large business firms may not have the kind of capital available for developing and implementing large-scale modern technologies. As a result, there may be a need for government with its financial resources to facilitate the development and implementation of new technologies, especially through the indirect approach of tax breaks, rather than through outright government expenditures.

Likewise with regard to hiring practices, business firms may not have much incentive for hiring welfare recipients, locating in high unemployment areas, or developing outreach programs to attract previously discriminated groups, unless there is some kind of government subsidy to do so. Engaging in those hiring practices may be beneficial to society, but not necessarily to the individual business firm, and business firms are oriented toward being profitable, not toward being idealistic. In other words, hiring a welfare recipient produces an external benefit-minus-cost, but not necessarily an internal one. If society wants those external benefits-minus-costs, then it should be willing to pay for them in the form of a tax reduction. That is especially true if a relatively small tax reduction can produce a relatively large increase in output, and also a reduction in other societal costs like welfare payment costs.

One effect of marketplace competition that is contrary to the new productivity is the stimulus that it gives to American business to ask for tariff protection from foreign competition. That kind of government policy runs contrary to a policy of stimulating new technology for increased productivity, as contrasted to sheltering American business from foreign business firms which have adopted new technologies. In the long run, all nations would be better off if they were to follow incentive programs of stimulating their respective national productivities so each country would be doing well whatever it does best relative to other countries.

DECISION SCIENCE AND PRODUCTIVITY IMPROVEMENT

Decision science can be defined as a set of methods for deciding which of various decisions or policies will maximize or increase benefits minus costs in achieving a given set of goals in light of the relations between the alternative decisions and the goals. Decision-science methods tend to fall into five categories that relate to benefit-cost analysis, decision theory, optimum-level analysis, allocation theory, and time-optimization methods.

Basic benefit-cost analysis involves making an optimum choice among discrete alternatives without probabilities. Discrete alternatives in this context mean alternatives where each one is a lump-sum project in the sense that a government agency can meaningfully adopt all or nothing of a project, not multiple units and not fractions of units. Each project is thus basically a yes-no matter. Under those circumstances, an agency that is interested in maximizing the good that it does should spend its whole budget for each of the alternative projects in the order of their benefit/cost ratios. This situation can be illustrated in choosing the optimum combination of a set of notification procedures for notifying defendants to appear in court, or a combination of dam building projects. Other examples include excluding illegally seized evidence, allowing abortions, or allowing teacher-led prayer in public schools.

Optimum level analysis involves finding an optimum policy where doing too much or too little is undesirable. These situations involve policies that produce benefits at first, but then the benefits reach a peak, and start to fall off. The object in such situations is to find the point on a policy continuum where the benefits are maximized. These situations may also involve policies that reduce costs at first, but then the costs reach a bottom, and start to rise. The object then is to find the point on a policy continuum where the costs are minimized. That situation can be illustrated by the problem of deciding the optimum percentage of defendants to hold in jail prior to trial, the optimum level of pollution, or the optimum speed limit on city highways.

Allocation theory or optimum mix analysis involves allocating scarce resources across activities, places, people, or other objects of allocation. The overall goal is generally to allocate one's scarce resources in such a way as to (1) use all the available budget, while (2) equalizing the marginal rates-of-return of the activities or places so that nothing is to be gained by switching from one activity or place to another. That kind of allocation recognizes that a good activity or place should not be given too much because after a while the diminishing marginal rate-of-return becomes smaller than what can be gained by shifting a dollar or unit of effort to another normally less productive activity or place. This situation can be illustrated by allocating the resources of the Legal Services Corporation between routine cases handling and law reform activities, or allocating anti-crime dollars of the Law

Enforcement Assistance Administration across a set of cities.

Time-optimization models involve decision-making systems designed to minimize time consumption. Time-optimization models often involve variations on optimum choice, risk, level, or mix analysis, but applied to situations in which the goal is to minimize time. Some time-optimization models are peculiar to a temporal subject matter such as (1) queuing theory for predicting and reducing waiting time and backlogs from information on arrival and service rates, (2) optimum sequencing for determining the order in which matters should be processed so as to minimize the average waiting time, and (3) critical-path analysis for determining what paths from start to finish are especially worth concentrating on with regard to delay reduction efforts.

In general, public policy evaluation based on decision science methods seems capable of improving decision-making processes so that decisions are more likely to be arrived at which will maximize or at least increase societal benefits minus costs. Those decision-making methods may be even more important than worker motivation or technological innovation in productivity improvement. Hard work means little if the wrong products are being produced in terms of societal benefits and costs. Likewise, the right policies are needed to maximize technological innovation, which is not so likely to occur without an appropriate public policy environment.

SOCIETAL PRODUCTIVITY AND PUBLIC POLICY PROBLEMS

Societal productivity affects every public policy problem, and public policy is highly important to substantially improving societal productivity. With regard to 43 societal policy problems, a typical list of the top five problems might include defense, inflation/unemployment, crime, civil liberties, and health. Others might have a different set of the top five. The important point is that societal productivity is relevant to whatever policy problems might be included. For example, a key problem in the realm of defense policy relates to how to develop more effective defenses for the United States at reduced costs. Both liberals and conservatives question how effective our defenses are, and they both question even more the extent to which we are efficiently buying defense. Increased productivity in that context does not just mean having an MX missile system at as low a cost as possible. It also means making the right decisions in terms of benefits minus costs in choosing the MX system over alternative defense systems. On an even higher level, one can talk about how wasteful any defense expenditures are in comparison to using the money for societal goods and services if we could develop alternative means of decreasing the probability of an attack on ourselves or our allies.

The inflation of rising prices and wages would be no problem if productivity were increasing simultaneously so that people would be receiving more benefits for the increased prices and so that workers would be producing more output for the increased wages. There would likewise be no unemployment problem and a substantial reduction in poverty if we could arrange for people to be employed more productively in a more organized economy. Such an economy would see to it that all people had jobs which they could perform, including older people, women, minorities, handicapped people, less-educated people, and others. There is obviously much waste in the crime field, not in the relatively trivial sense of police officers sleeping in squad cars, but in the more important sense of society's resources being wasted on prisons, police activities, and losses due to crime which could possibly be prevented through a more productive societal anti-crime program that provides more productive alternatives to crime-committing. Productivity in the civil liberties context especially refers to how to stimulate more freedom of speech and unconventional advocacy which will encourage the development and diffusion of innovative ideas. On the matter of health, a key problem is how to enable society to be more productive through the distribution of better health care in order to prevent and cure ailments that decrease societal productivity.

PUBLIC POLICY AND IMPROVING SOCIETAL PRODUCTIVITY

On the point that public policy is important to substantially improving societal productivity, even conservatives recognize that without an appropriate public policy environment, business would be unable to innovate and improve its ability to produce. Appropriate public policies from a conservative perspective might emphasize:

1. Police protection of property.
2. Enforcement of contract rights through the courts.
3. Maintenance of a money system.
4. Limited liability for corporations.
5. Protection of patents, copyrights, and trademarks.
6. Uniform standards concerning weights and measures.
7. Census and other statistical information.
8. Good roads, harbors, airports, and other infrastructure transportation facilities.
9. Protection of U.S. business activities abroad.
10. Loans to various business activities including housing, farming, exporting, and small business.
11. Special rates for business bulk mail.
12. Business bankruptcy proceedings which allow creditors to collect something and businesses to get a fresh start.
13. Special tax treatment in terms of business deductions.

14. Government purchases from business.
15. Government policy that benefits the economy as a whole including monetary and fiscal policy.

Appropriate public policy for stimulating societal productivity from a liberal perspective might emphasize the need for the government to:

1. Encourage the stimulus of international competition by refraining from adopting tariffs or other restrictions on international trade.
2. Play a greater role in long-term societal investment decisions in partnership with business and labor the way that Japanese government does.
3. Stimulate better relations between business and academia by subsidizing two-way exchanges of personnel, relevant conferences, mid-career training, and information systems whereby business is better informed of relevant developments in academia, and academics are better informed of business needs.
4. Help pay for the dismantling and replacement of obsolete industrial equipment.
5. Put more emphasis on positive incentives to get business to do socially desired activities instead of relying on regulation, litigation, and negative sanctions which generate negative relations between business and government.
6. Have a more vigorous policy of providing job security, retraining, and loans to start new business/jobs, so as to lessen the anxieties of American workers who feel threatened by technological innovation.
7. Actively pursue means for reducing arms expenditures between the U.S. and the Soviet Union in order to free billions of dollars in potential capital for implementing productive new ideas.

Instead of talking about public policy toward increased productivity from a conservative and liberal perspective, one could discuss the subject in terms of the key elements of productivity. Those elements are generally referred to as land, labor, capital, and management, and the organization of those elements. Land or natural resources is an important element, but it is not so subject to being improved through public policy, though the government can encourage conservation and the development of synthetic natural resources. On the matter of labor, some of the productivity improvement suggestions have included (1) the need for more education especially with regard to technical skills, (2) the need for more worker input into making management decisions, and (3) more sensitivity to worker morale among public employees. It is, however, often felt that workers can be more productive with good technology or capital equipment with which to work even if they lack strong motivation, as compared to strongly motivated workers who lack good technology.   To stimulate good technology, both liberals and conservatives endorse tax-break incentives.   Conservatives may, however, have more faith in across-the-board tax cuts like the 30 percent tax cut of the Reagan Administration.   Liberals tend to advocate ear-marked tax breaks which require specific productivity-increasing activities in order to earn the tax breaks.   A key problem in American technology may be the need for business to better implement innovative ideas.   The U.S. does seem to do well on creativity, especially in university research but may not be as efficient in implementing new ideas as the Japanese are.

Good management and leadership is important for choosing decisions that will maximize productivity.   There may be a need for better training of both public and private managers with regard to practical decision-making methods.   On the matter of stimulating more productive organization, that may mean stimulating more competition in the private sector, especially where business units can be relatively small and efficient.   The matter of having a more productive organization of labor, capital, and management often raises the issues of governmental versus private implementation.   Those issues in the past have taken the form of emotional disputes over socialism versus capitalism.   In recent years there has been a movement on the part of socialists to concede the need for more decentralization of decision-making, and to show more concern with increasing national income as a way of reducing poverty, rather than emphasizing income redistribution.   Likewise, there has been a movement on the part of capitalists to concede the need for more governmental coordination at least in the ways mentioned above, and to show more sensitivity to the need for equality of opportunity, with both coordination and equality directed toward increased productivity.

POLICY ANALYSIS AND PARTNERSHIP

In order to make these new productivity ideas more effective, it may also be necessary for the government to be more productive in choosing among alternative governmental programs in fields like housing, transportation, poverty, economic regulation, criminal justice, etc.   Doing so may require the development and implementation of methods for more meaningfully evaluating alternative programs and policies regarding their ability to achieve their goals effectively and efficiently.   Those methods are being increasingly developed in inter-disciplinary policy analysis programs and social science departments at universities across the country.   Government budget cutbacks have been a stimulus to that development in recent years, since budget cutbacks often necessitate an evaluation of existing programs to determine which ones should be cut.   Unfortunately, budget cutbacks have generated a negative atmosphere in policy evaluation emphasizing the need to reduce government output in light of reduced budgets. What may be needed in the public sector is a more positive attitude emphasizing the need to try to get more government output from those reduced budgets. In other words, a reduced budget can be viewed like a half-empty bottle, emphasizing what is missing and the need to cut back on what can be accomplished. In the alternative, it can be viewed like a half-full bottle, emphasizing what is there and the need to maximize what can be accomplished with the resources available.

In light of the above analysis, one can conclude that we may indeed be entering an area of new productivity involving (1) a partnership using tax reduction incentives to encourage productive behavior, (2) the private sector of business firms taking advantage of those incentives to increase their productivity, and (3) the not-for-profit sector including the academic world seeking to develop new knowledge relative to improved technologies, industrial psychology, public administration, and other relevant fields. That kind of productive partnership can mean increased societal benefits and reduced societal costs, which in turn can greatly expand the cornucopia of societal goodies, and lead to the next cycles of equalization and growth further down the line of American political history.

SOME CONCLUSIONS

"The New Productivity" in the context of this chapter refers to a set of ideas including:

1. Productivity should include all cost items, not just labor items.
2. Productivity should include both monetary and non-monetary benefits and costs.
3. Productivity should be thought of in a societal sense, not just in terms of individuals, business firms, government agencies, and other sub-societal units.
4. Productivity should be partly stimulated by a careful allocation of government subsidies and tax breaks.
5. The new productivity implies enabling people to be better off through an increase in the total national product, as contrasted to a re-distribution approach.
6. The new productivity is part of a cycle of alternating periods of growth and equality in American history.
7. The new productivity seeks to decrease inflation by providing more for one's money, and to decrease unemployment by enabling workers to produce and earn more in less hours, thereby making more jobs available.
8. The new productivity applies to stimulating productivity in all segments of society including public aid recipients, union members, white collar workers,

public sector employees, and corporate executives.

9. An emphasis on technological innovation and diffusion.
10. A motivation to increase the ability of the United States and other countries to compete well in international markets.
11. An emphasis on the development of new and useful ideas through university research.
12. An emphasis on developing better decision-making methods.
13. An emphasis on productivity in public policy-making so as to deal more effectively with social problems.
14. Productivity improvement as a bi-partisan and liberal-conservative joint activity.

PART TWO:

INCENTIVES FOR ACHIEVING

HIGHER GOALS

3

THE THEORY OF INCENTIVES

The purpose of this chapter is to bring out the usefulness of a benefit-cost perspective in generating ideas for encouraging socially desired behavior in a variety of different situations. The illustrative situations emphasized are tradition criminal behavior, business wrongdoing, and public officials who do not comply with relevant rules.

In this context, a benefit-cost perspective means viewing the behavior of individuals as being motivated by a desire to maximize their benefits minus costs. Those benefits and costs may be non-monetary as well as monetary. They may depend on the occurrence or nonoccurrence of some key event such as not getting caught when engaged in wrongdoing.

A benefit-cost perspective can be contrasted with a regulatory one, where socially desired behavior tends to be mandated by government orders, with an emphasis on administrative agencies and courts for enforcement, rather than the manipulation of incentives that make people want to comply. The perspective can also be contrasted with a rehabilitative one, where the emphasis is on the need to change the values of wrongdoers rather than to try to convince them they are acting contrary to their values, or better yet change the situation so their values cause them to want to behave in a socially desired way.

A benefit-cost perspective logically leads to saying that if an individual, group or society wants to encourage desired behavior, it should think in terms of (1) increasing the benefits of doing the right thing, (2) decreasing the costs of rightdoing, (3) decreasing the benefits of doing the wrong thing, (4) increasing the costs of wrongdoing, (5) increasing the probability of being detected and negatively sanctioned if one does the wrong thing, (6) increasing the probability of being discovered and positively rewarded if one does the right thing.

By thinking in those terms, one can often generate relevant ideas that might otherwise be overlooked, thought of less quickly, or thought of in a less organized way. One can also avoid ideas that may not be so relevant in the sense of not substantially affecting relevant benefits and costs.

There are a variety of ways of classifying the applications of benefit-cost analysis to encouraging socially desired behavior. One is in terms of the subject matters, including criminal behavior, business wrongdoing, and non-complying government officials. A second is in terms of the purpose, including having a deterrence problem for which suggested approaches are needed, or having suggested approaches for which a discussion of their effectiveness is needed. Another classification involves situations in which the benefits and costs of rightdoing are independent, rather than merely the complements of the benefits and costs of wrongdoing. The situation is complementary if the benefits of rightdoing mainly involve avoiding the costs of unsuccessful wrong-doing, and the costs of rightdoing mainly involve missing out on the benefits of successful wrongdoing.

TRADITIONAL CRIMINAL BEHAVIOR

Traditional criminal behavior provides a good example of the use of the general scheme to suggest and organize approaches for encouraging rightdoing. Since the benefits and costs of rightdoing are complementary here to those of wrongdoing, there are basically only three approaches rather than six. One can (1) increase the probability of being arrested, convicted, and imprisoned, (2) decrease the benefits from successful wrongdoing, and (3) increase the costs of unsuccessful wrongdoing. Each of those three general approaches generates two sets of specific approaches, a relatively conservative or prosecution-oriented set and relatively liberal or defendant-oriented set.

With regard to increasing the probability of being arrested, convicted, and imprisoned, a conservative orientation might emphasize reducing due process restrictions. Thus, one might argue in favor of making arrests, stops, or searches easier on the basis of mere suspicion rather than the higher standard of probable cause of wrongdoing. Likewise, convictions could be made easier by allowing evidence that is based on an illegal seizure, a confession without warnings, or questionable hearsay. Imprisonment upon conviction could be guaranteed by abolishing probation, suspended sentences, and community-based corrections. On the other hand, a more liberal orientation might emphasize increasing the probability of arrest, conviction, and imprisonment by developing more professionalism on the part of police, prosecutors, and other criminal justice personnel. That might include automatic suspensions of police officers who engage in illegal searches on the first occasion and automatic dismissals on the second occasion, especially if illegally seized evidence tends to decrease the chances of obtaining convictions.

With regard to decreasing the benefits of successful wrongdoing, a conservative orientation was reflected in the policies of the Law Enforcement Assistance Administration under Richard Velde. It emphasized what is sometimes referred to as hardening the targets. In the context of store robberies, this might mean developing systems of computerized credit via pushbutton telephones so as to minimize the cash carried in the cash register or by customers. It might also mean building bulletproof glass walls through which sales people transact business with customers in order to decrease the access of a would-be robber to whatever is in the cash register.

A more liberal orientation, although not necessarily mutually exclusive with target hardening, might emphasize decreasing the peer recognition benefits received by many successful store robbers. More specifically, the typical robber of certain types of stores or the typical mugger may tend to be someone between about age 15 and 25 who engages in such behavior at least partly because it brings him a kind of prestige among fellow teenage gang members. What may thus be helpful in decreasing the benefits of successfully knocking over a gas station or a mom and pop grocery store is to somehow change how prestige is obtained among such people. The Office of Economic Opportunity Community Action Program attempted to do that among the Black Peacestone Rangers on Chicago's south side in the 1960's by redirecting their aggressiveness onto rent strikes, consumer boycotts, election campaigning, and picketing government agencies. That type of anti-poverty gang work was, however, stopped largely as a result of the negative reaction of Senator McClellan's investigating committee which some people interpreted as being more bothered by that kind of community action than by the robbing and mugging it may have decreased.

On the matter of increasing the costs of unsuccessful wrongdoing, a conservative orientation might emphasize having longer prison sentences, more use of the death penalty, and more severe prison conditions. A liberal orientation, on the other hand might equally recognize the need for increasing the costs of noncompliance, but instead emphasize a different set of costs, namely, the opportunity costs one suffers as a result of being arrested, convicted, and imprisoned, or even just arrested. Middle class business executives do not rob stores or mug people in parks. They probably do not refrain from doing so because of fear of lengthy and severe imprisonment since they may be likely to receive probation if a first offense is involved. A more important reason for their restraint is probably the fear of losing the opportunities that are available to them in the middle class business world.

What may be needed is to give typical would-be store robbers more alternative opportunities that they risk losing if they are arrested for robbery or other crimes. This may require changing our educational institutions, neighborhood housing patterns, hiring procedures, and other socio-economic institutions in order to make those alternative opportunities more meaningful. If the teenage gang member did have more employment opportunities, he would not only suffer greater opportunity costs from getting arrested, but he also would receive less incremental benefits from an extra dollar obtained from a store robbery and he would have less need for anti-social peer recognition. Clearly, however, the opportunity costs approach to increasing the cost of noncompliance is a much larger social undertaking than the approach which emphasizes longer and more severe sentences.

One can see from the above example that a benefit-cost model can be suggestive of ideas that might otherwise be overlooked, less emphasized or be less clearly organized in the absence of such a model. Two caveats however are necessary. First, the model is no substitute for thinking and for understanding the subject matter since the model only provides general categories into which the specific approaches can be placed. Second, the general categories are logically deduced from the model, but the specific approaches reflect value judgments and empirical facts, not deductive logic. In other words, it logically follows that criminal behavior can be reduced by decreasing its benefits and increasing its costs, but target hardening and more severe sentences are not logically more meaningful than changing peer group values and emphasizing social opportunity costs.[1]

BUSINESS WRONGDOING

Business wrongdoing provides a good example of the use of the general scheme when one starts with a set of suggested solutions to a deterrence problem and then analyzes their effectiveness in light of the model. The sub-field of business pollution especially lends itself to that approach. A number of incentives have been unsystematically proposed for encouraging compliance

---

[1] On manipulating benefits and costs to decrease traditional criminal behavior, see Alfred Blumstein (ed.), *Deterrence and Incapacitation: Estimating the Effects of Criminal Sanctions on Crime Rates* (Washington, D.C.: National Academy of Sciences, 1978); Franklin Zimring and Gordon Hawkins, *Deterrence: The Legal Threat in Crime Control* (Chicago: University of Chicago Press, 1973); Jack Gibbs, *Crime, Punishment, and Deterrence* (New York: Elsevier, 1975); and Gary Becker and William Landes (eds.), *Essays in the Economics of Crime and Punishment* (New York: Columbia University Press, 1974). One should note that many anti-crime activities cannot be meaningfully categorized as liberal or conservative. For example, both ideological orientations endorse the idea of increased public participation to reduce crime occurrence, especially with regard to people being encouraged to report crimes, although not in a reckless manner in which noncrimes are frequently reported or people are falsely accused of wrongdoing.

with environmental standards. They include pollution taxes, injunctions, civil penalties, fines and jail sentences, tax rewards and subsidies, selective government buying, publicizing polluters, and conference persuasion.

The idea of a pollution tax is often mentioned as an especially effective incentive. Its effectiveness is largely due to the fact that it would directly increase the cost of noncompliance since the tax would be proportionate to the amount of pollution done by the business taxpayer. A common formula with regard to water pollution involves determining the total cost needed to keep a river segment at a given level of water quality, and then assessing each business firm on that river segment a portion of the total cost equal to the ratio between the firm's pollution and the total pollution in the river segment. By reducing its pollution, each firm thereby lowers its tax assessment, and that lowered assessment represents an increased benefit of compliance. The effectiveness of pollution taxes is also enhanced by virtue of automatic monitoring systems which are often a part of such proposals. Those systems increase the probability of the above costs and benefits occurring by making the assessment and collection of the tax or fee relatively automatic, as compared to proposals that require more active judicial action to enforce.

Proposed judicial action against polluters tends to be of three kinds, injunctions, civil penalties, and criminal sanctions. Like pollution taxes, the effectiveness of all three tends to depend on how they influence the costs of noncompliance (and the complementary benefits of compliance) and also the probability of those benefits and costs occurring. Injunctions to cease or suspend operating are the most costly to the polluting business firm, but they have the lowest probability of occurring. If an injunction is requested by a government agency, a private group, or an individual, then a judge would normally be quite reluctant to order a steel mill or other manufacturing establishment to shut down in view of the economic damage such a decision might mean to the employees, consumers, stockholders, and the community of the business firm. Civil damages are normally easier to obtain, especially if they are brought under a legal procedure that limits defenses available, such as in workmen's compensation actions. Civil damages are, however, normally less costly to the business firm than injunctions, unless a large class action is involved which decreases the probability of success. Criminal penalties in the pollution context are almost exclusively fines, rather than jail sentences. Such fines are easier to obtain than injunctions since they are not so economically disruptive to third parties, but they are more difficult to obtain than civil damages since they involve the more stringent due process standards associated with criminal law. Such fines also tend to be in the middle between injunctions and individual damages with regard to the costs to the polluting firm if imposed, although fines can range from low easily absorbed business expenses to assessments comparable to pollution taxes on up to the unlikely possibility of highly punitive fines.

Other proposals place emphasis on decreasing the money saved by non-compliance, and simultaneously decreasing the cost of compliance, rather than increasing the cost of noncompliance. Such proposals include tax rewards and subsidies. For example, installing equipment to decrease air, water, and other forms of pollution is normally an expensive cost of compliance. Government policy, though, can ease that cost by providing accelerated business deductions or credits for doing so, or the government can provide outright grants or no-interest, long term loans to further reduce the cost of compliance. Those benefits are likely to occur if such government programs are instituted. In other words, business firms are likely to make the changes if the government in effect makes them cost-free or combines a cost-reducing program with a program that provides enforced penalties for noncompliance. Large government subsidies to private industry, however, may not be so likely to get through the legislative process because of opposition from those who feel business should be doing more on its own, just as pollution taxes are not so likely to get through the legislative process because of opposition from those who feel they are too much of a burden on business.

Other proposals are likely to be less effective than the ones mentioned above because of their lack of influence on the key benefits, costs, and probabilities of the benefits and costs occurring. For example, selective government buying power in theory rewards non-polluters for complying (a benefit of compliance) and makes polluters suffer an opportunity cost (a cost of noncompliance). In practice, however, there are too many polluting firms that are not greatly affected by government purchases. Legislators and government purchasing agents also find it difficult to have pollution criteria override criteria relating to the cost and quality of the products purchased.

Likewise government publicizing of the names of polluters in order to get private consumers to engage in selective buying also has a low probability of the benefits and opportunity costs occurring, especially where the product is not a name brand or not a product bought by ultimate consumers. Conference persuasion is an especially ineffective approach although it was a major part of water pollution enforcement prior to 1972. Merely trying to convince business polluters of the social harm they are doing is not likely to encourage any legally desired behavior since it causes no increase in the costs of noncompliance, decrease in the benefits of non-compliance, or change in the probability of either of those costs or benefits occurring.

Although pollution is a good example to illustrate the model applied to business wrongdoing, it can also be applied to other forms of business regulation such as consumer fraud, worker safety, product safety, anti-trust practices, unfair management or union practices, stock manipulation and landlord abuses.[2]

NONCOMPLYING PUBLIC OFFICIALS

Noncompliance by public officials can take a variety of forms to which the model can be applied to suggest ideas for encouraging legally desired behavior. A good example where all six elements in the model are applicable is the situation of encouraging criminal court personnel (especially prosecutors and assistant state's attorneys) to make time-saving decisions that conclude trials quickly, rather than time-lengthening decisions that involve pospone-ments and delay. To increase the benefits of doing the right thing, the system can reward assistant state's attorneys with salary increases and promotions for reducing the average time consumption per case. To decrease the costs of doing the right thing, one could establish a computerized system that informs assistant state's attorneys concerning actual and predicted times at various stages for all cases to minimize the trouble to the attorneys to keep track of cases. They could also be provided with more investigative and preparation resources.

To decrease the benefits from doing the wrong thing, the system can provide for more release of defendants from jail prior to trial so that lengthening the pre-trial time will not make the jailed defendants more vulnerable to pleading guilty. By having so many defendants in jail awaiting trial, the prosecutor is benefited by delay since delay does increase the willingness of such defendants to plead guilty in return for probation or a sentence equal to the time they have already served awaiting trial, rather than wait longer for a trial. To increase the costs from doing the wrong thing, speedy trial rules can be adopted which provide for the absolute discharge of defendants whose cases extend beyond the time limits through no fault of their own. This is a heavier cost than merely releasing the defendant from pretrial detention since an absolute discharge means the defendant cannot be later tried for the incident for which he or she was being held.

To increase the probability of being detected and negatively sanctioned for delaying cases, the speedy trial rules can allow fewer exceptions such as suspending their application "for good cause" or "exceptional circumstances." Those exceptions decrease the probability that the penalty costs will be imposed. To increase the probability of being discovered and positively

---

[2]On manipulating benefits and costs to decrease business wrongdoing, see Frank Grad, George Rathjens, and Albert Rosenthal, *Environmental Control: Priorities, Policies, and the Law* (New York: Columbia University Press, 1971); William Baumol and Wallace Oates, *The Theory of Environmental Policy* (Englewood Cliffs, N.J.: Prentice-Hall, 1975); and Richard Posner, *Economic Analysis of Law* (Boston: Little, Brown, 1977).

rewarded if one does the right thing, the same computerized system that easily informs assistant state's attorneys what cases are running behind can also inform the head prosecutor which assistants are doing an especially good job so they will be more likely to receive the salary increases and promotions mentioned above.

On a more general level, one could talk about increasing the compliance of governmental administrators to judicial precedents and legislative statutes. Doing so might involve (1) increasing the probability of being caught and sanctioned, (2) increasing the severity of the sanctions, and (3) decreasing the benefits of continuing the former non-complying behavior. The probability of being caught and sanctioned can be increased by encouraging citizen suits as is done to some extent in the fields of environmental protection and equal employment partly to serve as a check on government agencies in those fields. Whistle-blowers reporting wrongdoing within government can also be protected by civil service rules. Catching wrongdoers is also increased if wrongdoing is clearly defined, as is increasingly occurring in the field of school desegregation by way of HEW guidelines.

The severity of the sanctions to obtain administrative compliance can include reprimands which may not be much of a cost to the average adminis- trator, but can be significant when directed by a court toward an agency lawyer. On a higher level of severity is the sanction of decreasing or blocking appropriations, as has sometimes been done by courts when dealing with racially discriminatory police examination procedures or public housing site selection. An especially severe sanction might be to hold an administrator in contempt of court subject to a jail sentence, as has occurred with public aid administrators who do not comply with maximum waiting periods for processing public aid cases. Such contempt sanctions, though, are less effective against government union officials who lead strikes contrary to federal or state law.

Decreasing the benefits of continuing the former non-complying behavior may require changing the approval of the constituents of the non-complying public official. For example, if the official refuses to comply with desegregation orders because he perceives that is what his or her constituents want, those non-complying benefits can be decreased by convincing local business interests how detrimental such non-compliance might be to local business expansion. Likewise, if an official refuses to comply because he or she perceives non-compliance is what immediate superiors or peers want, then the system should seek to win over those supportive elements. An example is when the Supreme Court or the Department of Justice seems to be talking to police chiefs in order to change police behavior with regard to interrogations and searches. A key benefit from non-compliance is the satisfaction one receives from doing things in their customary way. Courts and legislatures should therefore emphasize successive incremental changes as has been done in increasingly providing counsel for the poor in criminal cases starting with capital punishment cases in the 1930's, some felony cases in the 40's and 50's, the rest of the felony cases in the 60's, and misdemeanor cases in the 70's.

Numerous other applications of the model could be applied to non-complying public officials in the judicial, administrative, or legislative realm. For example, one could talk about how to encourage judges to be more sensitive to avoiding errors of holding defendants in jail who would appear for trial if released, as contrasted to errors of releasing defendants who might not appear. A similar sensitivity problem may exist (1) at the police arrest stage, (2) the decision to incarcerate a convicted defendant or rely on community-based probation, and (3) the decision to release on parole. The model can also be applied to discussing how to obtain greater compliance on the part of administrators like school board officials with regard to court desegregation, school prayers, and disciplinary procedures. The model can also be applied to legislators with regard to discouraging corrupt behavior. That type of application may involve a combination of proposals directed simultaneously at legislators, business firms, and bribe-offering individuals, thereby combining all three types of applications dealt with in this chapter.[3]

LIMITING ONE'S OPTIONS

The previous analysis contains useful ideas for using positive and negative incentives to encourage individuals to make the right choice when faced with a choice between socially desired and socially undesired behavior. That analysis should, however, be carried an important step further to at least mention the meaningfulness of trying to limit the options for would-be wrongdoers so they do not have such a choice.

As a specific example, we could use the problem of socially wasteful littering of bottles and cans. The basic choice is to litter or not to litter. We can try to discourage littering by placing penalties on doing so. That does not seem to be very effective because neither the wrongdoers nor those responsible for enforcing the rules take littering very seriously. A $100 fine for littering is therefore not so likely to be a deterrent and is seldom enforced. The enforcement could be increased by having special enforcement units in which promotions and other rewards are allocated strictly on the basis of anti-littering

---

[3]On manipulating benefits and costs to decrease noncomplying public officials, see Harrell Rodgers and Charles Bullock, *Law and Social Change: Civil Rights Laws and Their Consequences* (New York: McGraw-Hill, 1972); Samuel Krislov and Malcolm Feeley, *Compliance and the Law* (Beverly Hills, Calif.: Sage, 1970); and S. Nagel and Marian Neef, *Decision Theory and the Legal Process* (Lexington, Mass.: Lexington-Heath, 1979).

enforcement. This is in contrast to having the enforcement by regular police who are likely to consider anti-littering to be almost beneath their dignity in comparison with more serious crimes. Special enforcement units, though, are not likely to be adopted because the policy-makers also do not take littering that seriously. The individual littering case is not a serious matter. The sum total of all littering, however, does add up to millions of dollars in public clean-up expense.

We could also try to discourage littering or encourage non-littering by offering rewards for turning in used bottles and cans. That is probably a more effective approach than punishments, as rewards often are. One problem, however, is that the money received may have to be quite substantial in order to make the program fully effective. That might require a large deposit on each bottle, which could be the equivalent of an undesirable regressive tax on lower-income people. It can also be politically unpopular to try to pass legislation that requires large deposits. The bottle manufacturers are often able to defeat such legislation because of the burden the deposits might have on the public. An alternative would be to require the manufacturers to give rewards or bounties for returned bottles and cans without a deposit. They would fight that even more strenuously. They would fight less strenuously if the rewards came out of taxes, but that would possibly be even more politically unpopular than deposits.

As a third sometimes-mentioned alternative to the littering problem, one could simply prohibit the manufacturing of certain containers that are not bio-degradable, and that are especially responsible for expensive littering. If such a solution were technologically and politically possible, it would solve that kind of littering problem. The would-be wrongdoer would no longer be faced with the choice of whether to throw the bottle by the roadside, which is socially undesirable, or to put it in a wastebasket or return it to the grocery store, which is socially desirable. That choice would no longer exist if those bottles no longer exist. It is conceivable that beer bottles, for example, could some day be replaced by bio-degradable plastic containers similar to milk cartons that could be sealed so as to keep the beer from going flat. The development of such a container would be encouraged by prohibiting the present containers or by offering government subsidies for the development of new containers. The new containers would be especially likely to be adopted if they are less expensive for the manufacturers to make than the old containers. The important point from the perspective of encouraging socially desired behavior is not the technology of beer bottles or the politics involved in banning them. The important point is that if a technologically and politically meaningful way of eliminating a wrongdoing/rightdoing choice can be adopted, then it probably should be in preference to the punishments/rewards or incentives approach, although they are not mutually exclusive for different aspects of the same problem.

Another possibly good example of the options-limiting approach versus the incentives approach to encouraging socially desired behavior is in the field of gun control. People who advocate gun control think its adoption will result in a reduction of serious crimes. They generally do not link gun control to a rewards/punishments framework. One could, however, say that by not having access to a gun, the amount of crime benefits achievable in a robbery are likely to be less than with a gun. Bank robbers normally always have guns, and bank robbery is probably the highest form of robbery in terms of the amount of money at stake. Muggers are less likely to have guns, and mugging is probably the lowest form of robbery. Even a mugger is more likely to be successful with a gun than with a knife, club, or other weapon. The main way in which effective gun control is likely to reduce crime, though, is by decreasing the options of would-be criminals who would not think of engaging in certain kinds of crime without a gun. Effective gun control in this context refers to gun control that does substantially decrease the availability of guns to would-be criminals. One could also argue in favor of gun control by saying it eliminates the decision-choice of whether or not to shoot one's spouse, friend, or other antagonist in an emotional dispute. The choice may then become one of whether or not to punch the person which is generally a much less serious crime.

If one is going to talk about limiting the options of would-be wrongdoers, that can be approached in at least two ways. One way is to talk about making the wrongdoing decision physically impossible, or quite difficult, which is the case if there are no beer bottles available to be littered, or guns readily available to be used in robberies or emotional disputes. A second way is to talk about making the wrongdoing decision psychologically impossible or quite difficult to conceive. The main reason the average person never shoots anybody is not because guns are so unavailable. Rather, it is because the average person has been so socialized against deliberately killing other people not in self-defense that doing so is virtually an unthinkable alternative. What this analysis gets back to is the importance of a well-socialized conscience. Many people downplay the idea of a conscience on the grounds that everyone has his or her price such that for the right amount of money, they would even kill someone. If, however, the right price is a totally unfeasible figure, like $10,000,000, then for all practical purposes the alternative is unfeasible, which is like saying it is unthinkable.

CONCLUSIONS ON ENCOURAGING SOCIALLY DESIRED BEHAVIOR

From this analysis, one can see that a benefit-cost perspective may be useful for generating, organizing, and analyzing ideas for encouraging socially desired behavior. The perspective merely involves viewing the behavior of individuals as being motivated by a desire to maximize their benefits minus costs of both a monetary and non-monetary nature, taking into consideration the probability of the occurrence of events on which these benefits and costs depend. From that perspective, one can predict that people will change their behavior if the perceived expected benefits minus costs become greater for the new over the old behavior. From that perspective, one can prescribe that if society or public policymakers want to encourage socially desired behavior, they should arrange for such behavior to have a higher perceived expected value than the undesired behavior. What may be needed now are more researchers and practitioners to apply this kind of perspective to a variety of behaviors that are considered undesirable in order to encourage more socially desired behavior.

One can conclude this analysis by thinking of encouraging socially desired behavior as being like an obstacle course where society wants to place barriers in the way of people making wrong choices and facilitators in the direction of people making the right choices. The analysis brings out three general kinds of barriers/facilitators. First in time is to socialize children into treating various kinds of wrongdoing as so unthinkable that it makes no difference whether engaging in the wrongdoing behavior is physically possible, and it also makes no difference what the immediate rewards and punishments are. Second in time is to decrease the physical possibility of wrongdoing behavior to provide a barrier to those who have not previously been well socialized. Third in time is to provide punishments for wrongdoing and rewards for rightdoing with regard to those kinds of decisions that have not been already well handled by the socialization process or the structuring of the environment so as to limit the options. In a society that knows what kind of wrongdoing it wants to discourage and what kind of rightdoing it wants to encourage, those three approaches should be capable of achieving those goals when meaningfully implemented.[4]

---

[4]A leading exponent of the general theory of making wrongdoing physically difficult is C. Ray Jeffrey, *Crime Prevention Through Environmental Design* (Beverly Hills, Calif.: Sage, 1977), although he is also concerned with reduction in crime benefits by hardening the targets of criminal behavior. Leading exponents of the general theory of socialization of legal norms are June Tapp and Felice Levine (eds.), *Law, Justice, and the Individual in Society: Psychological and Legal Issues* (New York: Holt, Rinehart & Winston, 1977).

4

APPLICATIONS TO ALL FIELDS OF PUBLIC POLICY

Public policy is often defined in a highly general way that makes it virtually synonymous with government decisions or with what government does. Sometimes public policy is defined in terms of the results of those decisions, thereby emphasizing the allocations of things of value which the government makes, or who gets what as a result of government decisions. The purpose of this chapter is to view public policy not in terms of its form or its effects, but more in terms of its potential. In that sense, public policy can be viewed as incentives for encouraging socially desired behavior. In the context of developing countries, public policy can be viewed as incentives for societal improvement.

An appropriate way to show the potential incentives role of public policy is to go through a varied list of social problems and to discuss each one in terms of public policy incentives for lessening the social problems. The list should be chosen in a roughly random way so as not to appear to be slanted in the direction of making the potential of public policy look good. The *Encyclopedia of Policy Studies* has chapters on 22 specific policy problems, divided into five sections dealing with (1) political problems, (2) economic problems, (3) sociology-psychology problems, (4) urban-regional planning problems, and (5) natural science-engineering problems. These problems exist in both developed and developing areas, although not necessarily in the same form. We can take two problems from each section to illustrate public policy as incentives for societal development or for lessening social problems.[1]

Before getting into the specific social problems, one should note that public policy has the potential for encouraging socially desired behavior by working through five different related approaches. They are:

1. Increasing the benefits of doing right.
2. Decreasing the costs of doing right.
3. Increasing the costs of doing wrong.
4. Decreasing the benefits of doing wrong.
5. Increasing the probability that the benefits and costs will occur.

That checklist logically leads to such questions as who are the doers, and what benefits and costs are involved. The answers depend on the specific subject matters to which we now turn.[2]

PROBLEMS WITH A POLITICAL SCIENCE EMPHASIS

Perhaps the most basic problem for a developing country or area is to encourage good government in the sense of competent, dedicated people and in the sense of stimulating innovative, useful ideas for dealing with social problems. Using the five-part checklist, public policy can encourage competency and diversity by such means as:

1. Increasing the compensation of meritorious government workers.
2. Decreasing the communication costs of people with innovative ideas by providing them with access to mass media.
3. Increasing the possibility of removal or demotion from government for those who do not satisfy competency standards.
4. Confiscating the gains of people in government who corruptly benefit from

---

[1] Public policy evaluation in the context of developing areas is discussed in Howard Freeman, Peter Rossi, and Sonia Wright, *Evaluating Social Projects in Developing Countries* (Paris, France: Organization for Economic Cooperation and Development, 1980); I. Little and J. Mirries, *Project Appraisal and Planning for Developing Countries* (New York: Basic Books, 1974); and Hugh Schwartz and Richard Berney (eds.), *Social and Economic Dimensions of Project Evaluation* (Washington, D.C.: Inter-American Development Bank, 1977).

[2] For other material dealing with public policy from an incentives perspective, see Alfred Blumstein (ed.), *Deterrence and Incapacitation: Estimating the Effects of Criminal Sanctions on Crime Rates* (Washington, D.C.: National Academy of Sciences, 1978); Barry Mitnick, *The Political Economy of Regulation* (New York: Columbia University Press, 1980); Louis Tornatzky et al., *Innovation and Social Processes: National Experiment in Implementing Social Technology* (Elmsford, N.Y.: Pergamon, 1980); William Hamilton, Larry Ledebur, and Deborah Matz, *Industrial Incentives: Public Promotion of Private Enterprise* (Washington, D.C.: Aslan Press, 1984); S. Nagel, "Using Positive and Negative Incentives" in *Public Policy: Goals, Means, and Methods* (New York: St. Martin's, 1984).

wrongdoing.

5. Decreasing the risks of whistle blowers who report wrongdoing and providing bonuses for those who report rightdoing.

The realm of political science is sometimes divided into internal and external government problems. External or foreign policy tends to be dominated by problems of how to encourage peaceful interaction on the part of other countries especially neighboring countries. Relevant public policy incentives in that regard might include:

1. Increasing the benefits of mutual trade by developing agreements to benefit from each others specialties.
2. Decreasing the costs of mutual trade by lowering barriers in the form of tariffs, quotas, complicated customs arrangements, and other restrictions.
3. Increasing the cost of wrongdoing by developing internationally imposed penalties.
4. Decreasing the benefits of wrongdoing by emphasizing that aggressive interaction will result in the acquisition of nothing of value by virtue of policies that provide for destruction of oil wells and other resources if necessary.
5. Detection systems to determine that wrongdoing is occurring or is being prepared for.

PROBLEMS WITH AN ECONOMICS EMPHASIS

At the macro-economics level, public policy is primarily concerned with decreasing unemployment and inflation, or increasing employment opportunities and price stability. Devices such as manipulation of the money supply or taxing-spending differences are not so meaningful if unemployment and inflation are increasing simultaneously. An economy can also become distorted by trying to order business firms not to justifiably raise prices or by trying to order unemployed workers into certain jobs. An incentives approach might include such devices as:

1. Tax incentives to business firms and labor unions for keeping prices and wages down. Also monetary incentives to employers to hire the unemployed and monetary incentives to the unemployed to accept training and jobs.
2. Decreasing the costs of finding jobs and workers through better information systems.
3. Increasing the costs of violating price-wage guidelines and work incentives by withdrawing benefits and (in rare cases) by fines and other negative

penalties.
4. Confiscating the benefits of price-wage violations by special taxes on the gains.
5. More accurate information on prices, wages, and unemployment in order to allocate the benefits and costs more effectively.

At the micro-economics level, public policy is concerned with relations between business and consumers, labor, and other business firms. Those subjects have been traditionally dealt with through economic regulation as manifested in such U.S. government agencies as the Federal Trade Commission, the National Labor Relations Board, and the Anti-Trust Division of the Department of Justice. An incentives approach might be substantially more effective in either a developed country or a developing country, including such devices as:

1. Providing tax incentives to business firms to develop better relations with consumers, labor, and other businesses.
2. Decreasing the costs of such activities by providing appropriate government subsidies.
3. Increasing the penalties where the lives or safety of people is jeopardized,as with dangerous products and working conditions.
4. Confiscating the gains that come from violating guidelines concerning consumer protection, worker protection, and the protection of a competitive environment.
5. Hotline systems for facilitating the reporting of wrongdoing, and award systems for encouraging the reporting of rightdoing.

PROBLEMS WITH A SOCIOLOGY-PSYCHOLOGY EMPHASIS

In the realm of social problems, poverty may be the most serious one for both developing and developed countries. That problem, however, is closely related to the macro-economic problem of providing job opportunities briefly discussed above. Other key social problems include crime and ethnic group relations. On the matter of crime, the incentives approach might involve doing things like the following.

1. The main benefit of complying with the law should be that doing so gives one access to opportunities that are cut off to law violators. That means legitimate career opportunities must be provided to those who would otherwise turn to crime.
2. One cost of doing right may be a loss of prestige among youthful gang members who consider criminal behavior an indicator of toughness. There

is a need for working to redirect such peer group values so that toughness can be displayed in more constructive ways.

3. The costs of doing wrong can include negative incentives of longer prison sentences, but it may be more meaningful to emphasize the withdrawal of career opportunities which would otherwise be present.
4. Provisions should be made for facilitating the confiscating of the property gains of criminal wrongdoing, and decreasing the vulnerability of the targets of crime to lessen the benefits obtained.
5. The probability of arrest and conviction can be increased partly through more professionalism among law enforcement personnel.

On the matter of relations among races, religions, and other ethnic groups, the incentives approach can encourage more equitable treatment on the basis of individual merit through such means as:

1. Tax incentives to employers, schools, landlords, and others who deal with racial minorities to more actively seek out well-qualified minority members.
2. Decreasing the costs of such affirmative action by having better information systems directed toward both the suppliers of opportunities and toward the minority members who are interested in advancing themselves.
3. Increased penalties for racial discrimination including the publicizing of the convicted discriminator as a deterrence to others.
4. Confiscating gains from discriminating in the payment of wages or the provision of housing.
5. Periodic reporting of affirmative action activities so that benefits and penalties can be appropriately allocated.

PROBLEMS WITH AN URBAN-REGIONAL PLANNING EMPHASIS

The social problems most closely associated with urban-regional planning are housing and environmental protection. The housing field is one of inadequate provision of decent housing for the poor and the lower middle class. Incentives to lessen that social problem might include:

1. Tax incentives and subsidies to building contractors to construct more housing, especially for low income tenants or owners. On the demand rather than supply side, there may be a need for rent supplements to enable low income tenants to afford what is available.
2. One of the costs of renting to poor people may be the extra maintenance expense which could be reduced by educating tenants in property maintenance and by giving them more of a stake in the housing through equity arrangements, or at least representation in the decision-making.

3. Increasing the costs of wrongdoing could include penalties imposed on landlords who do not provide housing that satisfies minimum decency levels, and also penalties imposed on tenants who are destructive or negligent.
4   Decreasing the benefits which landlords receive who illegally provide substandard housing by having them pay rebates, or having their property subject to attachment to cover the benefits they have wrongfully received.
5. Encouraging tenants to report both good and bad behavior on the part of landlords, and encouraging tenants to report vandalism on the part of fellow tenants and others.

As for environmental protection, that is an area in which there has been substantial experimentation with a variety of incentives. They include:

1. Providing tax incentives designed to encourage adopting pollution-reduction devices by business firms and municipal agencies. Tax incentives can include pollution taxes which are levied in proportion to the amount of polluting done.
2. Subsidies designed to reduce the cost of expensive retro-fitting and new facilities.
3. Penalties for wrongdoing other than fines, such as publicizing brand-name wrongdoers, facilitating damage suits by people suffering environmental injuries, the withdrawal of benefits, and (as a last resort) injunctions that close polluting firms.
4. Confiscating the profits made as a result of not introducing required pollution controls.
5. Better pollution monitoring systems and bounties for reporting pollution violations, plus enforcement agencies that do nothing but pollution enforcement.

PROBLEMS WITH A NATURAL SCIENCE OR ENGINEERING EMPHASIS

A key problem among engineering-related problems is how to encourage the development of new energy sources and the conservation of existing energy. Relevant incentives include:

1. Increasing the benefits of doing right by tax reductions for adopting energy saving devices like improved insulation, special thermostats, and coal burning furnaces. Offering government purchase guarantees as an incentive to develop a feasible electric car.
2. Decreasing costs of doing right by providing subsidies to municipal governments in order to reduce their costs of energy-relevant enforcement

of housing and building codes.

3. Increasing the costs of doing wrong by publicizing the gasoline consumption qualities of different cars. Also charging vehicle taxes in proportion to gasoline consumption.
4. Decreasing the prestige benefits of driving gas guzzling cars by making small car driving a manifestation of patriotism.
5. Compiling data on the characteristics of alternative energy sources and energy saving devices so as to allocate better the rewards, penalties, and other incentives.

Energy policy is mainly a physical science problem. The key biological science problem in public policy is how to encourage better health care on the part of both providers and recipients. This is an especially important problem in developing societies where there is generally more concern for biological survival than in more developed societies. Relevant incentives might include:

1. Health-care providers can be subsidized to provide low-cost care on a mass basis. Recipients can be given cash incentives to submit to vaccinations and birth control.
2. The cost to health-care insurers can be reduced per insured person by requiring universal public participation.
3. The cost of wrongdoing can be increased by requiring higher health-care insurance premiums for people who are at fault in having bad health records such as smokers or those who have excessive cholesterol rates.
4. Sometimes infant formulas are diluted in developing countries in order to make the formula go further. That would not be a benefit if there were no need for it as a result of adequate provision of infant milk and food supplements.
5. There is a need for better record-keeping concerning the quantity, quality, and prices of the health-care providers and concerning the health of individuals so that public policy can better target the positive and negative incentives.

The problem of encouraging technological innovation is an especially important problem because technological innovation has large multiplier effects by virtue of its spillover into providing job opportunities, better products and work places, less expensive housing, anti-pollution devices, and other high technology ways of dealing with social problems. Applying the checklist here might involve noting:

1. Government subsidies may be especially important for technological innovation because private capital may not be available in sufficient

quantities and may not be so willing to wait for risky returns.

2. There are wasteful costs in re-inventing the wheel, which means public policy should strive to inform those who can benefit from new technologies as to what is available.

3. Penalties can be imposed upon firms that do not modernize such as automobile manufacturers or steel mills. The penalties can at least consist of not being provided with bail-out money or tariffs if they are threatened by more modern competition.

4. As for decreasing the benefits of doing wrong by not adopting new innovations, there are few benefits with the exception of not having to adapt or retool.

5. There is a need for more coordination in the allocation of subsidy benefits and tax incentives for technological innovation which may necessitate having a coordinating agency like the Japanese Ministry for International Trade and Investment.

SOME CONCLUSIONS

The incentives approach to public policy should be supplemented by a structures approach whereby public policy is viewed as also providing social structures that encourage socially desired behavior. For example, one can decrease crime through the above-mentioned incentives which cause people to choose right from wrong when faced with a decision dilemma. It would, however, be better to structure social relations so that people are seldom faced with such decision dilemmas. Gun control is an example of such structuring. If gun control does effectively remove a large quantity of guns from circulation, then the likelihood is less that an individual will be faced with deciding whether or not to shoot someone. On a broader level of structuring, one might note that if people have been socialized into considering killing other people as a virtually unthinkable activity, then they will also seldom, if ever, face a decision dilemma of whether or not to kill someone. It would not enter their minds to even entertain the dilemma, let alone decide in favor of the wrongdoing position. One can also appropriately structure relations in dealing with other social problems, as well as crime.

The incentives approach to public policy is as applicable to a socialist government as to a capitalist government. The key difference is that under a socialist government, the incentives are generally directed toward government managers rather than private entrepreneurs. In the field of environmental protection for example, the Soviet Union is just as confronted with how to get factory managers to adopt anti-pollution devices as is the United States. Under either system, factory managers have been traditionally rewarded in terms of the demand for their products and the lowness of their production costs.

Adopting anti-pollution devices does not increase demand/income or reduce expenses. In fact, it increases expenses. Thus either economic system requires public policy incentives to get relevant decision makers to operate contrary to the traditional reward system by adopting expensive anti-pollution equipment.

The incentives approach is applicable to developing areas in either developing or developed countries. The essence of the incentives approach is manipulating the benefits and costs of rightdoing and wrongdoing in order to encourage socially desired behavior. That includes the kinds of changes that are needed in order to desirably develop a developing area. The development of such areas may especially mean providing incentives for internal or external capital and innovators. It also generally or often means providing for good government, foreign policy, unemployment/inflation, economic regulation, crime control, ethnic relations, housing, environmental protection, and energy.

If public policy is important in providing these kinds of developmental incentives, then public policy studies is also important. Policy studies is largely the study of how to make public policy more effective and efficient. Thus the question of how can policy studies be useful to developing areas is closely related to questions of how can public policy be useful. One can perhaps conclude that policy studies can be most useful by further exploring the ways in which public policy can provide incentives for societal development and improvement.

PART THREE:

IMPROVING CONSTITUTIONAL

EFFECTIVENESS

5

BASIC HUMAN RIGHTS

.

The purpose of this chapter is to describe some of the consequences to a society of providing various controversial basic legal rights.

BASIC CONCEPTS

A right can be defined as (1) a behavior which a society tolerates a person to engage in without subjecting him to an injunction or penalty for doing so, or a (2) benefit which a society affirmatively confers upon a person that cannot be withdrawn unless there is a change in the societal rules. Rights can thus be "tolerated rights" which a society allows or affirmative rights which relate to benefits that a society grants.

Rights can also be controversial or non-controversial depending on whether their exercise arouses much or little dissension within the society. Thus, the tolerated right to breathe is generally non-controversial but the tolerated right to advocate radical ideas often raises controversy. Likewise, the affirmative right to receive mail from the post office is generally non-controversial, but the affirmative right to receive a minimum income as provided for in welfare legislation often raises controversy.

Rights can be legal or human rights. Legal ones are found in statements promulgated by government bodies with regard to how people (including government officials) ought to behave toward each other or be subject to sanctions. These statements manifest themselves in constitutions, statutes, judicial precedents, or in administrative regulations or a adjudications. Human rights represent statements similar in content to those found in legal rights but which philosophers find present in religious literature, in the inherent nature of man, or in an inductive analysis of the legal rights present in a variety of societies. This chapter will only explicitly deal with the consequences of legal rights, although what is said is applicable to human rights to the extent they overlap in content.

Legal rights can be basic or non-basic. Basic legal rights are those embodied in a society's governmental constitution or in statutes that can be supplemented although they are unlikely to be repealed. This chapter will emphasize the consequences of controversial basic legal rights in an American context although what is said is generally applicable to other societies as well.[1] The rights that will be particularly discussed are those that relate to (1) freedom of speech and religion, (2) equality of treatment, (3) safeguarding the innocent from conviction and harassment, and (4) the right to basic economic security. The consequences to be discussed are not so much the effects on the individuals who exercise these rights, but rather the effects on the total society. Available behavioral science or empirical research relating to these effects will be cited wherever appropriate.[2]

FREEDOM OF SPEECH AND RELIGION

The right of free speech in the American context can be defined as allowing, without penalty, both popular and unpopular viewpoints to be advocated or communicated in any media of communication so long as the communication does not involve hard-core pornography, untruthful defamation, obtaining money under false pretenses, invasion of privacy, or the likely promotion of bodily injury. In the United States this is a tolerated right rather than an affirmative right in that it does not include providing free access to the communication media with the exception of the narrow FCC equal-time rules.

What are the effects on a total society of providing the right of free speech? There are three basic effects which philosophers have tended to emphasize.[3]

---

[1]For empirical studies of basic legal rights in a non-American context see David Bayley, *Public Liberties in the United States* (Chicago: Rand McNally, 1964); and references under Constitutional Law in Charles Szladits, *A Bibliography on Foreign and Comparative Law Books and Articles in English* (Dobbs Ferry, N.Y.: Oceana Publishers, 1955 to present).

[2]Behavioral materials that deal with the social consequences of general legal rights include Stephen Wasby, *The Impact of the United States Supreme Court: Some Perspectives* (Homewood, Ill.: Dorsey Press, 1970); Theodore Becker, *The Impact of Supreme Court Decisions: Empirical Studies* (New York: Oxford, 1969); and James Levine, "Methodological Concerns in Studying Supreme Court Efficacy," 4 *Law and Society Review* 583-611 (1970).

[3]For a summary and bibliography of the philosophical, non-behavioral aspects of free speech see Thomas Emerson et al., *Political and Civil Rights in the United States 1-28* (Boston: Little, Brown, 1967), and the 1969 Supplement. The rest of Emerson's Volume 1 clarifies what free speech covers.

First, in matters of empirical science, free speech allows the truth to have a better chance of getting accepted. The suppression of Galileo and his Copernican observation that the earth revolves around the sun rather than vice versa is a case in point.

Second, in matters of normative policy, free speech allows the most effective means toward given ends to have a better chance of getting accepted. For example, suppression of the slavery abolitionists delayed the improved labor productivity per labor expense and the improved capital equipment which free labor promoted.

Third, free speech provides a check on corrupt and inefficient leadership and administrative personnel. Even dictatorships recognize the value of encouraging critics of administrative inefficiency even though they do not encourage criticism of top national officials or fundamental government policy.

Free speech is indirectly responsible for higher standards of living to the extent that free speech promotes scientic discovery and dissemination more effective means toward given societal goals, and more efficient governmental personnel. This partly explains why Table 5-1 shows a positive correlation between the level of free speech permissiveness and the level of modernity in the 84-country sample used.[4] Some of the positive correlation is also due to the reciprocal fact that higher standards of living create a more tolerant middle class which allows still more freedom of speech.

Some critics of free speech argue that it leads to political instability and revolution. The empirical data tend to show just the opposite relation. Table 5-2 shows a positive correlation between being a country that has a permissive free speech policy and being a country that has a high degree of stability. This relation is partly attributable to the fact that free speech facilitates non-violent change, particularly by providing more peaceful outlets through which potential revolutionaries can make themselves heard and win converts without resorting to revolution. The positive relation between free speech and non-violent change is also partly attributable to the fact that free speech and non-violent change are partly co-effects of having a large tolerant middle-class. The correlation between permissiveness and stability is, however, not as high as the correlation between permissiveness and modernity.

Freedom of religion is a legal right that has two aspects. One aspect says

---

[4]The free speech, modernity,and political stability data come from Ivo Feierband and R. Feierband, "The Relationship of Systematic Frustration, Political Coercion, International Tension, and Political Instability: A Cross-National Study" (Paper presented at the annual meeting of the American Psychological Association, 1966). See their paper for further details on the criteria for categorizing the countries. Other empirical studies in the free speech area include James Levine, "The Bookseller and the Law of Obscenity: Toward an Empirical Theory of Free Expression" (Northwestern University Ph.D. Dissertation, 1967); and Samuel Stouffer, *Communism, Conformity, and Civil Liberties* (New York: Doubleday, 1955).

TABLE 5-1. RELATIONS BETWEEN PERMISSIVENESS AND MODERNITY

Level of Modernity	Level of Permissiveness			TOTAL
	COERCIVE	MIDLEVEL PERMISSIVE	PERMISSIVE	
Modern	Argentina, East Germany, Czechoslovakia, USSR **(4)**	Austria, France **(2)**	Australia, Canada, Belgium, Denmark, Finland, Iceland, Ireland, Israel, Luxembourg, Netherlands, New Zealand, Norway, Sweden, Switzerland, United Kingdom, United States, Uruguay, West Germany **(18)**	24
Transitional	Albania, Bulgaria, Cuba, Dominican Rep., Egypt, Hungary, Korea, Nicaragua, Paraguay, Poland, Portugal, Romania, Spain, Union S. Africa, Venezuela, Yugoslavia **(16)**	Brazil, Ceylon, Chile, Colombia, Cyprus, Ecuador, El Salvador, Guatemala, Greece, Honduras, Japan, Lebanon, Panama, Peru, Syria, Thailand, Turkey, Tunisia **(18)**	Costa Rica, Italy, Mexico **(3)**	37
Traditional	Afghanistan, China, Ethiopia, Haiti, Morocco, Saudi Arabia, Taiwan **(7)**	Bolivia, Burma, Cambodia, Ghana, Indonesia, India, Iran, Iraq, Jordan, Laos, Liberia, Libya, Malaya, Pakistan, Philippines, Sudan **(16)**	**(0)**	23
Total	27	36	21	84

NOTE: The above table is based on an analysis of 84 countries as of 1948-1960.

TABLE 5-2. RELATIONS BETWEEN PERMISSIVENESS AND POLITICAL STABILITY

Degree of Political Stability	Level of Permissiveness			TOTAL
	COERCIVE	MIDLEVEL PERMISSIVE	PERMISSIVE	
Stability	Czechoslovakia Nicaragua East Germany Paraguay Ethiopia Poland Portugal Spain Romania Union S. Africa Saudi Arabia USSR Taiwan Yugoslavia (7)	Austria Cambodia Libya Philippines Tunisia (5)	Australia Netherlands Canada New Zealand Costa Rica Norway Denmark Sweden Finland Switzerland Iceland United Kingdom Ireland United States Israel Uruguay Luxembourg West Germany (18)	30
Midlevel Instability	Afghanistan Nicaragua Albania Paraguay Bulgaria Poland China Spain Dominican Rep. Union S. Africa Egypt USSR Haiti Yugoslavia Morocco (15)	Burma Iran Ceylon Japan Chile Liberia Ecuador Malaya El Salvador Pakistan France Panama Ghana Jordan Greece Sudan Thailand (17)	Belgium Italy Mexico (3)	35
Instability	Argentina Cuba Hungary Korea Venezuela (5)	Bolivia India Brazil Iraq Colombia Laos Cyprus Lebanon Guatemala Peru Honduras Syria Indonesia Turkey (14)	(0)	19
Total	27	36	21	84

NOTE: The above table is based on an analysis of 84 countries as of 1955-1961.

93

there shall be no governmental interference with religion and the other aspect says there shall be no governmental aid to religion. The American version allows exceptions to the no interference principle for dangerous religious practices like rattle snake ceremonies, and exceptions to the no-aid principle for indirect or minor aid like bus fare reimbursement to parochial school children.[5]

The effects of the no-interference right are similar to the effects of the free speech right since religious activity is a form of communication. In the field of religious speech, it may be even more important to let all viewpoints be heard since truth and effectiveness are so much more difficult to determine in this field. The field of religion also tends to be more highly emotional and small interferences can lead to strong resentments and to severe social conflict especially in a religiously heterogeneous society. Indeed, the Thirty Years War of the Protestant Reformation represented a greater per capita loss of life to the nations involved than any political war in European history.

Violations of the right to have the government give no aid to religion can produce many effects that even members of the aided or dominant religion might consider socially dysfunctional. First, aid can lead to interference toward the religion aided. This is why the Catholic hierarchy in the past opposed federal aid to parochial schools for fear that such aid would lead to restrictions on religious teaching in the parochial schools. Second, aid can easily lead to real or perceived favoritism since it is almost impossible to allocate aid equally among religions, partly because there is not likely to be agreement on whether equality should be measured by population, need, or some other criteria. Third, government aid can have the effect of decreasing church and home initiatives as John F. Kennedy noted in supporting the Supreme Court's ban on school prayers. Fourth, in a country that has many religious denominations, being in the safe majority in one place does not guarantee that one will be in the safe majority in other places, and thus what may be viewed as beneficial aid to religion in one part of the country may be viewed by the same religion as detrimental aid in other places. Fifth, aid-like interference can also generate strong resentments and severe social conflicts as is shown by the repeated anti-clerical conflict in France over French government aid to the Catholic church.

EQUALITY OF TREATMENT

---

[5]Studies dealing with the impact of decreasing government aid to and interference with religion as manifested in prayers in the public schools include William Muir, *Prayer in the Public Schools: Law and Attitude Change* (Chicago: University of Chicago Press, 1967) and Richard Johnson, *The Dynamics of Compliance: Supreme Court Decision-Making From a New Perspective* (Evanston, Ill.: Northwestern University Press, 1967).

Equal treatment under the law in the American context mainly relates to prohibitions on ethnic group discrimination, particularly discrimination against blacks. Discrimination refers to denying someone, because of his or her race, various opportunities for which they would otherwise be qualified. Discrimination can take many forms including (1) governmental discrimination with regard to criminal procedure, school access, and voting; or (2) private discrimination with regard to housing, public accommodations, and employment.[6] A form of discrimination exists when the dominant group forces segregation or involuntary separation on the minority group, but not when minority group members voluntarily choose to live together or to be distinctive. What are the effects of discrimination on the total society particularly the dominant racial group, not just the group discriminated against?[7]

Discrimination probably has a substantial effect on decreasing the gross national product by failing to make full use of the actual and potential skills that blacks have. Long established discrimination by the building trade unions is a good example. Likewise housing discrimination may prevent qualified blacks from living near suburban job openings to which they might otherwise lack meaningful access. Past school discrimination and inferior black school facilities might greatly lessen the chances that potential black professionals will achieve their potentiality.

Another kind of societal economic effect comes from segregated school and housing facilities. Segregated school systems may involve duplicate costs like the special Texas black law school or the Tennessee black medical school which were established with only a few students to avoid integrating white southern universities, although these two schools may have recently become economically viable institutions. Segregated housing patterns combined with employment discrimination can lead to ghetto slums with their dispropor-tionately high costs for police, fire protection, and welfare recipients. These unnecessarily high costs of segregation should especially trouble conservative taxpayers.

Discrimination against a minority group frequently has a depressive effect

---

[6]A detailed description of the right to be free of discrimination is provided in Volume 2 of Thomas Emerson et al., *Political and Civil Rights in the United States* (Boston: Little, Brown, 1967) and the 1969 Supplement.

[7]For behavioral science approaches to the effects of racial discrimination, see "The Effects of Segregation and the Consequences of Desegregation," 37 *Minnesota Law Review* 427 (1953), and G. Grier and E. Grier, *Equality and Beyond* (New York: Quadrangle, 1966). For the effects of anti-discrimination legislation, see Monroe Berger, *Equality by Statute* (New York: Doubleday, 1967); and Leon Mayhew, *Law and Equal Opportunity* (Cambridge, Mass.: Harvard University Press, 1967). For the effects of school integration, see James Coleman et al., *Equality of Education Opportunity* (Washington, D.C.: Office of Education, 1966) (Also known as the Coleman Report); and on housing integration, see Wilner, *Human Relations in Interracial Housing* (Minneapolis: University of Minnesota Press, 1955).

on weaker members of the majority group. Thus low wages paid to blacks tend to keep down the wages of whites in occupations that blacks might enter. Black strike-breaking labor can also deter more aggressiveness on the part of white unions. Likewise, depressed standards of police behavior in dealing with blacks are sometimes hard to change when the police deal with whites especially poor whites.

Psychologically speaking, discrimination against blacks can create a false sense of superiority on the part of some whites. This may partly account for the lack of education and occupational ambition of many whites southerners who have their race to fall back on to compensate for their lack of education and job status. Discrimination can also cause guilt feelings and anxieties on the part of whites, especially if their behavior and attitudes toward blacks conflict with democratic ideals which are preached in their society, thereby creating the American Dilemma. Discrimination can, of course, have severe psychologically disturbing effects on blacks, but the emphasis in this impact analysis is on the effects on the total society in general and the majority whites in particular.

With regard to American foreign and military policy, domestic discrimination decreases the ability of the United States to win influence in Africa, Asia, and Latin America. Domestic discrimination may also decrease the morale of blacks in the armed forces, especially in a war against non-Caucasian people, and it may increase interracial friction within the armed forces as indicated by numerous clashes in the late 1960's.

An especially important effect of discrimination is the antagonism and hatred that it generates on the part of blacks toward whites. Such emotional incidents can spark into intra-ghetto riots and possibly eventually into inter-neighborhood riots.   Discrimination also divides whites themselves between those who advocate faster removal of discriminatory barriers and those who advocate retention or slower removal. This intra-white hostility sometimes manifests itself in student and other youthful protest activities.

Miscellaneous effects of discrimination include the loss of new manufacturing developments by discriminatory communities, which business executives consider to have an undesirable environment for raising their families. Discrimination by reducing black income can also reduce black consumer purchasing power thereby hurting white business concerns. Finally, the presence of discrimination often deters non-discriminatory behavior on the part of whites who do not want to discriminate, but who feel compelled to comply with what they perceive to be the dominant viewpoint unless the dominant viewpoint is made illegal by anti-discrimination legislation.

In addition to mentioning various phenomena that behavioral scientists tend to agree are effects of discrimination, some alleged effects that have no scientific acceptance should also be mentioned. For example, the absence of discrimination may indeed lead to increased intermarriage. No accepted biological study, however, has shown that the children of a racially mixed marriage are in any sense biologically defective. In fact, by lessening the skin-color purity of the races, there may be a lessening of friction between the races. In addition, the children of a racially-mixed marriage are likely to have access to more societal opportunities than children with a wholly black background.

It is sometimes alleged that integrating schools will have the effect of lowering the learning level of white students without necessarily raising the level of black students. The Coleman Report, however, tends to show that economic class integration or racial integration along class lines (i.e., poor blacks with middle-class whites, poor whites with middle class blacks, poor blacks with middle class blacks, or poor whites with middle class whites) does not generally lower the learning level of middle class children, but does raise the learning level of the poorer children.

Some whites in more frank moments correctly allege that their jobs would be in jeopardy if discrimination barriers were dropped. In this regard, dropping discrimination against blacks is like dropping tariff discrimination against foreign products. It might mean a temporary relocation of marginal less-efficient persons, but the total national economy benefits from the lowered consumer prices and from the more efficient use of its labor. Likewise in the long run, removing inefficient racial discrimination can raise the gross national product, decrease governmental costs attributable to slums and duplicative facilities, increase depressed wages, make for more efficient geographical allocation of industry, and increase consumer purchasing power as have been previously mentioned.

Although this discussion of equal protection under the law has emphasized racial discrimination, many of the same social consequences described would apply to much of the discrimination which is based on sex, religion, ancestral nationality, economic class, or other characteristics which usually lack sufficient correlation with ability to be meaningful criteria for allocating employment and other social opportunities.

SAFEGUARDING THE INNOCENT FROM CONVICTION AND HARASSMENT

In the American context, the basic legal rights designed to safeguard the innocent from conviction and harassment include approximately ten different rights. They relate to all the stages of criminal procedure from the legislative process passing criminal laws through arrest, trial, and sentencing. They include the right to (1) no retroactive or vague criminal statutes or statutes declaring named persons to be guilty of wrongdoing, (2) arrest or search only where there is substantial likelihood of guilt, (3) no involuntary confessions or self-incrimination, (4) release pending speedy trial, (5) hired or provided counsel at trial and before, (6) formal notice of charges, (7) unanimous decision by a group of one's peers, (8) questioning adverse witnesses and calling one's own witnesses, (9) no excessive punishment, and (10) no repeated prosecution for the same matter.[8]

The effect of these rights, where they are applied, is to lessen the likelihood that an innocent person will be convicted or harassed. This effect can be easily supported by people who are unlikely to commit crimes, but who recognize the possibility that they or other innocent people might find themselves in a situation or business practice when they could be falsely suspected or accused of some kind of wrongdoing. These rights also decrease the likelihood that guilty persons will be convicted of a greater crime than was committed, or that they will receive punishment or treatment disproportionate to the crime. This effect can also be easily supported by most people who recognize that if the guilty are over-convicted or over-sentenced, this breeds unnecessary bitterness and general disrespect for the law rather than rehabilitation or deterrence. These rights also make it more difficult to convict the guilty, but most people probably recognize that it is more detrimental to their self-interest and the orderly functioning of society for one innocent person to be convicted than for one or even a few guilty persons to go uncaught for a specific crime. In general there would be no need to have these rights if there was some accurate automatic way of separating the innocent from the guilty.

In regard to specific rights, the right to a hired or provided lawyer is probably the most important for preventing wrongful convictions and harassment.[9] Having a lawyer aids the investigation of the facts, negotiation with the prosecutor, examination of witnesses, presentation of legal and factual arguments to the judge and jury, and the preparation of an appeal. A lawyer also provides psychological support to the defendant and an air of objectivity which the defendant himself could not provide. All the other procedural rights become less meaningful without an attorney to inform the defendant of his rights and to call violations to the attention of the courts, including violations that might occur at the police interrogation stage. Of the basic legal rights, only free speech may be more important, because without free speech violations of rights could not be readily called to the attention of a larger public.

---

[8] A description of the nature of the safeguards to protect the innocent from conviction and harassment is given in David Fellman, *The Defendants Rights* (New York: Rinehart, 1958) and William Lockhart, Yale Kamisar, and Jesse Choper, *Constitutional Rights and Liberties* (St. Paul, Minn.: West, 1970).

[9] Behavioral studies of the consequences of having counsel include Leon Silverstein, *Defense of the Poor* (Boston: Little, Brown, 1966); Nathan Lefstein and Vaughn Stapleton, *Counsel in Juvenile Courts* (Washington, D.C.: National Council of Juvenile Court Judges, 1967); and D. Wenger and C. Fletche, "The Effect of Legal Counsel on Admissions to a State Mental Hospital: A Confrontation of Professions" (Paper Presented at the annual meeting of the American Sociological Association, 1967).

Right to counsel has some important effects on the legal system besides protecting the innocent. The American adversary system presumes that both sides will be vigorously represented so that the neutral judge can arrive at the truth somewhere between the adverse positions; but if only one side is represented, the system may not function effectively. If the poor generally lack lawyers in prosecutions, evictions, repossessions, or other cases, their respect for the law will decrease although right to counsel currently extends only to criminal, not civil cases. Counsel for the poor and other alienated groups can also help to bring orderly reform of the law as an alternative to disorderly or violent change. In addition, widespread availability of counsel can serve to educate those who otherwise would be without counsel, and such education may prevent them from getting into legal trouble with creditors, landlords, and other people with whom they deal.

While it is generally agreed that brutal or random arrests, searches, and confession-obtaining techniques have adverse social effects (by creating an unduly fearful population and disrespect for the police), there has been some controversy over how to deter such police tactics. One cannot expect the prosecutor to be very vigorous in prosecuting police who have been zealously trying to help him. Likewise private damage suits are costly, time-consuming, embarrassing to the plaintiff, unlikely to result in victory because of police discretion and generally unsympathetic juries. If victorious, they are unlikely to result in a deterring damage-judgment because of the officer's lack of money, the difficulty of assessing damages, and a tendency of the city to pay the judgment. Internal police administration in these matters tends to be more protective than disciplinary. As a result of the lack of more effective alternatives, the courts have chosen to exclude illegally obtained evidence from the courtroom in hopes that doing so will encourage the police to operate more within the law when making arrests or searches and when obtaining confessions. Behavioral studies have shown this exclusionary rule has changed some police behavior.[10]

Some important behavioral research has recently shown that regardless of the nature of the crime or the defendant's prior record, he or she is more likely to be convicted if there is no release pending trial.[11] The chances of conviction are increased because (1) being in jail awaiting trial decreases one's ability to

---

[10]Empirical research on protecting the right to be free from unreasonable arrests, searches, and interrogation techniques include Richard Medalie et al., "Custodial Police Interrogation in our Nation's Capital: The Attempt to Implement Miranda," 66 *Michigan Law Review* 1347-1422 (1968); S. Nagel, "Testing the Effects of Excluding Illegally Seized Evidence," *Wisconsin Law Review* 283-310 (1965); and Edward Green, "Race, Social Status, and Criminal Arrest," 35 *American Sociological Review* 476-490 (1970).

[11]Anne Rankin, "The Effect of Pretrial Detention," 39 *New York University Law Review* 641-55 (1964).

investigate and prepare a defense, and because (2) defendants make a relatively bad impression on the judge and jury when brought for each trial session from the prisoners lockup area, rather than on their own through the regular courtroom entrance. Denying pre-trial release for want of bail money also has the effect of discriminating against the poor, increasing jail costs, promoting loss of jobs, and increasing the likelihood that the innocent will spend time in jail and that the guilty will spend more time than their sentence or the law provides.

Studies have shown that careful screening of defendants to determine their roots in the community followed by reminders of their court dates has the effect of producing a higher percentage of pre-trial releases and a lower percentage of those who do not show up in court than the traditional money bond system does.[12] Other behavioral studies have provided useful information with regard to how court congestion can be reduced so that released and failed defendants can be tried and convicted or acquitted sooner.[13]

There has been more behavioral research on the consequences of criminal procedure rights than on any of the other basic legal rights. The effects of criminal jury trials rather than bench trials has been well researched revealing that juries are more likely to acquit in 17 percent of the cases, although there is agreement in 75 per cent, and the judge is more likely to acquit in 2 percent, with the jury being undecided in 6 percent.[14] The unanimity requirement, the multiple decision-makers, and the less upper-class composition of juries probably accounts for their lesser propensity to convict compared to judges. Studies have also been made of the effect of various punishments especially capital punishment, although the right to be free from capital punishment has not yet been established in American legal rights.[15]

Although no behavioral research has been done on some of the other procedural rights, the effects of their presence or absence can be readily hypothesized. Vague or retroactive criminal statutes obviously cannot have a meaningful deterrent effect if the statute does not clearly refer to future behavior. Likewise, it is common sense that if a prosecutor could repeatedly prosecute a defendant for the same matter, he or she might eventually get a conviction of an innocent person or an over-conviction of a guilty person, to say nothing of the obvious harassment involved. Without clear notice of the

---

[12]Charles Ares et al., "The Manhattan Bail Project: An Interim Report on the Use of Pretrial Parole," 38 *New York University Law Review* 67-95 (1963).

[13]Hans Zeisel et al., *Delay in the Court* (Boston: Little, Brown, 1959); and J. Navarro and J. Taylor, *Data Analysis and Simulation of a Court System for the Processing of Criminal Cases* (Washington, D.C.: Institute for Defense Analysis, 1967).

[14]Harry Kalven and Hans Zeisel, *The American Jury* (Boston: Little, Brown, 1966), p.56.

[15]Hugo Bedau, *The Death Penalty in America* (New York: Anchor, 1967).

charges against defendants and the right to call their own witnesses and to question opposition witnesses, an innocent defendant would clearly tend to have a much more difficult time establishing his innocence.

THE RIGHT TO BASIC ECONOMIC SECURITY

The right to basic economic security is a relatively modern right at least in the American context. It is embodied in statutes rather than in the Constitution. To the extent it is provided, however, there can constitutionally be no arbitrary classifications of recipients, or the equal-treatment right will be violated. Likewise, there can be no deprivation of government economic benefits unless the recipient is provided with due process to give him an opportunity to show the illegality of the deprivation.

Relevant statutes in American law include (1) the National Labor Relations Act of 1935 which provides the right to join labor unions which can aid in providing economic security (2) the Fair Labor Standards Act of 1938 which provides for the right to a minimum wage, maximum hours, safe working conditions, and freedom from child labor; (3) the Social Security Act of 1935 which provides for aid to the aged, disabled, unemployed, and to dependant children; and (4) the Employment Act of 1946 which declared that the American people have the right to expect the federal government to provide maximum employment, production, and purchasing power.[16]

Sometimes critics of these rights talk in terms of a conflict between freedom and economic security. On the contrary though, freedom of speech was very important in revealing the harm that was being done to society by the absence of these economic rights. Likewise basic economic security is necessary to make freedom of speech meaningful, because those lacking economic security are generally not in a financial position to take advantage of expensive forms of communication, and economic insecurity also makes one less tolerant of deviant ideas and less adaptable to social change except change that will mean personal economic benefits. There is clearly a close relation between economic security and equal treatment with regard to race relations, since (1) being black and being poor are positively correlated, and because (2) those who discriminate often do so out of economic insecurity, and (3) being poor makes one more subject to discrimination.

An important general effect of increased economic security is to lessen

---

[16]Empirical studies of the statutes relating to the right to basic economic security are described in H. Koontz and R. Gable, *Public Control of Economic Enterprise* (New York: McGraw-Hill, 1956), 487-590, 758-794; G. Bloom and H. Northrup, *Economics of Labor Relations* (Homewood, Ill.: Irwin, 1954); M. Lee, *Economic Fluctuations* (Homewood, Ill.: Irwin, 1955) 421-538; and Gary Steiner, *Social Insecurity: The Politics of Welfare* (Chicago: Rand McNally, 1966).

economic anxieties that workers might have. Such anxieties can interfere with morale and efficiency and thereby lower the gross national product. Too much security, however, might cause a worker to lessen attempts to improve himself.

All four of the key New Deal statutes mentioned above have had important specific consequences for American society, just as related statutes have in other countries. Statistics show a substantial increase in union membership subsequent to the passage of the Nation Labor Relations Act, and a substantial decrease in strikes for union recognition as contrasted to strikes for more favorable contract terms. Other statistical studies have shown that unions do produce higher wages, shorter hours, and safer conditions at least for union members.

For non-union members, the Fair Labor Standards Act has provided similar although lower benefits. These economic effects have directly benefited a large segment of the population and indirectly benefited the total economy, particularly by virtue of the more efficient use of capital and labor which raising the price of labor has encouraged, and also by the economic stimulus stemming from increased purchasing power to the extent wages have increased more than prices. Strengthening unions has also had political effects by increasing the likelihood that legislation will be passed favoring union interests.

The Social Security Act has encouraged earlier retirement for the aged and therefore earlier advancement for the young. The aid to dependent children provisions have spawned a tremendous bureaucratic apparatus, and in that regard may soon be replaced by the Family Assistance Bill of 1971.

The Employment Act has not eliminated unemployment or price inflation, but its encouragement of greater government spending and lower taxes in time of unemployment and the reverse in time of inflation (combined with other governmental regulatory devices) has dampened the business cycle to some extent. Provisions in the Social Security Act that provide payments to the unemployed, dependent children, and the retired also help to level-off business cycles because these payments increase in times of recession and decrease in times of prosperity.

In general, this chapter has attempted to describe and footnote some of the broad consequences of providing various basic legal rights. There is clearly a need for more behavior research on the impact of rights. Such social science research is needed to supplement the more philosophical discussion of the definitions, justifications, identifications, and relations of both human rights and legal rights. Such research will also help to build further bridges between philosophy and the behavioral sciences. It is hoped that this chapter has pulled together some of the relevant ideas and literature for others to build upon.

6

GOVERNMENT STRUCTURES

The main purpose of this chapter is to discuss the relevance of basic governmental structures to the effectiveness of public policy outputs in achieving their goals. The examples are largely from the American government context, but references will be made to other nations as well. The chapter is divided into four parts dealing with (1) the main controversial issues in structuring governments, (2) the relations among alternative government structures, (3) the mutual effects of government structures on domestic and foreign policy, and (4) the effects of American government structures on societal productivity.[1]

---

[1]There seem to be no books, book chapters, or articles that systematically deal with the relations between governmental structures and public policy. In the American government context, there are three kinds of textbooks that are somewhat relevant. They include:

(1) Textbooks that devote the first half to government structures and the second half to government policies, or at least have a lot of policy-substance chapters. An example is John Ferguson and Dean McHenry, *The American System of Government* (New York: McGraw-Hill, 1977). Earlier editions, though, contain more policy chapters before it became popular to have separate policy-substance books. Also see John Straayer and Robert Wrinkle, *Introduction to American Government and Policy* (Columbus, Ohio: Charles Merrill, 1975).

(2) Textbooks that discuss government structures from a public-choice perspective which emphasizes the use of deductive models for explaining the behavior of government officials, but occasionally talk in terms of the behavior or structures that will maximize given goals. Examples are Peter Aranson, *American Government: Strategy and Choice* (Cambridge, Mass.: Winthrop, 1981), and Wayne Frances, *American Politics: Analysis of Choice* (New York: Goodyear, 1976).

(3) Textbooks that are highly evaluative of government structures in an ideological sense. They tend to be explicitly liberal/Marxist/socialistic or sometimes conservative/ capitalistic. Examples would be Edward Greenberg, *The American Political System: A Radical Approach* (Cambridge, Mass.: Winthrop, 1977); Duane Lockard, *The Perverted Priorities of American Politics* (New York: Macmillan, 1971); and Richard Saeger, *American Government and Politics: A Neoconservative Approach* (Glenview, Ill.: Scott Foresman, 1982).

CONTROVERSIAL ISSUES IN STRUCTURING GOVERNMENT

There are five basic dimensions that are especially relevant in discussing governmental structures. They deal with:

1. Relating the national government to the state or provincial governments.
2. Relating the chief executive to the legislature.
3. Relating the courts to the executive-legislative branches of government.
4. Relating the political parties to each other.
5. Relating the government to the people.

FEDERALISM

On the matter of national-provincial relations, there are basically three alternatives. They consist of:

1. A unitary form of government, where all power goes to the national government to delegate as it sees fit to the states.
2. A confederate form of government, where all power goes to the states to delegate as they see fit to the national government.
3. A federal form of government, where a constitution specifies that some powers go to the national government and some powers to the state governments.

Unitary government is the prevailing form in the world. England represents a good example. Examples of confederate governments include the American Articles of Confederation in the 1780's and the Southern Confederacy in the 1860's. Contemporary United States represents a good example of the federal form of government. The U.S. as of 1980, however, is more nearly unitary than it was as of 1880 or 1780 although the long-term trend has its ups and downs. Increased national government has resulted from socio-economic forces such as increases in (1) severity of wars, (2) interstate and international business, (3) big labor and other pressure groups that seek aid and require regulation, (4) urbanization and resulting loss of self-sufficiency, (5) periods of severe inflation and recession, and (6) competition with foreign ideologies. It has also resulted from such enabling factors as (1) expanded sources of national government revenue for carrying on increased government programs, (2) improved managerial techniques for handling large-scale government operations, and (3) changing constitutional interpretations. The growth has also resulted from an ideological or additudinal shift from a prevailing attitude favoring minimal government toward an attitude that government has many positive responsibilities. The increased national government represents absolute growth and growth relative to the states, but state government activities have also increased.[2]

SEPARATION OF POWERS

On the matter of executive-legislative relations, the basic alternatives are:

1. A parliamentary form of government, whereby the legislature chooses the chief executive.
2. A monarchic or autocratic form of government, whereby the chief executive chooses the legislature or advisory body, or has none.
3. A presidential form of government, whereby the people choose the chief executive and the legislature independently of each other.

Parliamentary government is the prevailing form. England also represents a good example. Examples of monarchic autocracy include Saudi Arabia and the past feudal versions of western European countries Contemporary United States represents a good example of the presidential form of government. The U.S. as of 1980, however, involves more power to the chief executive relative to the legislature than was the case as of 1880 or 1780, although the long-term trend has its ups and downs. Increased chief executive power has resulted from the same socio-economic forces, enabling factors, and ideological shift as the increase in national government power. Increased power of chief executives over legislatures represents absolute growth, but is also relative in the sense that the power of legislatures has also increased.[3]

JUDICIAL POWER

On the matter of judicial power, there are basically two alternatives:

1. A system of concurrent review, whereby the legislature, the chief executive, and the courts are considered as having equal responsibility for upholding the constitution.

---

[2]Discussions of federalism include Daniel Elazar, *American Federalism* (New York: Crowell, 1972); William Riker, *Federalism: Origin, Operation, Significance* (Boston: Little, Brown, 1964); and Kenneth Wheare, *Federal Government* (New York: Oxford University Press, 1963).

[3]Discussions of separation of powers include Peter Odegard and Victor Rosenblum (eds.), *The Power to Govern: An Examination of the Separation of Powers in the American System of Government* (White Plains, N.Y.: Fund for Adult Education, 1957); Howard Ball, *Constitutional Powers Cases on the Separation of Powers and Federalism* (St. Paul, Minn.: West, 1980); and Alexander Hamilton, James Madison, and John Jay, *The Federalist Papers* (New York: New American Library, 1961), Chapter 13.

2. A system of judicial review, whereby the courts (particularly the highest national court) are considered as having authority to declare legislative and executive acts to be unconstitutional.

England represents concurrent review. The U.S. represents judicial review, although the form of judicial review has changed. Prior to the 1930's judicial review emphasized declaring economic regulation unconstitutional, but showed little sensitivity to civil liberties. Since the 1930's judicial review has left economic regulation to legislative discretion, and has declared much legislation unconstitutional as being in violation of civil liberties.

The retreat on declaring economic regulation unconstitutional is largely due to the same social forces that are responsible for increased power to the national government and to the executive branch. The more aggressive position on protecting civil liberties is due to (1) the growth of a more educated population which is more adaptable to change and more capable of recognizing the value of minority viewpoints, (2) middle class tolerance as contrasted to the greater anxieties of the rich in an unbalanced society especially the newly rich, and as contrasted to the poor who cannot afford to be so tolerant of minority competition, (3) the pressure of interest groups like the ACLU and the NAACP, (4) urbanism and its accompanying greater tolerance of deviant behavior, and (5) the growth of greater diversity in the American population.[4]

POLITICAL PARTIES

Political parties are groupings of people working together to get their members elected to political office. In relating political parties to each other, the basic alternatives are:

1. A one-party system, where opposition parties are virtually non-existent, although the one party may have factions.
2. A multiple-party system, although the parties may be grouped into coalitions.
3. A two-party system, with the possibility of minor parties and factions within the two major parties.

The Soviet Union is an example of a one-party system, as are many

---

[4]Discussions of judicial review and judicial power include Alexander Bickel, *The Supreme Court and the Idea of Progress* (New York: Harper & Row, 1970); Richard Funston, *A Vital National Seminar: The Supreme Court in American Political Life* (Palo Alto, Calif.: Mayfield, 1978); and Donald Horowitz, *The Courts and Social Policy* (Washington, D.C.: Brookings, 1977).

developing countries. France and Italy have multiple-party systems. Both England and the United States have basically two-party systems. Interest groups/associations and direct public participation also supplement the political party system in converting portions of the public will into governmental policy-makers or policy.

British and American parties differ on the dimension of the degree of ideological difference between the political parties. The alternatives on that dimension are:

1. A relatively strong ideological difference, generally over matters of socialism versus capitalism.
2. A relatively weak ideological difference, generally over the in's versus the out's although with some differences as to sensitivity to less well-off groups within the society.

The American party system has always been oriented toward two parties, although there have been changes in the party names, the influence of third parties, and the degree of factionalism. Ideological differences become greater in times of domestic crises, although the long-run trend is toward more liberalism by both parties for reasons that relate to the growth of economic regulation and civil liberties.[5]

DEMOCRACY

On the relation between the government and the people, there are two basic alternatives:

1. A dictatorial system, where:
   a. The general public has relatively little impact on the government,
   b. and/or minority viewpoints are repressed.
2. A democratic system, where:
   a. The adult public has voting rights for determining office holders,
   b. and holders of minority viewpoints are allowed to try to convert the majority.

The Soviet Union qualifies as a dictatorial system in light of the above definition, although it may be less dictatorial since the death of Stalin. The U.S.

---

[5]Discussions of party systems include James Sundquist, *Dynamics of the Party System: Alignment and Realignment of Political Parties in the United States* (Washington, D.C.: Brookings, 1973); William Chambers and Walter Burnham (eds.), *The American Party Systems* (New York: Oxford University Press, 1975); and Everett Ladd and Charles Hadley, *Transformations of the American Party System* (New York: Norton, 1978).

qualifies as a democracy. Voting rights in the U.S., though, have not been so wide-spread until the twentieth century with regard to race, sex, and age. Free speech rights have also expanded under twentieth century Supreme Court interpretations for reasons mentioned in discussing judicial review.[6]

RELATIONS AMONG THE GOVERNMENT STRUCTURES

This chapter treats American government structures as policies in three different ways. One way emphasizes how they affect each other. The second way is as basic structural policies which affect domestic and foreign functional policies. The third way is as basic policies that facilitate and sometimes hinder societal productivity. As for the relations among government structures, there are five structures which means 20 relations, as is shown in Table 6-1. In that table, relation 1 deals with the impact of separation on federalism, and relation 2 deals with the impact of federalism on separation. Thus, each relation deals with the impact of the column category on the row category. The order of the relations is the order in which they are discussed in the text.

The first pair of those 20 relations is the mutual impact of separation of powers on federalism. The separation between the national legislature and the chief more power being exercised by the states than would be the case with a more cohesive national government. In the other direction, the divisiveness of 50 states weakens the total American government, and may thereby create a semi-vacuum into which steps the President and the executive branch in order to fill the need for more national leadership. The President by his national constituency represents national unity more than Congress, which reflects federalism by having two senators from each state.

The second pair of relations is judicial review and federalism. Judicial review has tended to restrict the power of the states. From 1880 to 1935, the Supreme Court declared unconstitutional many state statutes in the realm of economic regulation, arguing that those statutes interfered with interstate commerce, violated substantive due process, or impaired the obligation of contracts. From 1935 on, the Supreme Court has declared unconstitutional many state statutes restrictive of civil liberties on the grounds that those statutes violated the equal protection clause, due process, or the first amendment. The Supreme Court has been more willing to declare state legislation unconstitutional than congressional legislation. In the other direction, federalism has had an impact on judicial review by generating the existence of

---

[6]Discussions of democracy include Roland Pennock, *Liberal Democracy: Its Merits and Prospects* (New York: Rinehart, 1950); Henry Kariel, *Frontiers of Democratic Theory* (New York: Random House, 1970); and Henry Mayo, *An Introduction to Democratic Theory* (New York: Oxford, 1960).

TABLE 6-1. RELATIONS AMONG GOVERNMENT STRUCTURES

Effects

	Causes				
	Federalism	Separation of powers	Judicial review	Two-party system	Democracy
Federalism		1	3	5	7
Separation of powers	2		9	11	13
Judicial review	4	10		15	17
Two-party system	6	12	16		19
Democracy	8	14	18	20	

state supreme courts which also exercise the power of judicial review over legislation, although mainly state legislation and state constitutions. Until 1970, those state supreme courts were generally more conservative than the U.S. Supreme Court, especially on civil liberties matters. Since 1970, however, some state supreme courts have gone further than the U.S. Supreme Court in such areas as declaring capital punishment unconstitutional and declaring unconstitutional the inequalities that exist in educational funding across schools in different parts of a state.

On the relation between the two-party system and federalism, the two-party system influences federalism by providing a connecting link between the states and the national government. Thus the division between a state and the White House or Congress is lessened if they are controlled by the same political party, as they tend to be. In the other direction, federalism affects the two-party system by encouraging the development of more decentralized political parties than would otherwise be the case. Some states in effect have both a national party organization and a state/local party organization, especially where and when being a national Democrat or Republican has a different meaning from being a state one.

As for the relation between democracy and federalism, democracy affects federalism by providing elections at both levels of government. That has a partially unifying effect, although there are attempts in some states to keep the elections at separate times. In the other direction, federalism has adversely affected democracy by allowing for undemocratic states. Examples include the states of Mississippi, Alabama, Georgia, and South Carolina prior to the civil rights period of the 1960's when those states sought to disenfranchise blacks and poor whites.

Judicial review has affected separation of powers by decreasing the power of quasi-legislative regulatory agencies during the period from 1880 to 1935, but judicial review now readily allows such regulation. Separation of powers in turn influences judicial review in that Congress and the President are less likely to interfere with judicial review by court-curbing legislation when Congress and the President are split between the two major political parties than when they are united by one party, especially if the Supreme Court is dominated by the other party.

The two-party system affects separation of powers by decreasing the separation when the same party controls both the White House and Congress. The two-party system increases the separation when opposite political parties control each branch of government. Separation in turn influences the party system by in effect creating presidential and congressional political parties the way federalism encourages state political parties that are separate from the national parties.

Democracy affects separation of powers since the voters tend to demand participation in selecting both the President and Congress. Separation of powers, however, has adversely affected democracy by allowing less democratic parts of the country to have an undue influence in the American Congress. That was so for many years when southern senators and representatives from one-party areas had the power to block civil rights legislation by virtue of their seniority, committee chairmanships, and filibustering.

The two-party system affects judicial review since judicial review is stimulated when there is a party split between Congress and the Supreme Court, especially if congressional legislation is passed along party lines. Court-curbing activities are most likely to occur when the dominant party in Congress disagrees with the judicial review of the Supreme Court. As for the impact of judicial review on the two-party system, there have been some significant Supreme Court decisions, such as those on redistricting, the rights of minority parties to get on the ballot, the constitutionality of election financing laws, prohibitions on white primaries, and decisions on residence or other requirements for voting.

Democracy may have an impact on judicial review to the extent that the Supreme Court is influenced by the elections returns. That may have been the case in 1936 when the overwhelming victory of the Democrats may have been partly responsible for the changed voting behavior on the Supreme Court. Presidential election returns also make a difference by way of choosing the president, who then chooses members of the Supreme Court. In the other direction, judicial review has been a big factor in promoting democracy by way of numerous Supreme Court decisions that have protected the minority-rights aspects of democracy. One might also note that judicial review is undemocratic in the majority-rule sense when exercised by non-elected judges with long tenure. It is, however, democratic in the minority-rights sense when exercised to allow minority viewpoints to try to convert the majority.

As for the relations between democracy and the two-party system, those two structures are partly related by definition. Democracy requires allowing minority viewpoints which implies an opposition political party. Democracy, as so defined, is thus incompatible with a one-party system. Allowing minority viewpoints also allows for a healthy opposition party. The two-party system also helps to preserve democracy since the dominant party likes majority rule and the out-party likes minority rights.

MUTUAL EFFECTS OF GOVERNMENT STRUCTURES ON PUBLIC POLICY

Public policy can be classified in a variety of ways. One classification is in terms of domestic policy and foreign policy. The most controversial issues in American domestic policy over the last generation have related to matters of government regulation and the providing of public goods. Government regulation has included both economic and non-economic regulation. The traditional economic matters emphasize inflation/unemployment, union-management relations, and consumer/anti-trust matters. The non-economic matters emphasize regulation that relates to nondiscrimination and environmental protection. Providing public goods includes public education, public health, and public aid.

Foreign policy issues tend to be divided into regions of the world, but for the past generation, most of those issues have related to competition between the United States and the Soviet Union in those regions or to competition between American democratic capitalism and Soviet dictatorial communism.

Table 6-1 shows ten relations between the five governmental structures and the two functional policy areas. Five of those relations deal with the impact of the structures on the policies, and five with the impact of the policies on the structures. There are thus 20 relations in all, with the first ten relating to domestic policy, and the second ten relating to foreign policy.

The figure also seeks to clarify that socio-economic forces are also important in influencing governmental policies and governmental structures. For example, the growth of large-scale economic units has been a key force in shaping domestic policy by virtue of the loss of intimate contact between workers and employers and between consumers and producers. Likewise, the growth of nuclear missile warfare has been a key force in shaping foreign policy by virtue of its generating a partial stalemate of military power between the U.S. and the Soviet Union. Domestic and foreign policy can in turn influence the socio-economic forces such as the growth of large multi-national businesses. Socio-economic forces also affect the structural variables, both directly (as for example when the Supreme Court responds to the historical context in which it operates), and indirectly by their effect on domestic regulation and foreign policy which in turn influence government structures.[7]

DOMESTIC POLICY

Federalism has had some important effects on governmental regulation. It has made government regulation more decentralized than it would otherwise be (e.g., telephone company regulation). It has provided testing grounds for new forms of government regulation in particular states (e.g., workmen's compensation in Wisconsin). It has also provided a less uniform regulatory program than a unitary governmental system would, with accompanying

---

[7]On the relations between societal structures and societal functions, see Don Martindale (ed.), *Functionalism in the Social Sciences: The Strength and Limits of Functionalism in Anthropology, Economics, Political Science, and Sociology* (Philadelphia: American Academy of Political and Social Science, 1965); and James Charlesworth (ed.), *Contemporary Political Analysis* (New York: Free Press, 1967), 72-107.

TABLE 6-2. EFFECTS OF GOVERNMENT STRUCTURES ON PUBLIC POLICY

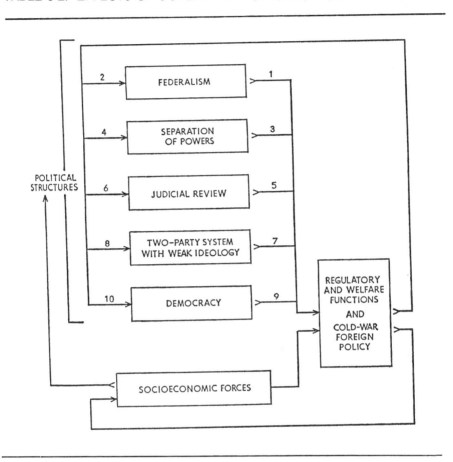

possibilities of intergovernmental conflict (e.g., trucking regulation) and of intergovernmental vacuums (e.g., union-management regulation).

Government regulation also has a feedback effect on federalism. Increased responsibility has tended to increase the power of both the federal and the state governments, but relatively speaking the increase has been substantially greater at the federal level because, to be effective, so many regulatory programs require interstate regulation (e.g., programs designed to prevent depression and inflation).

Just as federalism has produced relatively uncoordinated regulatory programs in terms of intergovernmental relations, separation of powers has likewise produced relatively uncoordinated regulatory programs in terms of interbranch relations. *Separation of powers* makes possible the control of Congress and the Administration by opposed political parties or opposed ideologies, which leads to at least temporary inaction (e.g., the lack of a vigorous relief and recovery program between 1930 and 1932).

On the other hand, increased government regulation has tended to weaken separation of powers by concentrating more quasi-legislative and quasi-judicial power in the hands of administrative agencies, where quicker and more expert action can generally be taken than in Congress or the courts (e.g., transportation rate-making or the adjudication of stock brokerage violations).

Judicial review has had the effect of slowing the increase in governmental regulation (e.g., the child labor cases), but not preventing it.

On the other side of the picture, the increase in government regulation has grown so large that this phenomena, along with personnel and social changes, has probably been a major cause of the withdrawal of the federal courts from nullifying economic regulatory legislation since 1937.

The check and balance provided by the *two-party system* has probably tended to make regulatory programs operate more efficiently than they otherwise would. The out-party is constantly trying to find and reveal to the public examples of waste, corruption, and unresponsiveness on the part of the in-party. However, the two-party system has meant that the planning of regulatory programs must be more short run than would be so with a one-party system. Federal economic programs, for instance, generally cannot be planned for more than one presidential administration ahead because of the possibility of a change in the party occupying the White House. The relatively weak ideological split in the American party system, however, has meant that when the out-party comes in, it will not drastically change all the economic programs of the former in-party. It has also meant that campaign disputes over regulatory issues generally tend to be fought along pragmatic lines rather than along ideological lines of socialism versus capitalism.

Viewed from the other side of the conceptual scheme, increased government regulation and regulatory issues have probably sharpened the differences between Democrats and Republicans. In the early 60's, for instance, the sharpest inter-party disputes were over Keynesian fiscal policy, Medicare for the aged, and President Johnson's anti-poverty program. Upsurges in economic regulation during the Wilson and Roosevelt administrations clearly sharpened inter-party differences.

The *democratic aspects* of universal adult suffrage combined with relative freedom for unpopular viewpoints has enabled substantial economic reforms to be introduced without violent revolution. In both England and the United States, socialistic reformist philosophies were able to win acceptance without generating reactionary repression.

Probably the most controversial relation shown in Table 6-1 is the impact of economic regulation on democracy. If one defines democracy so as to include the right to operate a business for profit as the owner sees fit, without being subject to government regulation, then government regulation by definition has decreased democracy.

If, on the other hand, one defines democracy in terms of universal adult suffrage combined with freedom for unpopular viewpoints to make themselves heard, then most regulatory programs of the 20th-century have directly or indirectly helped to increase American democracy. Surely, universal adult suffrage can be more effectively exercised by workers who have the time to familiarize themselves with politics instead of merely working long hours at a bare subsistence wage starting in early childhood. Maximum hour laws, minimum wage laws, and child labor laws have helped to free workers so they can gain increased political familiarity. Business regulation legislation has probably helped (along with the mass media and increased education) to decrease the undue power that business concerns exercised over state and federal legislatures in the past.

FOREIGN POLICY

The mutual relations between governmental structure and American foreign policy are similar to the relations between structure and domestic functions in some ways, but different in others. *Federalism*, for instance, has affected American foreign policy by making it more provincial and isolationist than it would otherwise be if the state governments had less influence on the national government. Federalism has especially served to embarrass the national government on occasions when state or local governments acted contrary to American foreign policy, such as the Little Rock school desegregation riots, New York's attempt in the 1930's to disrupt the American acceptance of Czarist bank deposits in New York banks in payment of Russian debts, and the New Orleans lynching of Mafia-associated Italians in the 1900's.

The cold war and increased American international activity, however, have greatly strengthened the national government relative to the states since only the national government conducts diplomatic relations and provides for the common defense.

Separation of legislative and executive powers has hampered presidential foreign policy-making in comparison with such countries as Great Britain, where the chief executive is always the leader of the dominant legislative party. A classic example of the lack of coordination occurred is the post-World War I period when Congress and the President could not agree on the role the United States should play in the Versailles Treaty and the League of Nations.

The cold war, however, has increased the importance of the President by virtue of his access to secret diplomatic and intelligence information, his ability to make relatively quick decisions combined with the increased need for such decisions, his power to recognize revolutionary governments, and his status, along with the Vice-President, as the only elected official with a national constituency.

Judicial review has had little, if any, effect on American   foreign policy. The Supreme Court has held that American treaties and foreign policy actions must conform to the Constitution, but the Supreme Court has never held a treaty to be unconstitutional.

On the other hand, treaty-making has had some effect on judicial power because a treaty becomes the law of the land, and it thus gives the courts a weapon by which contrary state laws can be declared illegal. This weapon could become more important if the United States signs the United Nations Declaration on Human Rights, although practically all its provisions have already been incorporated explicitly or by interpretation into the federal Constitution or federal statutes.

The American *two-party system* lessens the united front that the United States might otherwise maintain in comparison with the one-party communist system. This inter-party friction to the extent it exists could have been a factor in Nazi Germany's feeling that the United States could be beaten.

On the other hand, the cold war has promoted a substantial quantity of bipartisanship in Congress that might otherwise be absent.

The *democratic structure* of American government affects American foreign policy by being a partial factor in determining with whom and against whom the United States is allied. It also shapes the process whereby American foreign policy is made by placing more emphasis on debate and consensus.

A view of the relation from the other direction however, shows that the cold war and an intense foreign policy in general do tend to reduce the aspects of democracy that relate to the freedom to disagree. There tends to be a decreased tolerance of political nonconformists, particularly nonconformists whose ideology may be interpreted as leaning in the same direction as the ideology of the enemy powers. Nevertheless, the cold war has strengthened

American democracy by encouraging the political and economic upgrading of depressed economic and ethnic groups in order to unify the country and in order to improve the national image. Some of the New Deal activity with regard to providing for the right to join unions and with regard to social insurance programs was probably motivated partly by ideological competition with the Soviet Union. Likewise, the cold war has provided incentives for the passage of civil rights laws, which have broadened the base of American democracy.

RELATING SPECIFIC POLICIES TO GIVEN STRUCTURES

Substantive public policies can be grouped on various dimensions that relate to the government structures with which they are especially associated, much as the following:

1. Some policy fields mainly involve policy-making by judicial decision-makers, such as the field of civil liberties, personal liability, and contractual rights. Other policy fields involve presidential decision-making, such as foreign and defense policy. When it comes to taxing and spending policy, then Congress, the state legislatures, and the city councils are most important.
2. On the dimension of level of government, policy matters of zoning, sanitation, police, fire, and schools, are particularly local matters, although often with federal money. The state level tends to control criminal justice, property rights, and family relations. The national level is particularly relevant to foreign/defense, unemployment/inflation, and civil liberties policy.
3. On the dimension of citizen participation in policy-making, there is relatively little participation in the policy fields that are national and thus appear aloof. There is relatively much in the fields that are local, such as public housing, public schools, and public parks. Interest groups tend to be more important in those fields where citizen participation is less important, such as economic regulation, including anti-trust, consumer protection, and union management relations.
4. Another dimension is the extent to which there is private exercise of public functions. That especially occurs in local matters like hospitals, transportation, and communication, and less so in national matters like foreign defense and postal policy.

EFFECTS OF GOVERNMENT STRUCTURES ON PRODUCTIVITY

Societal productivity in this context means maximizing societal benefits minus societal costs through public policies that are effective, efficient, and equitable. American government structures both facilitate and hinder the achievement of that general goal. Discussing the productivity effects of those structures helps clarify the advantages and disadvantages of the structural alternatives in a more modern context than referring to Montesquieu, Locke, Hobbes, Rousseau, and other political thinkers who were frequently referred to at the time of the adoption of the American Constitution. The material in the previous section emphasized how American government structures influence the substance and process of American domestic and foreign policy. The material in this section emphasizes how those structures influence the productivity of those policies and thus of society, although similar examples can sometimes be used for both matters.[8]

FEDERALISM

Federalism facilitates productivity in various ways. One way is by providing a testing ground for trying out new ideas. Good examples include the contrived experiments of the 1970's, including the housing experiments conducted by the Department of Housing and Urban Development. In one such experiment, HUD arranged for rent supplements for the poor in a number of communities. In some of the communities, landlords were informed as to what maximum would be tolerated by HUD in order to protect poor people and the taxpayers from being overcharged. In other communities, landlords were not informed as to what maximum would be tolerated. In accordance with true experimentation, the communities were randomly allocated to each of these two alternative policies. It was interestingly found that the communities which in effect had rent control standards tended to charge higher rents under the rent supplement program than communities with no rent control standards. The explanation was that the landlords interpreted the standards as allowing or even encouraging them to raise their rents to the maximum without risking any loss of rent-supplement tenants. In the other communities, landlords were reluctant to raise their rents for fear they would lose tenants who reliably paid the rent as a result of the rent supplements and who tended to take reasonably good care of the property as a result of the selection criteria for determining who gets rent supplements.

Other examples include the attempts by the Law Enforcement Assistance Administration to fund special pre-trial release projects in various communities

---

[8]An analysis of the effects of government structures on societal productivity is partly related to an analysis of the advantages and disadvantages of alternative government structures, although those analyses use a variety of criteria other than societal productivity. See Herbert Levine, *Political Issues Debated: An Introduction to Politics* (Englewood Cliffs, N.J.: Prentice-Hall, 1982); Charles Dunn, *American Democracy Debated* (Glenview, Ill.: Scott, Foresman, 1982); Neal Riemer (ed.), *Problems of American Government* (New York: McGraw-Hill, 1952); and Leslie Lipson, *The Great Issues of Politics* (Englewood Cliffs, N.J.: Prentice-Hall, 1981).

and then to make comparisons across communities with different types of projects or with no projects at all. One could point out that federalism is not essential for such inter-place experiments since unitary governments also have diverse cities that can be the basis of such experiments. A federal form of government, however, does encourage diversity and an experimental tradition across both states and cities more so than a unitary government is likely to do.

Federalism provides multiple policy-formation places for generating new ideas. In the American context, that means 50 state governors and 50 state legislatures. They are more likely to generate new innovation concerning public policy than if they were just employees in 50 field offices of a national government department. The semi-autonomy of the 50 states generates independence which leads to innovation. Innovation in turn leads to increased productivity, although only a small portion of innovative ideas may be productivity successes. Examples include new technological and management science developments in dealing with crime, fire-fighting, pollution, transportation, and other urban policy problems. State highway departments, for example, do some times develop new ideas relevant to road-building, and state universities certainly are a source of a great deal of innovation. One might, however, point out that state government agencies as contrasted to state universities, have not been as innovative in developing new technologies as private contractors have been. That may reflect a lack of adequate incentives in state bureaucracies, but they are more likely to be innovative under a federal system than under a unitary system.

One of the main ways in which federalism encourages societal productivity is by the healthy competition among the states for attracting business firms and population. The competition is healthy when it is based on offering better governmental services. It is not so healthy in terms of societal benefits and costs if it is based on allowing business firms to operate with child labor, racially discriminatory practices, or unsafe working conditions. Those socially undesirable forms of competition, though, tend to be eliminated or lessened by federal legislation which provides more uniform standards where they seem to be socially desirable. To a considerable extent, people move from one state to another for reasons of economic opportunities, educational opportunities, and climate/scenery. State governments can definitely influence educational opportunities by how much money they choose to allocate to schools. They can also influence economic opportunities by offering business firms legitimate tax breaks for locating in their respective states, especially where the business firm and the state have mutually beneficial interests. States can even influence the scenery factor by how much money they choose to devote to improving their recreational environment.

On the other hand, federalism can interfere with societal productivity by generating some wasteful duplicative effort and conflicting governmental regulations. The duplicative effort of maintaining 50 state governments may not involve very much incremental cost over the governmental presence that would otherwise have to be maintained if there were 50 or even 10 national government regions or sub-regions. More important, the costs of excessive duplication may be substantially less than the costs of not obtaining the opportunities for innovation that come from 50 heads rather than one. As for conflicting inter-state regulations, the Supreme Court attempts to deal with that by declaring them in violation of the free flow of interstate commerce. When business firms object to so-called conflicting state regulations, they are generally objecting to the idea of being subject to economic regulation, regardless whether it is uniform or non-uniform regulation.

SEPARATION OF POWERS

Just as 50 state governments plus one national government are more likely to lead to innovative ideas than just one national government with or without 50 regional offices, so also is innovation likely to be increased by having executive and legislative branches of government that are independent of each other, with both separately seeking to appeal to voters. Separation of powers was originally defended as a conservative check-and-balance idea. It could also be defended as a way of increasing innovation. However, requiring that new ideas be adopted by two branches of government and two legislative houses can delay the implementation of new ideas.

There is clearly a healthy competition between federal executive agencies and Congress in seeking to develop technically competent units that can evaluate and propose new policies for achieving given goals. Within the 1970's, four congressional agencies have greatly improved their competence in that regard, namely, the General Accounting Office, the Congressional Budget Office, the Office of Technology Assessment, and the Congressional Research Service. The competence of congressional staffs for doing policy analysis has also improved. On the executive side, more systematic policy evaluation is now being done by the Office of Management and Budget, the White House Domestic Staff, and specialized evaluation units within HUD, HHS, DOE, Labor, Defense, etc. Those developments are partly attributable to executive agencies taking the lead and Congress feeling the need to keep up by improving its own policy evaluation competence. If the chief executive were an extension of the legislature by way of being a parliamentary prime minister, there would be less likelihood of those developments, which are conducive to better governmental policies and societal productivity.

Many recent concrete examples can be given of the development of diverse ideas between Congress and the White House. For example, since 1965 there have been substantial differences between the branches of government concerning foreign policy in Viet Nam and in Latin America. There have been substantial differences on how to deal with energy problems, inflation-unemployment, and social welfare matters. That has been true when Congress and the president have been dominated by different political parties as in the Nixon and Ford administrations. It has also been true when the Democrats have controlled both branches of government, as in the Johnson and Carter administrations. It is also true in the Reagan administration, with the White House and the Senate under Republican control, and the House of Representatives under Democratic control. The key question is whether the productivity benefit of multiple sources of ideas outweighs the productivity detriment of slowness in getting the new ideas adopted. The system in effect represents a compromise between innovation and stability with innovation especially coming in times of the domestic crises of a depression/recession or a period of upheaval in the demands of relatively worse off groups within society, as indicated by the innovative policy periods of the 1930's and the 1960's.

JUDICIAL REVIEW AND JUDICIAL POWER

Whether or not judicial review has been conducive to societal productivity is a controversial issue. Judicial review did hold back the rights of workers and consumers from about 1880 to 1935, and it did expand the rights of minorities from 1935 to the present. Thus, the value of judicial review to societal productivity depends partly on whether one considers the expanded rights of workers, consumers, and minorities to be productive or counter-productive. The matter of minorities is discussed below under democracy. The matter of the relevance of worker and consumer rights is discussed here, although that is partly an issue of socialism versus capitalism, which was discussed in the previous chapters. Judicial review or judicial power can be discussed as an abstract structural matter (as was done with federalism and separation of powers) instead of in terms of the substance of its exercise. As an abstraction, it seems neither productive nor unproductive, unlike federalism or separation of powers. Its productivity is more meaningfully judged by looking to the substantive policies that it has eventually allowed or even endorsed.

By increasing the rights of workers, the Supreme Court and the judicial process have encouraged the adoption of labor-saving technology, which has thereby increased the productivity of labor and of society. This has been true with regard to workers' rights concerning child labor, minimum wages, maximum hours, unionization, occupational health and safety, and workmen's compensation. Many of those workers' rights have come from legislation, but the Supreme Court has played an important role in nullifying or legitimizing the legislation, and the courts in general have often developed rights through interpretation of statutes and/or common law principles.

On the other hand, one can argue that productivity increased most in the United States during the 1800's when the courts gave business largely a free hand in dealing with workers and consumers. A counter-argument is that when one starts with such a low base, it is easy to have big percentage increases. One can also argue that in the 1800's, the geographical frontier and the new immigration facilitated productivity increases. Some might also argue that the 1800's represented a stage in knowledge development when it was relatively easy to invent new things. It may be even easier, now, however, given the greater knowledge base that we have.

By increasing the rights of consumers, the courts have encouraged the development of better quality products. That has increased societal productivity in the sense of societal benefits minus societal costs. This has been true of consumer rights concerning labeling of products, product safety, rights to sue for negligent manufacturing, and rights to sue for breach of implied warranties. A counter-argument is to emphasize that the best way to get improvements in the quality of products is through the market place by people voting with their dollars. On the other hand, consumer sovereignty does not mean much in a relatively non-competitive economy. Consumers can also exercise their dollar-voting more effectively if informative labeling is required.

By increasing worker rights, workers may thereby have their morale lifted so they are in a more positive frame of mind about their work, and are thus possibly likely to be more efficient. If, however, workers are happier when they have more rights, then what about management being happier? In other words, the court decisions may lessen management incentives to develop new technologies, since the court decisions do make being an entrepreneurial business person less profitable than it otherwise would be.

Freeing capital from its obligations to workers and consumers does not necessarily mean that it will be invested in improved technology. The freed capital may just generate bigger profits, bigger executive salaries, and more corporate waste. By freeing capital, however, business is able to use at least some of it to develop new technologies. One must be willing to incur some waste in order to get productive new technologies. Much of the potential technology-money may go to profits and salaries, but if it goes to workers, it may be equally or even more unproductive.

THE TWO-PARTY SYSTEM

There is a close relation between the two-party system and democracy, as mentioned in discussing the relations among the governmental structures. Majority rule would not be very meaningful without political parties to serve as an intermediary between the people and the government. Political parties provide candidates for the majority to choose among in electing representatives to the government. Likewise, minority rights to attempt to convert the majority imply the right to form an opposition party for systematically expressing minority viewpoints. In view of those relations, the discussion below of the productivity of both the majority-rule and minority-rights aspects of democracy in effect serves as a main part of the discussion of the productivity aspects of the two-party system.

There are, however, some aspects of the system which are worth mentioning separate from the democracy discussion. The two-party system stimulates more innovation than a one-party system, although maybe less than a multi-party system. The two party system, however, is able to function more effectively and with more stability for carrying out the program of the dominant party than a multiple-party system, although maybe less than a one-party system. In other words, the two-party system represents a compromise between (1) the greater innovation but lesser efficiency of the multiple-party system, and (2) the lesser innovation but greater efficiency of the one party system.

The lack of relatively sharp ideological differences between the American parties allows new ideas to be developed and applied without too much fear that if there is a change in the political parties, everything will be wiped out. On the other hand, the lack of ideological differences means less competition and thus less choice for the voters, although there are still choices across individuals. Thus the American ideological differences provide more competition and choice than a one-party system or a system of non-ideological parties, but not so much contrast as to jeopardize desirable continuity when there is a change in parties.

DEMOCRACY

Democracy as defined above includes both majority rule and minority rights to try to convert the majority to minority viewpoints. As for the majority rule element, there are a number of points that can be made in favor of majority rule as being conducive to societal productivity, such as:

1. People almost genetically have a desire to exert control over their destinies. Democracy gives them at least the feeling that they are playing some part in controlling the government. Democracy thereby tends to make people feel happier in that regard, assuming all other things are held constant.
2. The more people who participate in government and politics, the greater is the leadership pool and the innovation potential. Thus, if an individual with valuable ideas and leadership qualities is in one of the disenfranchised groups in a society that does not enfranchise virtually all adult groups, then that person's abilities may not be put to good use.

3. A democratic form of government is more efficient because if it is not, it can be more easily voted out of office. A government that is not subject to being removed by majority rule may be less likely to improve itself. It may only change by shifting office holders through the equivalent of palace revolutions, but not change in terms of basic principles.
4. A democratic government in the hands of the people more quickly finds out about complaints, and it can thus better remedy the source of those complaints. By remedying those complaints and thereby obtaining more popular support, society is likely to have a more productive population than one that feels antagonistic toward the government and society.
5. Democratic governments tend to rely on an educated citizenry in order to function well, but they also tend to encourage citizens to become more politically enlightened by providing citizens with learning experiences through participating in governmental activities, especially on the local level.
6. Democracies are sometimes criticized because they move more slowly in making decisions by virtue of their governmental structures which require more approval by representatives of the people. That delay may, however, be more than justified if the decisions reached are more effective and efficient than they otherwise would be.
7. Democracies are also sometimes criticized because majoritarian rule can mean a lot of authority to those who are lacking in expert knowledge, a favorable orientation toward new ideas, or lacking in an attitude toward being especially productive. That may be a largely irrelevant point, though, if the leadership does tend to be reasonably knowledgeable, receptive toward innovation, and oriented toward societal productivity.

As for the minority rights element of democracy, there are a number of points that can be made in favor of minority rights to convert the majority as being conducive to societal productivity, such as:

1. In matters of science, the free circulation of popular, unpopular, and extremely unpopular ideas allows the truth to have a better chance of getting accepted. A dramatic example of where a dictatorial society was severely hurt by restricting freedom of scientific speech was Nazi Germany with regard to the development of nuclear weapons. In the 1930's Einstein physics was looked upon by Hitler as Jewish physics and not to be encouraged. As a result, Nazi Germany lost time in the development of nuclear energy and weapons. In the meantime, Einstein helped convince President Roosevelt to develop the atomic weapons which helped the United States win World War II. That was a high opportunity cost for Nazi Germany to pay. A dramatic example of where a dictatorial socialistic society was severely hurt by restricting freedom of scientific speech was Communist Russia with regard to development of hybrid

grains. In the 1950's, Mendelian genetics was looked upon by Stalin as Catholic biology and not to be encouraged. As a result, the Soviet Union encouraged an approach to growing crops that emphasized providing a good environment more than good genes. Environmentalism was in conformity with Stalin's interpretation of Marxism. Those were the years in which the Soviet Union fell from being a breadbasket of Europe to an importer of foreign grains to the substantial detriment of its economy and its international trade, from which it still may not have fully recovered.

2. In matters of policy rather than science, freedom of speech allows the most effective means in achieving given ends to have a better chance of getting adopted. A dramatic example of that from within the United States is the prohibition on advocating the abolition of slavery, which existed in the South in the 1800's prior to the Civil War. Those restrictions on that minority viewpoint may have helped delay the conversion of the southern economy from a slave economy to a free economy, and that delay may have facilitated the occurrence of the Civil War. More important, the legacy of prolonged slavery was probably a key factor in holding back the south for many years after the Civil War. Even now, the legacy of prolonged slavery may be a key factor responsible for at least some of the race relations problems of the United States. The occurrence of slavery is highly correlated with having a relatively unproductive, inefficient economy which provides little incentive for introducing modern labor-saving technology that can greatly raise standards of living. The poorest parts of the world are those that practice slavery, serfdom, peonage, and related forms of human bondage, and that generally place restrictions on advocating alternative economic systems.

3. Freedom of speech also provides a check on leadership that is corrupt, inefficient, and not complying with the legal system. The U.S. Supreme Court has recognized in some of its opinions that freedom of speech may be the most important right in the Bill of Rights. Without it, the other rights are less meaningful if one cannot inform others that the rights are being violated. Even the dictatorial Soviet Union at the height of the Stalin era encouraged people to speak out against corrupt and inefficient leadership, at least at the lower and middle leadership levels so long as the basic principles of Communism were not attacked. The government has provided a subsidized periodical called Krokodile that carries articles and reports critical of bureaucrats who are not properly carrying out five-year plans and other Soviet policies.

4. Freedom of speech tends to raise standards of living by ways of points 1, 2, and 3 with regard to developing better science, public policy, and the implementation of science and public policy. Some of the effect of free speech on higher standards of living is indirect by virtue of free speech leading to increased industrialization and education which in turn leads to higher standards of living. Cross-national studies that classify countries in terms of

being permissive, middling, or repressive with regard to free speech tend to show that the more permissive societies are the ones with the most industrialization and the highest standards of living.

5. One argument that sometimes is made against freedom of speech is that it creates an unstable society by encouraging agitation and possibly even violent change. The realities, however, are just the opposite. The same cross-national studies tend to show that the more permissive societies also have the highest stability and degree of change through peaceful means. The explanation is partly that free speech provides a safety valve which decreases the likelihood of resorting to violence. Free speech also tends to be highly correlated with having a large educated middle class, which in turn demands majority rule which tends to facilitate non-violent change. In the absence of majority rule, entrenched minorities sometimes have to be dislodged by means other than voting them out of office after an appropriate educational campaign.

SOME CONCLUSIONS

On the basis of the previous discussion, one can reach three sets of conclusions. They relate to evaluating government structures in historical terms, evaluating structures in more general terms, and the policy implications for improving government structures.

EVALUATING GOVERNMENT STRUCTURES IN HISTORICAL TERMS

On the basis of this analysis, one can conclude that the American government structures may be desirable from the perspective of promoting societal productivity, but that they are not necessarily transportable to other nations. In other words, those structures may be quite productive to the United States in light of its historical development, but they might not be so productive to any country like England or the Soviet Union in light of their historical development. For example, federalism is more meaningful to the U.S. than England because the U.S. is a larger, more diverse country that would be more difficult to govern as a unitary country. It also came into existence by building on 13 separate nations that formed a confederacy and for whom a federal form of government was as big a step as they would have been likely to take in light of that background.

Likewise, the absence of separation of powers in England reflects the fact that Parliament developed as a manifestation of middle class opposition to a feudal monarchy. The prime minister was originally spokesman for Parliament or the dominant party in Parliament. As the power of the monarchy receded, the prime minister became the chief executive, but his election by the Parliament rather than by the people was retained. The U.S. on the other hand chose to have an elected chief executive because it needed a chief executive, and a democratic procedure seemed more appropriate to the principles of the Declaration of Independence and the American Revolution than establishing an American monarchy.

Judicial review is also more meaningful in the American than in the English context. One cannot have a meaningful system of judicial review (whereby the courts determine whether the constitution is being violated by the executive or legislative branches of government) unless one has a constitution that is embodied in a reasonably clear and integrated document. That is true of the American constitution. The British constitution (in the sense of the fundamental principles of British government) is scattered among a variety of documents and traditions. American judicial review also owes its existence to the coincidental presence of Chief Justice John Marshall in the formative years of American government in view of his establishment of the principle in the convenient case of Marbury vs. Madison.

The U.S. party system does not have as sharp an ideological split as the English party system largely because the American population is not as sharply divided along class lines in view of the greater upward mobility in the U.S. In order to have a labor party, it is important to have a working class that identifies itself as a working class. In the U.S., however, people have traditionally considered themselves only temporarily in the working class until they or their children could through hard work and education become management people or enter the professions.

If the ideological differences are extremely sharp and antagonistic, then a one-party system is likely to develop because the party in power may find it difficult to tolerate the opposition party given that history of antagonism. That kind of phenomenon helps explain the one-party system of the Soviet Union where intense hatreds were developed between the conflicting ideologies prior to 1917. That kind of conflict also leads to a tradition of not tolerating vigorous advocacy of minority viewpoints. As less developed countries become better educated, however, the people tend to demand more popular input and more tolerance of ideological differences.

EVALUATING STRUCTURES IN MORE GENERAL TERMS

In general, the position that a nation chooses to take on each of the five basic dimensions tends to be reinforcing of the other positions. For example, federalism, separation of powers, judicial review, the two-party system, and democracy in the United States tend to be supportive of each other, as indicated by the analysis of the relations among the government structures in Table 6-2. Likewise, in England, the unitary system, parliamentary government, concurrent review, the two-party system, and democracy tend to be internally consistent given the smallness, the homogeneity, and the history of England.

Within the Soviet Union, the nominal federal system, parliamentary system, concurrent review, the one-party system, and the absence of democracy also tend to be internally consistent given the largeness, the heterogeneity, and the history of the Soviet Union. If those structures were to operate inconsistently within a country, they would be likely to undergo change, regardless whether the inconsistency is among the structures or is between the structures and the society or the economy.

Within the American, English, or Russian context, the structures do play a part in influencing policy decisions. In the U.S., they tend to make for more decentralization, less coordination, more constitutional constraint, more sta- bilized political competition, and more popular support than would be the case if the U.S. chose opposite positions on those five dimensions. English and Russian policy, on the other hand, tend to be more centralized, more coordin- ated, and less constrained by constitutionalism. English policy, however, differs from Russian policy partly because of the two-party competition in England and the greater influence of the public and minority viewpoints.

Although the structures that a policy system adopts and maintains are likely to be internally consistent and are likely to influence public policy, not all structures seem to be equally productive in terms of facilitating policy choices that are likely to maximize or achieve societal benefits minus societal costs. A political climate more conducive to the development of innovative ideas is produced by federalism, separation of legislative-executive powers, judge-made laws, two or more political parties, and democratic tolerance of minority viewpoints. Innovation may be the key to large-scale productivity-improvement on the theory that operating with the previous pool of ideas may stagnate a society no matter how well those ideas are applied. Implementation, however, is also important. Japan represents a society that implements ideas well, which are obtained from elsewhere, but Japan has not been one of the world's innovators. The United States has been highly innovative in its universities, small businesses, and some aspects of government research work, but it has recently been slow in implementing new ideas, especially when doing so requires adoption by so many governmental entities. What may be needed are a set of governmental structures that allow for multiple policy-formation foci, but at the same time provides for governmental institutions specifically oriented toward the implementation of new ideas for increasing societal productivity.

POLICY IMPLICATIONS FOR IMPROVING GOVERNMENTAL STRUCTURES

The countries of the world that seem to be moving most rapidly as of 1982 in terms of productivity improvement include Japan, West Germany, and Sweden. Their governmental structures do not differ greatly from the United

States. All four countries are democracies with two-party or two-bloc systems. West Germany is a federal government, whereas the other two are unitary. Sweden has no judicial review, whereas the other two have some aspects of judicial review, partly imposed by the United States after the end of World War II. All three have parliamentary forms of government that may facilitate coordination which the United States lacks and which would be helpful in implementing new ideas. The possibly greater reluctance of the U.S. to implement new ideas in the private and public sector may, however, be more attributable to such factors as:

1. American business has traditionally had captive domestic markets that provided a disincentive to implement new ideas, whereas those other countries have been more accustomed to international competition.
2. American business and American public opinion tend to look for profits within a short time frame, which interferes with implementing expensive new ideas that are not likely to pay for a while.
3. American business may be less respectful of the new ideas of American academics than business people are in Japan, West Germany, and Sweden.
4. American business has had less of an incentive to start over by virtue of not having been bombed out as happened to West Germany and Japan.
5. Long-term expensive investment may have to come from the government, but American business may be more resistant to governmental activity in business decisions.
6. American labor may be more resistant to implementing new ideas because of a greater feeling of insecurity than Japanese workers have.
7. The United States spends a larger dollar amount and percentage amount for defense than any of those countries. Those expenditures can be seriously interfering with the ability of the United States to implement expensive new ideas.

If the above factors are holding back American implementation of new ideas for increasing societal productivity, then what role can the government play to lessen their adverse influence? Relevant policies corresponding to the above seven factors include:

1. The government can encourage the stimulus of international competition by refraining from adopting tariffs or other restrictions on foreign trade. Allowing international competition will stimulate American business, as well as provide benefits for American consumers.
2. There is a need for the American government to play a greater role in societal investment decisions in partnership with business and labor the way the Japanese government does. The government does not have to report

yearly profits to stockholders the way corporate officers do, thereby facilitating a long-term and more national perspective.

3. American government should seek to stimulate better relations between business and academia by subsidizing exchanges of personnel through visiting professorships and visiting executiveships, as well as through subsidized conferences, mid-career training, and better information systems.

4. It is unreasonable to think that the American government would bomb out an industry, but the American government can pay for the dismantling and replacement of obsolete equipment.

5. American government needs to put more emphasis on positive incentives to get business to do socially desired activities instead of relying on regulation, litigation, and negative sanctions, which inevitably generate negative relations between business and government.

6. American government needs to have a more vigorous policy of providing job security, retraining, and loans to start new businesses/jobs, so as to lessen the anxieties of American workers who feel threatened by the implementation of new ideas.

7. American government needs to more actively pursue means for reducing arms expenditures between the U.S. and the Soviet Union in order to free billions of dollars in potential capital for implementing new ideas.

None of those suggestions require that the United States abandon its presidential form of government for a better coordinated parliamentary form of government in order to be able to implement desirable new ideas more easily. Perhaps a parliamentary form of government would produce greater societal productivity if all the other variables were held constant. The impact, however, seems relatively trivial in comparison to the more important governmental activities mentioned above. It also seems relatively trivial in comparison to the productivity benefits of federalism, having two or more major political parties, and allowing popular minority viewpoints to have an opportunity to try to convert the majority. One also needs to be politically realistic and recognize that there is virtually no chance of changing from a presidential form of government to a parliamentary form, given how well entrenched the presidential form is, and given its consistency with the democratic desire of the people to elect the President.

In conclusion, the United States does seem to have a set of political structures that are reasonably conducive to societal productivity. What seems to be needed is not a changing of those structures, although they are constantly evolving to better fit changing times. Rather what is needed is a recognition on the part of American government policymakers that the American government has positive responsibilities for stimulating societal productivity. Those responsibilities may manifest themselves in the form of tax breaks for big business when a conservative administration is in power. They may manifest themselves in the form of an expansion of the public sector when a liberal administration is in power. The important development going into the 1990's is the recognition by both sides that societal productivity is too important to be left to society and the economy alone without the help of meaningful public policy-making.

PART FOUR:

COORDINATING PUBLIC

AND PRIVATE SECTORS

7

A BETTER DIVISION OF LABOR

A broad level issue in the discussion of public policy (at least since ancient times) has been the division of labor between the government and private enterprise in administering societal activities. This is partly the traditional issue of socialism (or collectivism) versus capitalism (or individualism). Until recently, the debate has focused on who should own the major means of production and distribution. The contemporary debate tends to place more emphasis on how should the government and public policy stimulate either public or business administrators to be more productive for the good of society. The matter of alternative incentives for encouraging socially desirable behavior is the subject of the previous chapter. This chapter is more concerned with who should administer public or societal activities, regardless who has ownership rights.

The chapter is divided into two main parts. The first part deals with developing criteria for who should administer public functions between public (or government) and private (or business administration). That part is especially concerned with showing examples of good and bad public and private administration. One purpose is to get across the idea that whether public or private administration is most appropriate depends on a number of pragmatic circumstances, and cannot be resolved by ideological dogma. The second part of the chapter is concerned with alternative forms of public involvement and developing criteria for deciding among the alternative forms. Those forms can include total non-involvement, government subsidies, private litigation, regulation, and government ownership in the order of degree of involvement.[1]

WHAT IS A PUBLIC FUNCTION?

Before discussing who should administer public functions, it seems appropriate to discuss what is a public function. A public function is an activity that a majority or substantial quantity of the people in a society agree needs to be provided on a collective basis rather than on an individual basis. An example is having an army to defend the society from attack. This can be contrasted to having each individual citizen own nuclear weapons so he or she can be the equivalent of a one-person army. That would be intolerable in terms of the danger that citizens would present to each other. Having an army can also be contrasted to having each individual own a rifle and be available on call to defend the nation from nuclear attack or against a conventional army. That would be a rather useless defense force in the 1990's, even if it worked in 1775 at Lexington and Concord.

Just because some activity like having an army is decided to be a public or societal function does not mean it has to be administered by the government. There is no inherent reason why General Motors or Westinghouse could not be given a contract to hire an army and procure weapons to defend the United States. We do not resort to privatization when it comes to having an army because it is probably not benefit-cost effective. The cost would be far higher than we could pay draftees or even semi-patriotic volunteers. The benefits of successful combat would also be less since mercenaries are less likely to sacrifice their lives than soldiers imbued with saving their country.

Having a national army may be the most widely accepted public function. At the opposite extreme might be an activity like having houses of ill-repute. Most people, at least in American society, seem to feel that houses of ill-repute should not be provided either by the government or by the private sector. This does not mean that people are in favor of police crackdowns on non-obtrusive, one-on-one prostitution. The issue regarding houses of ill-repute in the United States is not whether such houses should be government institutions or private businesses. Rather the issue is whether they should be provided to people at all. The answer is generally no, with the exception of Nevada and possibly a

---

[1] For further details on the public-private controversy in a contemporary context, see Emanuel. S. Savas, *Privatization: The Key to Better Government* (Chatham, N.J.: Chatham House, 1987); Martin Rein and Lee Rainwater (eds.), *Public/Private Interplay in Social Protection: A Comparative Study* (Armonk, N.Y.: M.E. Sharpe, 1986); Dennis Thompson (ed.), *The Private Exercise of Public Functions* (Port Washington, N.Y.: Associated Faculty Press, 1985); and Richard Hula (ed.), *Market Based Public Policy* (London: Macmillan, 1987). Also see the symposium issues on privatization of the *Journal of Policy Analysis and Management* (Summer, 1987), the *Public Administration Review* (November/December, 1987), and the *Proceedings of the Academy of Political Science* (1987).

few other places. On this matter, it is up to each individual to make his or her own arrangements to buy, sell, or otherwise obtain sex without expecting society to provide either government or private enterprise brothels. At one time, private enterprise brothels were quite popular, but they have disappeared at least partly because of such technological developments as the telephone (which has facilitated the call girl business) and the automobile (which has facilitated the street-walker business).

Between the national army (which is well-accepted) and the house of ill repute (which is well-rejected), there are a number of activities that people feel a properly functioning society should provide. There may, however, be disagreement as to whether they should be government-provided or provided by private enterprise. An example is airline service. All civilian passenger airlines in the United States are privately owned. Virtually all passenger airlines elsewhere in the world are government owned. One could have a government-owned airline that is managed by a private managing company, although there does not seem to be such an airline in existence. Like passenger airlines, other examples of societal activities that are sometimes government owned and sometimes privately owned include electric power companies, telephone companies, and steel mills, but seldom garden plots, small retail operations, or services like barbering.

An interesting new phenomenon is the government-owned facility that is privately managed. This is the case with some prisons in the United States. The government owns the prison, but it gives a contract to a private company to hire management personnel and guards to administer the prison. It is also the case with some public housing projects which are owned by the government, but managed by a private real estate management company. One can also have the opposite counterpart which is a privately owned facility that is operated by the government. An example would be a privately owned apartment building which the government rents and manages for use as a public housing project. One could likewise have a building that consists of nothing but government offices and government administrators, but the building is owned and leased by a private landlord.

Thus, we can classify activities in terms of whether people consider them essential to a properly functioning society or either non-essential or detrimental. We can then classify the ones that are considered essential public functions into those that are or should be government provided, and those that are or should be provided by private enterprise. We can further sub-classify the government-provided functions into those in which government employees do the providing, or those in which the government hires a private entity to do the providing. We can likewise sub-classify the private-enterprise activities into those that have no government involvement at all and those in which there is government involvement in the form of subsidies, liability rules, regulation, or some combination of all three forms of government involvement in private-enterprise activities.[2]

WHO SHOULD ADMINISTER PUBLIC FUNCTIONS?

In order to answer the question as to who should administer public functions, it would be helpful to describe some examples where public administration is generally recognized as being more successful, and some examples where it is generally recognized as being less successful than private administration. From those examples, we should be able to see some general principles or criteria for deciding who should administer public functions.

EXAMPLES OF GOOD PUBLIC AND BAD PRIVATE ADMINISTRATION

Legal services for the poor is an example in which public administration has been reasonably effective, efficient, and equitable in comparison to private administration. In this context, public legal services refers to the Legal Services Program of the Office of Economic Opportunity which was established in 1965 and followed by the Legal Services Corporation in 1976. Private legal services for the poor refers to the charitable legal aid programs that existed prior to 1965 and even now to a lesser extent, along with proposed government reimbursement programs operated like Medicare-Medicaid.

Quantity of cases processed and quantity won is a measure of effectiveness in this area. Prior to 1965, legal aid programs in middle-sized cities like Champaign-Urbana handled only a small quantity of cases compared to the large quantity subsequently handled by the Legal Services Program. In the years 1964 and 1965, the Champaign County Legal Aid Program handled 50 and 49 cases respectively. In 1966, the Champaign County Legal Services Program was handling about 100 cases every month, and successfully closing them through advice, negotiation, or sometimes litigation. The reasons for the increased effectiveness included (1) maintaining a regular location rather than scattered volunteers, (2) publicizing the availability of legal services, (3) establishing trust with poor people, including militant poor people, (4) specializing and acquiring expertise in poverty law problems, and (5) having some federal funds available for facilities, equipment, and salaries. One should also note that the cases handled by full-time salaried Legal Services lawyers

---

[2]For further details on the nature of public functions, see "Political Systems: The Ordering of Human Relations" in Melville Herskovits, *Man and His Works* (New York: Knopf, 1952), 327-346; "The Emergence of Government" in Robert MacIver, *The Web of Government* (New York: Macmillan, 1951), 3-60; and "Political Sociology" in Raymond Mack and Kimball Young, *Sociology and Social Life* (New York: American Book Company, 1968), 395-416.

tend to be more important precedents than the more routine cases handled by traditional legal aid or Judicare systems.

As for efficiency, meaning cost-saving, one would think legal aid volunteers would be more efficient. They do save the taxpayer money, but they do not necessarily save society money. An example of their wastefulness was having lawyers come to the county courthouse every Saturday morning to wait for poor people to show up with legal problems. Many mornings were spent with virtually no clients, given the low visibility and acceptability of the program among poor people. The Legal Services Program, on the other hand, has been able to get competent attorneys at low wages partly by drawing on their idealism, although they need replacing each year. Contracting out the legal services under a Judicare system analogous to Medicare is far more expensive. Judicare has been rejected for both civil and criminal cases in favor of less expensive public defenders and LSC attorneys who operate on relatively low salaries, rather than relatively high case-by-case fees.

As for equity, the traditional legal aid programs were not very evenly spread. They tended to exist only in big cities and only in downtown areas. They were not so available to the rural poor, or even the urban poor who did not come to the down town area. The OEO Legal Services Program and the LSC have prided themselves on their neighborhood law offices to reach out to poor neighborhoods and also rural legal services. The LSC can be found in white Appalachia, Indian reservations, black ghettos, Hispanic barrios, the rural South, and the rural North.

In addition to doing better on criteria of effectiveness, efficiency, and equity, the government-provided legal services for the poor also does better on political criteria. This includes public participation by members of the poverty community, the bar, and public officials. It also includes predictability as to what it takes to qualify in terms of objective poverty guidelines. It also includes procedural due process whereby those who feel they have been wrongly denied legal services can have a meaningful procedure available to voice their complaint and obtain a hearing. The salaried Legal Services Program also serves as a liberal symbol of concern for the legal rights of the poor, and as a conservative symbol designed to promote respect for the legal system.

There are those who object to legal services for the poor on the grounds that it disrupts landlords and merchants, takes cases away from other lawyers, or pushes radical causes. In the 20 years of federal legal services, however, there have been no scandals regarding padded bills or services charged that were not provided. This is in sharp contrast to the Medicare and Medicaid system of private medical services for the poor which has had numerous scandals involving doctors, nursing homes, pharmacists, dentists, and other health care providers. This is one reason the Reagan administration advocated a volunteer program to provide legal services to the poor, rather than a

Judicare program with government reimbursement to private-sector lawyers.[3]

EXAMPLES OF GOOD PRIVATE AND BAD PUBLIC ADMINISTRATION

Housing for the poor is an example in which the private sector has been reasonably effective, efficient, and equitable in comparison to public administration. In this context, public housing means government owned and operated housing projects for the poor. Private housing means rent subsidies to the private sector to enable the private sector to provide housing for low-income tenants.

On the matter of effectiveness, public housing has been a failure compared to rent supplement programs. In terms of quantity of housing made available, there has been little increased public housing in the United States since about 1970. In fact there have been some dramatic decreases, such as literally blowing up the Pruitt-Igoe Homes in St. Louis. They were considered bankrupt in the sense of consistently costing more to maintain than the monetary or non-monetary benefits could justify. On the other hand, the private sector is willing to make available almost unlimited housing to the poor, so long as poor people with rent supplements can pay the rent.

On the matter of efficiency, public housing projects have been extremely expensive per dwelling unit. They were originally designed to save money by being high rise, which decreases land costs and enables every floor to also be a ceiling with many common walls. The lack of more individualized dwelling units, however, has led to a lack of sense of ownership or even possession. That has led to vandalism and the failure to report it. Rent supplements, on the other hand, save money in such ways as (1) avoiding the initial building cost by using existing housing stock, (2) encouraging better care of the property, thereby lowering maintenance costs that might otherwise require higher rent supplements, and (3) increasing self-pride and ambition which lowers the costs of welfare and crime committing.

On the matter of equity, public housing has resulted in discrimination against poor whites and segregation of poor blacks. Whites have in effect been discriminated against as a result of public housing projects being located disproportionately in black neighborhoods where the projects have frequently become all black. Rent supplements, on the other hand, are as available to poor whites as they are to poor blacks. Also important is the fact that rent

---

[3]For further details on alternative ways of providing legal services to the poor, see Arthur Berney et al., *Legal Problems of the Poor: Cases and Materials* (Boston: Little, Brown, 1975); Legal Services Corporation, *The Delivery Systems Study* (Washington, D.C.: LSC, 1980); Lee Silverstein, *Defense of the Poor in Criminal Cases in American State Courts* (Chicago: American Bar Foundation, 1965); and S. Nagel, "Effects of Alternative Types of Counsel on Criminal Procedure Treatment," 48 *Indiana Law Journal* 404 (1973).

supplements can easily lead to racial and class integration, whereas big housing projects are not easily absorbed in white or middle class neighborhoods.

Public housing also does poorly on the political values of public participation, predictable rules, and procedural due process in view of how authoritarian and arbitrary public housing projects have traditionally been managed. This is in contrast to the greater dignity associated with rent supplements. The rent supplement program also serves as a liberal symbol of doing something important for the poor, while also being a conservative symbol of the meaningfulness of private-sector property.

It is relevant to note that although rent supplements are an example of good private administration of a societal function, that is not the case with the mortgage supplement program of the early 1970's. That program involved the federal government making funds available for poor people to buy homes through private real estate agents, rather than through HUD employees or other public administrators. The privately administered program became a scandal, worse than used-car fraud or the Medicare-Medicaid frauds. Real estate agents failed to inform low income buyers of the maintenance costs of bad heating, plumbing, and electrical systems. Trying to meet those costs frequently interfered with meeting even the low mortgage payments. As a result, foreclosures were frequent, analogous to used car repossessions, but with the federal government making good on whatever was owed. The greed factor became so great that it was not enough to double or triple collect on the same house through foreclosures. Assessors were bribed to inflate the value of the houses to further increase what was collected. The program was soon abandoned even though it began with strong liberal and conservative support, and might have succeeded if it were administered by salaried government employees, rather than by private real estate agents operating on commissions.[4]

CRITERIA FOR DECIDING WHO SHOULD ADMINISTER PUBLIC FUNCTIONS

Looking at the above examples, the most obvious criteria relate to what might be referred to as the three E's, the three P's, and political feasibility which is closely related to liberal and conservative symbols. Those criteria are:

1. Effectiveness. This relates to how well public versus private administration

---

[4]For further details on alternative ways of providing housing to the poor, see Henry Aaron, *Shelters and Subsidies* (Washington, D.C.: Brookings, 1972); Anthony Downs, *Federal Housing Subsidies: Their Nature and Effectiveness and What We Should Do about Them* (Chicago: NAHB and Real Estate Research Corporation, 1972); and Carter McFarland, *Federal Government and Urban Problems: HUD, Successes, Failures, and the Fate of Our Cities* (Denver: Westview, 1978).

achieves the basic public function of providing legal services for the poor, housing for the poor, or whatever the public function is.

2. Efficiency. This relates to getting the cost per unit down. Salaried government employees are normally less expensive than independent contractors charging on a per-item basis. Substantial cost can be saved, however, by relying on existing private sector facilities.

3. Equity. This criterion normally favors the government because it is usually not profitable for the private sector to be concerned with equitable distribution of services and products, rather than distribution in terms of where the money is. Special circumstances may, however, make a market-place solution more equitable across race and class, as in the case of housing for the poor.

4. Public participation. If this is an important goal, it is more likely to be provided by government agencies than by private firms.

5. Predictable rules and procedural due process. This is also more likely to be provided by government agencies who have constitutional obligations to do so, more so than the private sector.

6. Feasibility from a liberal and conservative perspective. If a program is liked by both liberals and conservatives, it is likely to be a success. The Legal Services Program is liked by both liberal and conservative lawyers, although not necessarily for the same reasons. Public housing projects are disliked by both liberals and conservatives, although again not necessarily for the same reasons.

The above list of criteria is arranged roughly in order of importance. The most important criterion is probably effectiveness, followed by efficiency, equity, and the three P's. Political feasibility is more a constraint than a criterion. Without it, a program cannot be adopted or continue, regardless how well it scores on the other criteria.

A key point is that there is nothing inherent in a publicly or privately administered program that makes it likely to be more or less effective or efficient. One has to analyze each public function separately. Legal services for the poor operates better in government hands, but housing for the poor operates better largely in the private sector. Note, however, that in both cases government money is needed to make the programs successful because the low income beneficiaries or charities cannot afford to sufficiently support either program. The main reason legal services operates better in government hands is because there are not enough volunteer attorneys to do the work needed, and paying for individual cases is too expensive. The main reason rental housing operates better in private hands is because there is plenty of private housing available, and the rent supplements are actually less expensive than providing comparable housing through government owned and operated projects.[5]

ALTERNATIVE FORMS OF PUBLIC INVOLVEMENT

There are five major forms of public involvement in the administration of public functions.

FIVE FORMS

Total Non-Involvement. This is not a form of involvement, but it is important to include in the list of possibilities. It largely means leaving the provision of the public function up to the private marketplace with no government subsidies, liability rules, or regulation.

Government Subsidies. This is a way of getting the marketplace to do what is considered socially desirable for which the ordinary income and expense incentives are insufficient or non-existent. An example would be subsidizing the adoption of anti-pollution equipment which would otherwise be too expensive to business firms or municipalities without producing any increased income. Another example would be paying for the retooling of the auto or the steel industry through special tax breaks that could include totally foregoing taxes to the extent of the cost of retooling. Such a subsidy may be necessary where the stock and bond market is not so willing to provide the capital for a large, risky venture that may take years to pay off.

Private Litigation. This means the establishment of liability rules by the government and the authorizing of courts or quasi-judicial agencies to grant hearings and court orders concerning alleged violations. Private litigation could be subsidized by rules that require the losing defendant to pay the lawyer costs

---

[5]For further details concerning policy goals and criteria for deciding who should administer public functions, see Frank Fischer and John Forester (eds.), *Confronting Values in Policy Analysis: The Politics of Criteria* (Beverly Hills, Calif.: Sage, 1987); William Dunn, (ed.), *Values, Ethics, and the Practice of Policy Analysis* (Lexington, Mass.: Lexington-Heath, 1983); and "Public Policy Goals" in S. Nagel, *Public Policy: Goals, Means, and Methods* (New York: St. Martin's, 1984), 33-122. For further details dealing with the criteria of effectiveness, efficiency, equity, public participation, predictability, procedural due process, feasibility, and symbolic criteria, respectively, see Judith Bentkover, Vincent Covello, and Jeryl Mumpower (eds.), *Benefits Assessment: The State of the Art* (Dodrecht, Holland: Reidel-Kluwer, 1986); George Downs and Patrick Larkey, *The Search for Government Efficiency* (New York: Random House, 1986); Douglas Rae, et al., *Equalities* (Cambridge, Mass.: Harvard, 1981); Roland Pennock, *Liberal Democracy: Its Merits and Prospects* (New York: Rinehart, 1950); Herbert Wechsler, *Principles, Politics, and Fundamental Law* (Cambridge, Mass.: Harvard, 1961); David Fellman, *The Defendant's Rights Today* (Madison, Wisc.: University of Wisconsin Press, 1976); Helen Ingram and Dean Mann (eds.), *Why Policies Succeed or Fail* (Beverly Hills, Calif.: Sage, 1980); and Murray Edelman, *The Symbolic Uses of Politics* (Urbana, Ill.: University of Illinois Press, 1964).

of the plaintiff.

Regulation. This means establishing rules concerning how the private sector is to behave in areas like occupational health and safety, environmental protection, equal employment opportunity, labor-management relations, and other fields covered by the regulatory agencies. One difference between regulation and private litigation is that under regulation, the government brings the legal action against violators. One difference between regulations and subsidies is that regulation is backed by negative sanctions like injunctions, fines, and jail sentences, whereas subsidies are rewards or reimbursements for doing right, rather than punishments for wrong-doing.

Government Ownership. This is the ultimate in public or government involvement. It is what is usually meant by government administration. The Legal Services Program, however, involves government administration generally with no government-owned facilities. Likewise, one could have government ownership of a factory, park, or school in which a private firm is hired to run it.

EXAMPLES OF ALL FORMS OPERATING IN THE SAME INDUSTRY

In almost any industry, all five forms of public involvement operate simultaneously. This is true of such basic industries as food, shelter, clothing, police protection, and garbage collection. To obtain insights for developing criteria for deciding among the five forms, we might somewhat randomly pick three industries to observe all five forms in operation, and especially to observe under what circumstances one form rather than another is used.

Air Transportation. In the air travel industry, doing nothing has in recent years been effective for getting prices down. The best way to have low prices is to have vigorous competition which may occur without subsidies, litigation, regulation, or ownership. Subsidies, however, make a lot of sense for getting an industry started or retooled such as the airmail industry. It required expensive subsidies in its early years to literally get off the ground.

Litigation can often be helpful for decreasing abusive practices such as suing the asbestos manufacturing companies for abusing the workers. That has not been necessary in the air travel industry because an airline that has more than a couple of accidents is likely to go bankrupt, be taken over, or change its name for lack of customers. Class action lawsuits with regard to over-booking may be an example of changing the behavior of the airlines through litigation, but regulation of over-booking by the Civil Aeronautics Board and later the Department of Transportation has been more effective.

Regulation is important in the air travel industry for licensing pilots and mechanics and for inspecting planes. Airline regulation illustrates two contrasting forms of regulation. Both forms label certain types of behavior as being undesirable, such as overworking workers. One form considers the behavior to be so undesirable as to flatly prohibit it. That is the case with pilots flying more than a certain number of hours which could jeopardize the safety of the passengers. The second form considers the behavior to be undesirable, but instead of prohibiting it, the behavior is allowed to occur but at an increased cost. That is the case with overworking people at the ticket counter who are required to be paid time and a half for overtime, but they are not prohibited from working more than 40 hours a week.

Government ownership manifests itself in the air travel industry in the form of governments owning all the airports across the country that handle major airlines and large jets. The main reason seems to be that airport safety is too important and unprofitable an activity to be left to the private sector.

Automobiles. Doing nothing or having a laissez-faire government policy is useful for getting auto prices down in the context of international competition. One of the main reasons for low auto prices in the United States, or at least lower than they otherwise would be, is competition from Japan, West Germany, and elsewhere. One of the main ways of adversely interfering with those low prices is for the government to institute tariffs, import quotas, or other policies which will lessen the international competition.

An example of a government subsidy in the automobile industry that someday may pay off is the government's offer to buy a huge quantity of electric cars from any manufacturer who can develop an inexpensive, feasible version. That offer is part of the federal air pollution legislation of the 1970's. The existence of the offer has already served to stimulate manufacturers and inventors to experiment more than they otherwise would. A feasible electric car has still not been developed because it requires a storage battery that is presently too large for an ordinary car. The alternatives of driving with a long extension cord or frequently stopping to get recharged are not feasible.

An example of litigation as a regulatory device in the automobile industry is the lawsuit against the Ford Pinto or the Chevy Chevette. The Pinto was put out of business by lawsuits from people severely injured as a result of a gas tank arrangement that too easily exploded. The Chevette was also put out of business by lawsuits which successfully established that the Chevette could roll over too easily compared to what one would expect from a normal car.

Regulation in the automobile industry is illustrated by standards for decreasing pollution exhaust. Without the federal regulations, there would be little incentive for automobile manufacturers to institute pollution devices or for auto users to buy them on their own. Regulation is also widespread with regard to speed limits, stop signs, stoplights, and numerous rules of the road which make driving probably the most regulated of all activities.

Government ownership is present in the field of auto transportation since virtually all highways and streets are owned by federal, state, or local governments. The days of private toll roads ended about 200 years ago. Even our strongest conservative advocates do not seem to advocate a return to privately owned highways supported by tolls that would go to private landlords, with a different landlord every hundred yards or so.

Telecommunications. The policy of leaving matters to a competitive marketplace has been very effective in reducing prices for long-distance calling. The cost of long-distance telephone calls is one of the few items that has decreased over the years in spite of inflation. One can now call anywhere in the United States during the off hours for approximately $7 an hour, which is substantially less than ten years ago, with faster service due to direct-distance dialing to almost anywhere in the world.

A good example of the role of government subsidies in the telecommunications field, is the development of communications satellites. Developing them was far too expensive and risky for private enterprise, especially since it meant developing the rockets to boost the satellites into orbit, not just developing the satellites. The advent of communications satellites has made it possible for the modern equivalent of Dr. Livingston to phone home from Malawi to Scotland in a matter of seconds, rather than have to wait for Dr. Stanley to spend a year finding him. Communications satellites also make it possible for the whole world to watch popular American TV shows simultaneously.

Litigation has been important in the telecommunications industry, but not to enable people to sue for damages for personal injuries. Instead litigation has enabled business firms like phone-equipment manufacturers and long- distance re-sellers to successfully sue AT&T for anti-trust violations. Those lawsuits have made possible the competition that has reduced the price of phone equipment and long-distance calling.

An example of regulation in the telecommunications field that many people consider desirable is the licensing of radio and TV stations regarding prime channels so as to rationally allocate the scarce space. One criterion used in awarding licenses is whether the station will provide opportunities for minority viewpoints to be heard and will give equal time to political candidates where their opponents have been given free time. Liberals support that kind of criterion. Conservatives support criteria that say licensees must not unduly engage in obscenity. It is interesting to note that the rationing of communications space has now become an international and extra-terrestrial matter by virtue of the competition to locate communications satellites in prime areas in the sky. Leaving those location problems to individualistic solutions could result in countries shooting down the communications satellites of other countries. That would not be as desirable as having meaningful criteria for allocating scarce space, such as giving the less expensive closer spaces to countries that have less ability to pay for the more expensive, further out spaces.

Government ownership manifests itself in telecommunications mainly in the form of some publicly owned TV and radio stations. In the United States, they are usually owned by state universities or public corporations that rely on tax support, contributions, and foundation grants. Those publicly owned stations provide programming that may be considered intellectually and culturally desirable, but are not sufficiently commercially profitable. Such programming is even more prevalent in Europe and elsewhere than in the United States. Like government-owned airports and roads, government-owned educational television stations (along with all the commercial ones) seem accepted even by conservatives who recognize the socialistic nature of a government owned television station. It is interesting that conservative William Buckley does most of his broadcasting on government-owned TV stations.

CRITERIA FOR DECIDING AMONG THE FIVE FORMS

From these three sets of examples, one can generalize some principles as to when non-involvement, subsidies, litigation, regulation, or government ownership might be best.

Non-involvement works best when the industry is highly competitive and competition is likely to achieve socially desired behavior. This is especially so regarding the pricing of products, since competition can bring prices down. This is not so regarding such matters as environmental protection, occupational health and safety, or equal employment opportunity. In fact, competition is likely to hurt the achievement of those societal goals. If competition is high, business firms may cut back on anti-pollution, safety devices, and affirmative action programs because they may involve extra expense which the firms cannot afford.

Sometimes competition is not furthered by non-involvement because the formerly competing firms may conspire to fix prices or may engage in mergers that result in too few firms to be competitive. Under those circumstances, anti-trust litigation or regulation may be needed to supplement non-involvement in order to promote competition for the benefit of consumers. The firms may also benefit from competition by virtue of increased sales due to lower prices, but especially by virtue of the stimulus it provides to innovation, including innovations that increase profits.

Subsidies are important where society wants business firms to provide unprofitable services to the poor, as with subsidies to the energy industry in the form of energy purchase supplements, or the housing industry in the form of rent supplements. Subsidies may also be needed where innovation is too expensive for private industry to undertake, as with communications satellites, the development of nuclear energy, and the development of the airplane industry. The fields that were mentioned as not being especially relevant to competition could be handled by subsidies such as pollution, workplace safety, and equal opportunity. That might meet with political opposition on the grounds that business firms should not be subsidized to do the right thing. Such subsidies would be analogous to paying them not to commit crimes. It might be noted that subsidies in the form of tax foregoing are more politically acceptable than subsidies in the form of outright cash gifts, with low interest loans in between.

Litigation may help individuals to obtain compensation for negligence and occasional intentional wrongdoing. It is not very effective in changing the behavior of business firms unless it becomes very expensive to them. Otherwise, the expense of paying damages may be substantially less than the expense of changing their behavior. By bringing a class action involving lots of injured people litigation awards can become quite expensive. The reason litigation has been more important in promoting safer cars than safer airplanes is because an unsafe airplane that crashes generates a big news story which decreases consumer purchases of that airline's services. An unsafe car does not generate big news, but a few million-dollar damage suits can do so. Litigation can also be more effective if the legislatures or courts establish rules of strict liability or no-fault liability. The plaintiff then merely has to show that the defendant's product was a factor in the accident and not prove that the defendant acted negligently. Anti-trust litigation is a special form of litigation separate from personal injury litigation, but often highly effective in changing behavior by restoring competition.

Regulation is most meaningful where there are serious problems present and competition, subsidies, or litigation do not seem so meaningful. This is the case where we are interested in preventing serious accidents before they occur rather than compensating people or bankrupting an airline afterwards. Thus, we flatly prohibit certain unsafe practices regarding pilots, airplanes, toxic chemicals, and drunk driving. Regulation is also especially appropriate where there are scarce resources to be allocated, such as food rations in wartime, prime channels on radio or TV, or possibly gasoline during an energy shortage. The alternative would be to allow the highest bidder to have the food, prime channels, or gasoline which society might consider to be an inequitable solution. Regulation is also important where certain forms of business behavior are socially desired, but the marketplace provides no income-receiving or expense-avoiding incentives to behave accordingly, and society does not want to buy the behavior through subsidies.

The main explanation or justification for government ownership in a basically free enterprise society is that there are certain services that society wants to have performed and private enterprise finds them too unprofitable to provide. That includes much of the Amtrak passenger service, a post office system that delivers mail to every rural location at the same low price, and city public transportation. The alternative would be heavy subsidies of the private sector which would probably cost the taxpayer more than providing the service through government ownership or government employees, as is also the case with legal services for the poor.

A second big explanation and justification for government ownership is that the activity could be very profitable to some parts of the private sector, but that other parts of the private sector do not want to be preyed upon. This is the case with government ownership of roads where conservative private businesses want government ownership, rather than pay tolls to other business people in order to transport their goods. Likewise, the privately owned airlines seem to prefer government-owned airports, rather than pay higher fees to privately owned airports in order to receive safety and other services that they now receive at government-owned airports.

A third explanation for government ownership is that the private-sector firms or firms may be perceived as guilty or likely to become guilty of monopolistic abuses requiring a government takeover to prevent, rather than use anti-trust action which may be considered less efficient. This explanation has been a key factor in government ownership of such supposedly natural monopolies as telephone, electricity, water, and other such companies. Monopolistic abuses can relate to consumers, workers, stockholders, and government relations. Consumer abuses can include over-charging, poor quality, unsafe products, and inequitable services. So-called natural monopolies are, however, being increasingly seen as capable of some control through competition, as with telephone and now electricity services as new forms of competition become technologically possible.[6]

---

[6]For further details concerning alternative forms of public involvement especially subsidies, liability rules, and regulation, see William Hamilton, Larry Ledebur, and Deborah Matz, *Industrial Incentives: Public Promotion of Private Enterprise* (Washington, D.C.: Aslan Press, 1984); Henry Manne (ed.), *The Economics of Legal Relationships: Readings in the Theory of Property Rights (and obligations)* (St. Paul, Minn.: West, 1975); Barry Mitnick, *The Political Economy of Regulation: Creating, Designing, and Removing Regulatory Forms* (New York: Columbia, 1980); Eugene Bardach and Robert Kagan (eds.), *Social Regulation: Strategies for Reform* (San Francisco: Institute for Contemporary Studies, 1982); and Alan Stone, *Regulation and Its Alternatives* (Washington, D.C.: Congressional Quarterly Press, 1982).

8

A BROADER PERSPECTIVE

This chapter is concerned with some broader aspects of having a better division of labor between the public and private sectors. If the division is handled well, it can favorably affect all policy problems, not just the matter of economic organization, or such important economic policy problems as unemployment and inflation. The division is also relevant to matters of crime reduction, racial discrimination, health, education, welfare, freedom of communication, international relations, environmental protection, and technology development. This is not an analysis of how capitalism or socialism causes any of these policy problems. It is a brief analysis of how a pragmatic mixed orientation can help deal with the problems better than either approach alone can.

The chapter is also concerned with a variety of additional issues which the basic controversy generates, such as (1) the role of benefit-cost analysis in making decisions concerning the division between the sectors, (2) the role of the not-for-profit sector, (3) the importance of providing job opportunities, (4) the relevance to creativity, (5) the relation to levels of government, and (6) the need to distinguish the division issue from the issue of big versus small units of operation, or broad versus narrow jurisdiction.

Taking a broader perspective also enables one to see relevant trends in a larger context. Those trends relate to increased involvement of the public sector, changing forms of government involvement, and the simultaneous increase in privatization. Those trends and additional issues can be well illustrated with the problem of foster care of neglected or delinquent children. The chapter further clarifies the distinctions between the public-private controversy and the socialism-capitalism controversy, and ends with an emphasis on individualizing the situations but with general criteria.

PUBLIC-PRIVATE CONTROVERSY ACROSS ALL POLICY PROBLEMS

The public-private controversy has usually emphasized the issue of who should supply various goods to consumers. The answers tend to be that the government should supply public education, postal services, police protection, fire protection, national defense, and other traditional government services. The usual answer also tends to say everything else should be supplied by the private sector.

The material presented in the previous chapter has implied that the issue is much broader than just providing various consumer services. In fact, all public policy problems need to be examined more closely from the perspective of the division of labor between the public and private sectors. Public policy problems would also benefit from more systematic analysis of the division of labor among national, state, and local governments and among legislatures, administrative agencies, and courts, but those are separate issues. One can see the importance of the public-private distinction more clearly if one goes through a list of the most important public policy problems.

ECONOMIC PROBLEMS

Perhaps the most important economic public policy problem is what to do about unemployment. The general answer is to finds jobs for the unemployed. That immediately raises the question of whether they should be primarily public-sector jobs or private-sector jobs. Government jobs are fine if they relate to normal governmental functions like the necessary building and maintaining of roads, schools, libraries, and other government facilities. Government jobs are not so meaningful if they involve padding payrolls to conduct routine activities that were being conducted before with less people. Jobs that are merely designed to put people to work doing anything represent a considerable opportunity cost when the same people could be doing something more constructive. There are likely to be more potential jobs available in the private sector, although monetary incentives may be needed to stimulate private employers to hire the unemployed. Monetary incentives may also be needed to stimulate the unemployed to move to where the jobs are or to get appropriate training. The best training may be on-the-job training with governmental monetary incentives to provide and accept the training.

Another important economic problem is what to do about inflation. The traditional approaches have involved decreasing the money supply by raising taxes, decreasing government spending, raising interest rates, requiring banks to maintain more reserves to back up their loans, and possibly price controls backed by fines and even jail sentences. Those approaches are basically government approaches with little room for private-sector discretion. At the opposite extreme would be total non-involvement by government on the theory that high prices will have to come down in order for goods to be sold. That is not so in an economy where competition is lacking to force prices down, and where business and labor may raise their prices in order to offset reduced sales or wages. The new middle position involves the use of incentives to encourage business firms and labor unions not to raise prices and wages. The incentives can include substantial tax breaks that make not raising prices and wages quite worthwhile.

SOCIAL PROBLEMS

A key social problem is the problem of crime reduction. This is a social problem that can be used to illustrate the five forms of government involvement. Total non-involvement may be the most appropriate way to deal with possession of small amounts of marijuana, sex crimes among consenting adults, and other victimless crimes.

An example of subsidies is the program to hire inner-city youth where the jobs they are to perform is to finish high school. If they do they job well, they get raises. If they do not do the job well, they get fired. Such a subsidy may be very benefit-cost effective if it reduces criminal behavior and increases the ability of inner-city youth to get jobs that are more profitable and meaningful than robbery, burglary, and other forms of criminal behavior.

Private litigation can supplement criminal prosecution as a means of decreasing wrongdoing among business firms. Regulation is the traditional way of dealing with crime whereby certain acts are labeled criminal and made subject to penalties, but the penalties may lack sufficient deterrent value if they are too difficult to impose. Government ownership of state-owned lotteries and pari-mutual betting may be eliminating the numbers racket and bookmaking.

Discrimination based on ethnic affiliation is a social problem that has been partly reduced in the past by such government incentives as the withholding of government purchases from private-sector firms. Withholding federal aid to education or for other local government functions can be effective in reducing school segregation or discriminatory hiring practices.

In the realm of health, education, and welfare, we have the perennial question of deciding among unregulated private-sector doctors, various forms of regulation, and government-salaried doctors. We also have public schools, private schools with government funding, and purely private schools. The welfare field is characterized by combinations of public aid, private charity, and government subsidies to the private sector to provide job opportunities for people who would otherwise be public aid recipients.

POLITICAL PROBLEMS

A key political problem is providing freedom of communication to stimulate the creative development of ideas and to comply with the First Amendment. The traditional liberalism has been non-involvement of the government in the market place of ideas. The newer liberalism involves government regulation to require the private sector to provide radio and TV time for minority viewpoints, and government funding of radio-TV stations partly to provide outlets for minority viewpoints.

International relations has traditionally meant relations between governments. Transnational corporations are increasingly playing a part in how governments relate to each other. Business firms that object to socialistic practices in developing countries may provoke hostile interaction by the dominant countries from which they come. Agreements among transnational corporations to set prices or divide markets may have more impact on international economics than treaties among nations. Regulating such transnational corporations involves a tradeoff between the desire to stimulate competition and the desire to control markets. American banks threatening to stop loans or demand repayment may be more disruptive than the State Department recalling an ambassador.

SCIENCE POLICY PROBLEMS

Environmental protection and conservation of nature is largely a governmental function. It is not profitable or equitable for private enterprise, including the maintenance of private parks, beaches, and wilderness areas. Pollution reduction is a good example of the use of innovative marketplace incentives, such as marketable pollution permits. They allow business firms to pollute, but such permits are expensive to buy from one's competitors. The expense and a desire to avoid subsidizing one's competitors stimulates pollution reduction.

The development of science and technology proceeds in the United States mainly through universities, although the major American universities are state-owned or recipients of substantial federal funding. In Europe, government institutes are important for the development of science. In Japan, private corporations play a larger role than they do in the United States. Perhaps the best approach in the development of science and technology and in other areas is a combination of involvement by the government and private enterprise.[1]

ASPECTS AND PRINCIPLES IN THE PUBLIC-PRIVATE CONTROVERSY

We have probably now covered the main issues in the public-private controversy by discussing what is a public function, the criteria for deciding who should administer public functions, the criteria for choosing among the forms of government involvement, and the broadness of the public-private controversy across policy problems. There are, however, other aspects and principles in the public-private controversy that should be addressed.

The concern for deciding whether a specific activity should be handled by the public sector or the private sector has stimulated a substantial amount of systematic benefit-cost analysis. Regardless what decision is reached in any specific situation, there are benefits to systematically thinking about how the situation should be handled. Even if the prevailing method is retained, that kind of thinking can lead to improvements in effectiveness, efficiency, equity, and the achievement of political values.

One should note the importance of the not-for-profit sector as a third alternative to government handling versus private enterprise for various public of people who would benefit from a temporary or long-term institution. Government institutions may be too expensive and too depressing, just like government public housing. Purely private institutions in this context may be unduly exploitative of people who cannot completely care for themselves. That is where the not-for-profit sector can provide the benefits of both lower cost and more sensitive, idealistic care.

Perhaps the most useful function that the private sector can perform is to provide additional job opportunities although often with the aid of government stimuli either through strings-attached incentives or through more traditional fiscal and monetary policies. Those job opportunities can make a big difference in all fields of public policy, such as health, education, and welfare. People would be more healthy and have less illness absenteeism if they had more constructive job opportunities. Students would stay in school and pursue higher education more if they could see the relations more clearly between such education and good job opportunities that might be available to them.

---

[1]For further details on the nature of public policy problems, including to some extent the public-private controversy as it applies to those problems, see Theodore Lowi and Alan Stone (eds.), *Nationalizing Government: Public Policies in America* (Beverly Hills, Calif.: Sage, 1978); Clarke Cochran et al., *American Public Policy* (New York: St. Martin's, 1986); Arnold Heidenheimer, Hugh Heclo, and Carolyn Adams, *Comparative Public Policy: The Politics of Social Choice in Europe and America* (New York: St. Martin's, 1983); Richard Siegel and Leonard Weinberg, *Comparing Public Policies: United States, Soviet Union, and Europe* (Homewood, Ill.: Dorsey, 1977); and S. Nagel (ed.), *Encyclopedia of Policy Studies* (New York: Marcel Dekker, 1983).

The welfare system would obviously benefit if people on various forms of welfare could have job opportunities instead of welfare, including the mothers of dependent children, the elderly on social security, and the disabled.

Creativity and innovation are especially important functions in an advancing society. On that activity, governmental institutions in the form of state universities or private universities with federal funding have a better record than private business does. The private sector generally cannot afford expensive basic research that may not pay off for some time, if ever. There is a need for more government funding to facilitate the transmission of innovative and useful ideas from academic science to business and government.

Government involvement not only takes different forms in terms of non-involvement, subsidies, liability rules, regulation, and ownership, but also different forms in terms of levels of government. In the United States and elsewhere, one can have any of those five forms of government involvement operating at the national, state, or local level. Government ownership or operation of a public function at the national level includes the post office, Amtrak, the TVA, and the activities of every cabinet-level department. At the local or municipal level, virtually every city or other local governing body now owns and operates public transportation systems, public parks, and public schools. All big cities operate municipal garbage collection rather than leave it to private contracting, although that is not necessarily so for smaller cities, including Champaign-Urbana. At the state level, there is less government ownership and operation, but it is present in state parks and all the activities that are associated with state government agencies.

The issue of public versus private administration should be distinguished from the issue of big versus small units of operation. There is no inherent reason why private has to mean big business or little business, or why government has to mean a big government agency rather than a smaller, decentralized government unit. The term "bureaucratic" is often used to refer to government operations that are characterized by (1) performing functions in a very literal way without considering the purpose behind the rules, (2) performing functions in an arbitrary way without complying with the reasonably objective literal rules, (3) taking a long time to process activities with a concern for unnecessary detail, and (4) resisting change which could improve the effectiveness and efficiency of the activities. Those characteristics could occur in a big business operation as well as a big government operation. They could also occur in an inefficient mom-and-pop grocery store.

One should also distinguish the public versus private issue from the issue of how broad the jurisdiction should be of each government unit or business unit. If the jurisdiction becomes too broad in terms of subject matter, then some matters are likely to be handled poorly. Overly diverse activities defeat the advantages of specialization and division of labor. This can occur when a state university takes on the activity of becoming a computer store or other functions that are not inherently part of teaching classes and doing research. This can also occur when a business firm tries to take on the functions of teaching college courses, instead of sending its personnel to a university.

SOME TRENDS RELEVANT TO THE PUBLIC-PRIVATE CONTROVERSY

The long-term trends are toward defining more activities as worthy of public involvement, including government involvement. Explanations for those long-term trends include (1) growth of big business, accompanied by the loss of face-to-face consumer-manufacturer relations and sometimes the growth of monopoly power, (2) growth of big labor and other pressure groups promoting government activities, (3) increasing severity of war and defense needs, (4) increasing severity and complexity of large-scale unemployment, inflation, and international trade problems, and (5) urbanization and the resulting loss of self-sufficiency, including the loss of the extended family caring for a variety of relatives.

The form of government involvement has been changing in recent years away from regulation and the threat of punishment for wrongdoing toward more use of incentives to encourage rightdoing such as subsidies, tax breaks, and low interest loans. There is also a trend toward more contracting out of government activities and the use of market supplements or vouchers, as contrasted to the activities being provided for by government employees. There is still a trend toward an overall increase in the percentage of the labor force that is employed by government and the percentage of the gross national income that is paid by government.

As for trends among the levels of government there is a trend toward the national government having an increasing percentage of the total government labor force and government revenues. When it comes to government ownership, however, there may be a trend toward more municipalization. This manifests itself in the public power field where in the 1930's the cry was for nationalization of the power industry. In the 1980's, there is more talk about cities operating their own power companies, partly because new technologies make that more feasible. There is also increased talk about having competing power companies. Thus, this area, like so many others, illustrates the state of flux of the public-private controversy.

An especially important and interesting trend is the fact that government involvement and privatization are increasing simultaneously. Government involvement in the economy and the general society is increasing for reasons mentioned above. Privatization is increasing because the government is finding that some of its increased activities can be more effectively, efficiently, and possibly equitably handled by contracting to the private sector. Thus, indicators of government involvement are increasing, such as government employment and tax revenues-expenditures. At the same time, there is more government contracting even for activities that have traditionally been solely government activities, such as the operating of prisons. In recent years, more government personnel and money has gone into federal, state, and local prisons as a result of baby boom crimes, court orders requiring improved prison conditions, and determinate sentencing which requires fixed terms that are higher than previous average sentences. At the same time, a number of states are contracting with private firms for the operation of prisons and various forms of community-based corrections.[2]

SOME CONCLUSIONS

FOSTER CARE AS A GENERAL ILLUSTRATION

The care of neglected children provides a good general illustration of some trends and principles relevant to the public-private controversy. Prior to the mid 1800's, the care of neglected children was barely a public function. Until the child welfare movement subsequent to the Civil War in America, children could be readily abused by their parents with virtually no legal penalties. There were almost no compulsory education laws or provisions for dealing with abandoned children over the age of about five other than to allow them to live in the streets. When public concern became more prevalent, charitable institutions began to provide facilities. Later public institutions became more available, although they frequently were nothing more than converted poor-houses, poor farms, tuberculosis sanitariums, or even old jails.

By the mid-1900's, it was recognized that institutional care in the form of either public or private orphanages was highly expensive per child with adverse effects on child development. This stimulated the foster-care movement whereby children would be placed with willing and able foster parents at considerably less cost to the state and with more personal care. As a result, orphanages became virtually nonexistent in the United States subsequent to 1950. As of about 1970, there has been an increased push for government-subsidized day care programs as a modern form of foster care, although for only part of the day. The government subsidy enables the mother of pre-school children to hold a job to the net benefit of the children, the mother,

---

[2]The field of prisons and community-based criminal corrections illustrates the trends regarding increased government involvement, new diversity of forms of involvement, a mixing of levels of government, and a simultaneous increase in privatization. For further details, see Judith Hackett et al., *Contracting for the Operation of Prisons and Jails* (Washington, D.C.: National Institute of Justice, 1987); and the symposium on "Privatization of Prisons," 40 *Vanderbilt Law Review* 813-902 (1987).

the day care employees, the mother's employer, the economy, and the taxpayer who otherwise might be supporting the children and mother on public aid. Thus, foster care and day care are good examples of programs that involve government funding, but with delegation to the private sector to administer the programs, rather than government employees.

A foster care program would not work for juvenile delinquents, as contrasted to neglected children. There would be a shortage of foster parents willing and able to take serious juvenile delinquents. The cost necessary to place them privately might be prohibitive in comparison to halfway houses or probation. Those arrangements are like outpatient treatment or community-based corrections. This is in contrast to the old-fashioned reform school, which (like the orphanage) may provide the worst of both possible criteria in terms of relatively high cost and low benefits. Thus, the comparison of dealing with neglected and delinquent children illustrates how a non-public function becomes a public function and how, through experimentation, society decides whether the function is better administered by the government or by the private sector.

In this context, a distinction needs to be made between unnecessary government employees and necessary government funding. A distinction also needs to be made be tween the commercial private sector (which would possibly involve franchised foster homes) and the not-for-profit private sector (in which foster care is done partly out of love for children, rather than as a money-making venture). Another distinction on the matter of neglected and abused children is the liberal-conservative distinction, which is different from the public-private distinction. Liberals tend to advocate rehabilitation of the parents, the children, and the community, including economic rehabilitation, although with an increasing trend toward de-institutionalization. Conservatives tend to be divided among those who advocate a punitive approach toward abusive or neglectful parents in conformity with a general emphasis on the power of punishment. They are unlike conservatives who advocate a non-involvement policy by the government in conformity with an emphasis on the power of the father and the husband in the traditional household.[3]

SOCIALISM VERSUS CAPITALISM

The public-private controversy should be distinguished from the socialism capitalism controversy. One distinction is that the public-private controversy

---

[3]For further details on foster care and neglected children as a general illustration of the public-private controversy, see Albert Wilkerson (ed.), *The Rights of Children: Emergent Concepts in Law and Society* (Philadelphia: Temple University Press, 1973); Francis Russo and George Willis, *Human Services in America* (Englewood Cliffs, N.J.: Prentice-Hall, 1986); and Robert Morris, *Rethinking Social Welfare: Why Care for the Stranger?* (New York: Longman, 1986).

covers all public functions, whereas the socialism-capitalism controversy is mainly concerned with the major means of production and distribution. Thus, the public-private controversy might refer to the contracting of watchman services by a government agency which now uses government employees, or the takeover of garbage collection services by a city that has now become too large for private scavengers. The socialism-capitalism controversy is more likely to argue over whether a government should take over the steel mills or the coal mines from the private sector or return them to the private sector.

Another distinction is that the public-private controversy tends to be more pragmatic in looking to the individual circumstances of the activity that is proposed for takeover or privatization. The socialism-capitalism controversy tends to react more on ideological grounds and to favor taking over virtually everything from a socialistic perspective or to favor privatizing virtually everything from a capitalistic perspective.

A further distinction relates to the criteria for choosing among the alternatives. The public-private alternatives tend to be decided by talking in terms of effectiveness, efficiency, equity, public participation, predictability, procedural due process, and feasibility, as was done in discussing legal services and housing for the poor. The socialism-capitalism alternatives tend to be decided by talking in terms of which alternative will achieve more gross national product, freedom, popular control, opportunity, security, and initiative, as is done in the classic and contemporary literature debating those alternatives.

The public-private controversy tends to accept a positive role for the government, especially with regard to funding various activities. The controversy is not over government involvement versus no involvement, but more over the form that government involvement should take. That often means talking in terms of subsidies, liability rules, regulation, contracting, but not necessarily ownership. On the other hand, public versus private ownership is the key concept in the socialism-capitalism controversy, or at least has been in the past.

On the matter of trends concerning the distinctions between these two controversies, the trend is toward blurring the distinctions as indicated by the following:

1. Socialists in government have become more concerned with routine governmental matters than they were when they were out of government writing Communist Manifestos about taking over the major means of production and distribution.
2. Socialists have become more pragmatic and less ideological, as indicated by the party platforms of the German Social Democrats, the British Labor Party, and both the Soviet and Chinese Communist parties.

3. Socialists are increasingly using concepts like effectiveness, efficiency, and equity, which are associated with public policy evaluation. Systematic program evaluation is increasingly occurring in both socialistic and capitalistic countries.
4. Ownership is lessening in importance in socialistic thinking. This is indicated by the recognition that ownership of the steel mills in Poland and elsewhere in Eastern Europe has possibly not been as oriented toward the interests of workers and consumers as private ownership of the steel mills in West Germany, Japan, and elsewhere in the western world. Who controls (and for what interest) may be more important than who owns the title to the property.[4]

INDIVIDUALIZING WITH GENERAL CRITERIA

The overall conclusion toward which this analysis points is the need for treating each public function and public policy activity separately in deciding the division of labor between the public and private sectors. There are general criteria which can be applied in deciding that division of labor, such as relative effectiveness, efficiency, equity, public participation, predictability, procedural due process, and feasibility. There are also less general criteria such as (1) the degree of idealism that is needed or would be beneficial in administering an activity, (2) observing how things have been traditionally handled, and (3) complying with constitutional rights, such as the right to counsel in criminal cases. Having general criteria for resolving specific activities does not mean that there is a general solution like a socialistic or a capitalistic solution.

One can possibly generalize further and say there is no inherently best way to deal with policy problems in terms of the national, state, or local governments, or solutions by legislative, administrative, or judicial action. What we have in the public-private controversy is a combination of (1) a pragmatic analysis which emphasizes doing what works best under individual circumstances and (2) a more general analysis which emphasizes looking for underlying criteria that explain or justify why different solutions are adopted under different circumstances.

---

[4]For further details on the socialism-capitalism controversy from the perspective of contemporary advocates of capitalism, see Milton Friedman, *Capitalism and Freedom* (Chicago: University of Chicago Press, 1963); and Irving Kristol, *Two Cheers for Capitalism* (New York: Basic Books, 1978). From the perspective of contemporary advocates of socialism, see Michael Harrington, *Why We Need Socialism in America* (New York: Dissent, 1971); and Paul Sweezy, *Socialism* (New York: McGraw-Hill, 1949). From a perspective that compares both viewpoints, see Robert Heilbroner, *Marxism: For and Against* (New York: Norton, 1980); and Edward Burns, *Ideas in Conflict: The Political Theories of the Contemporary World* (New York: Norton, 1960); and "Balancing Public and Private Sector Implementation" in S. Nagel, *Public Policy: Goals, Means, and Methods* (New York: St. Martin's, 1984), 185-204.

The socialism-capitalism controversy is too holistic to be practical, but pure pragmatism may overemphasize the trees at the expense of the forest. Between those extremes, we have individualized generalizations or the best of both deduction and induction. As has been said, whatever works best is best. Political science and policy studies, however, have an obligation to determine the criteria for predicting and explaining what is likely to work best.

PART FIVE:

PUBLIC POLICY SUBSTANCE

AND METHODS

9

SPECIFIC PUBLIC POLICY PROBLEMS

A public policy problem is an area of government activity in which there is a general consensus that government ought to be involved, but controversy as to what forms that involvement should take. A meaningful way of classifying specific policy problems is in terms of the scholarly discipline with which they are most often associated. All policy problems are inherently multi-disciplinary. The disciplinary classification used in this chapter and elsewhere in the book indicates the discipline that tends to offer the most courses or journal articles on the policy problem from among the basic disciplines of economics, political science, sociology-psychology, and natural science-engineering.

The problem of poverty, for example, clearly involves economic, political, and psychological aspects, but it is classified under sociology because sociology and social work departments tend to offer more courses on the subject than do other departments. The applied disciplines of management science, law, and urban-regional planning correspond roughly to the basic disciplines of economics, political science, and science-engineering. They also tend to cut across all policy fields since management science/operations research provides general methodologies for arriving at means for maximizing given goals, and public policy often manifests itself in the form of laws. Having a set of categories for grouping policy problems helps make public policy studies better organized rather than an A-to Z laundry list of policy problems. Using a disciplinary classification also brings out the fact that many disciplines are relevant to policy studies.

Problems with the political science emphasis include civil liberties, electoral policy, legislative reform, foreign policy, and defense policy. Problems with an economic emphasis include regulation of the economy, housing/land use, transportation/communication, and taxing/spending. Problems with a sociology-psychology emphasis include poverty/welfare, minorities/discrimination, crime/criminal justice, education, and population policy. Problems with a natural science or engineering emphasis include science/technology, health, environmental protection, energy, and agricultural policy.

PROBLEMS WITH A POLITICAL SCIENCE EMPHASIS

CIVIL LIBERTIES

The field of civil liberties policy is generally discussed in terms of three types of issues relating to free speech, equal protection, and due process. The equal protection aspects of civil liberties are emphasized below on "Blacks, Women, and Other Minorities," and the due process or fair procedure aspects are emphasized below on "Crime and Criminal Justice." The most important civil liberties issue, however, is the free speech issue which deals with how far should society go in allowing without penalty both popular and unpopular viewpoints to be advocated or communicated in any media of communication so long as the communication does not involve untruthful defamation, obtaining money under false pretenses, invasion of privacy, the likely promotion of bodily injury, or certain types of hardcore pornography.

Free speech is generally considered the most important constitutional right because without it, one could not adequately communicate existing defects and new ideas regarding the other policy problems dealt with below. Free speech increases the probability that the most effective means toward given ends will become accepted. It also provides a check on corrupt and inefficient leadership and administrative personnel. The Supreme Court has recognized its importance by applying the First Amendment to all levels of government and by narrowing the exceptions to free speech, especially over the last 50 years, although with intermittent plateaus and some retreats. The expansion of the right to express unpopular viewpoints may be largely attributable to having an increasingly more educated population which is more adaptable to change and more aware of how often currently accepted viewpoints were formerly unpopular. Free speech in America has traditionally only meant a hands-off policy by the government regarding unpopular ideas, and not an affirmative policy that includes providing free access to the communication media. That affirmative aspect, however, is increasing by way of FCC equal time rules, public broadcasting, and public campaign financing.

A special form of free speech in the United States is the freedom of popular and unpopular religions to carry on their activities without governmental interference. In the field of religious speech, it is especially important to let all viewpoints be heard since truth and effectiveness are so much more difficult to determine in this field. Along with the restriction of no governmental interference with religion goes the restriction of no governmental aid to religion since aid can also lead to interference, favoritism, decreased private initiative, retaliatory action, and intense divisiveness, especially in a multi-religious society.[1]

ELECTORAL POLICY

Governmental policy regarding who participates in the process of choosing policymakers is especially important since it indirectly influences all policy fields. Basic issues of electoral policy deal with eligibility to vote, procedures for registration and voting, nomination procedures, and campaign funding and methods. Voting eligibility has over the years dealt with expanding the franchise to include non-propertied persons, minority religions, blacks, women, young people, and new residents. Current trends involve increasing the franchise by making registration and voting easier such as through mobile registration units, postcard registration, election-day registration, and extended voting hours and places. The United States has traditionally expressed more concern about the error cost of allowing ineligible people to register or vote than about the error cost of deterring eligible ones from doing so, unlike other countries where registration and voting are relatively easy.

Nomination procedures have tended to move in the United States from nomination by a small group of politicians to nomination by conventions and by direct primaries which involve the potential participation of all party members or voters. Recent years have especially seen a concern for placing restrictions on campaign contributions and expenditures, along with increased support for governmental subsidies of campaign costs mainly to lessen the indebtedness of candidates to campaign contributors. In the election of the president there is a constant concern with proposals for changing the electoral college system to a system that would allocate each state's electoral college vote to the

---

[1] For books relevant to civil liberties policy, see Jonathan Casper, *The Politics of Civil Liberties* (New York: Harper and Row, 1972); John Gardiner (ed.), *Public Law and Public Policy* (New York: Praeger, 1977); Jay Sigler, *American Rights Policies* (Homewood, Ill.: Dorsey Press, 1975); and Stephen Wasby (ed.), *Civil Liberties: Policy and Policy-Making* (Lexington, Mass.: Lexington-Heath Books, 1976).

candidates in proportion to their popular vote, or simply elect the President on the basis of the popular vote alone.[2]

LEGISLATIVE REFORM

Like electoral policy, the field of legislative reform indirectly influences all policy fields. A key related issue has to do with the apportionment of legislative districts. Traditionally, metropolitan districts have involved more people per legislative representative than rural districts, but recent Supreme Court decisions have stimulated near-equality of people per legislative representative. Redistricting can still be done in such a way as to disproportionately favor one political party over another even with equal population, although that kind of gerrymandering may be reduced as a result of future Supreme Court decisions requiring some degree of closeness between the political party percentages in the electorate and in the legislature.

With regard to legislative procedure, the subject of legislative reform has generally referred to (1) reducing the role of filibustering and other delaying tactics which enable a minority of legislators to prevent the majority from voting on pending bills; (2) reducing the role of seniority in choosing committee chairpersons rather than election by committee members; and (3) having more frequent and longer legislative sessions especially at the state level. With regard to legislative personnel, legislative reform often refers to the need for (1) higher and more enforced ethical standards for legislators; (2) more staff and salary and longer terms to attract better legislators and enable them to serve more effectively; and (3) more restrictions on pressure-group activities so legislators can be more attuned to their wider constituencies.[3]

FOREIGN POLICY

Foreign policy problems have been especially important economic, demographic, psychological, technological, and ethical aspects, as well as relevance to other disciplines. Perhaps the most meaningful division of the issues is into those that deal with international conflict versus issues of international cooperation. The conflict issues relate to (1) conflict prevention mainly through

---

[2]For books relevant to electoral policy, see Richard Carlson (ed.), *Issues on Electoral Reform* (New York: National Municipal League, 1974); William J. Crotty, *Political Reform and the American Experiment* (New York: Crowell, 1977); and Edward Tufte (ed.), *Electoral Reform* (Symposium issue of the *Policy Studies Journal*, 1974).

[3]For books relevant to legislative reform, see Donald Herzberg and Alan Rosenthal (eds.), *Strengthening the States: Essays on Legislative Reform* (New York: Doubleday, 1972); Leroy Rieselbach (ed.), *Legislative Reform* (Lexington, Mass.: Lexington-Heath Books, 1977); and Susan Welch and John Peters (eds.), *The Impact of Legislative Reform* (New York: Praeger, 1977).

alliances and international organization, and to (2) conflict resolution mainly through negotiation and sometimes war. The cooperation issues relate to cooperation in trade, environmental protection, energy, communications, transportation, postal service, food, labor, health, education, and banking.

An alternative way of organizing foreign policy issues would be in terms of the country or region whose foreign policy is being studied, which is a kind of cross-national perspective that can be applied to any policy problem. A related organization of the issues would be to think of foreign policy just from an American perspective but to divide the issues in terms of the countries and regions with which the United States interacts. That kind of geographical perspective, however, tends to miss issues that cut across American relations with other countries and tends to focus unduly on current events rather than on matters of a more lasting nature.

Another meaningful way of organizing foreign policy issues involves emphasizing the goals and means of state departments or foreign ministries in dealing with other countries. These goals include winning allies, consumers for American products, sources of raw materials, and human rights for foreign nationals. The means include trade, economic aid, military aid, propaganda, subversion, the institutions of diplomacy, and international organization. Closely related to this division of goals and means are issues that relate to the structures, personnel practices, and administrative procedures used within the State Department and the government in general to make the means more efficient in furthering the goals, and to make both means and goals more responsive to elected officials and the public.[4]

DEFENSE AND ARMS CONTROL POLICY

Defense policy emphasizes developing a capability for deterring foreign aggression, and arms control policy emphasizes mutual reduction or restraint in armament development. Defense policy issues include: (1) balancing air, naval, and land power; (2) balancing massive strategic power versus the ability to fight limited wars or engagements; (3) balancing the ability to engage in conventional warfare versus guerilla and counter-insurgency activities; (4) civil defense with regard to shelter programs, anti-ballistic missiles, industrial relocation, and aftermath planning; (5) civilian control over the military; (6) intelligence gathering activities; (7) problems involved in recruiting, training, and retaining military personnel; (8) coordinating military capabilities with one's

---

[4]For books relevant to foreign policy, see Graham Allison, *Essence of Decision: Explaining the Cuban Missile Crisis* (Boston: Little, Brown, 1971); Richard Merritt (ed.), *Foreign Policy Analysis* (Lexington, Mass.: Lexington-Heath, 1975); and James Rosenau, *The Scientific Study of Foreign Policy* (New York: Free Press, 1971).

allies; (9) the development and implementation of new weapons technologies; (10) policy toward the use of atomic, chemical, and bacteriological weapons systems which are oriented toward civilian destruction; (11) administrative structures to facilitate rational responses to defense problems; and (12) internal security matters especially in time of war.

Arms control issues include: (1) provisions for monitoring compliance with agreements, which formerly meant debating the degree of on-site inspection but which now can be handled partly through satellite surveillance; (2) the extent to which there should be a mutual reduction in armaments or merely restraint in the development of new armaments; (3) the extent to which there has to be a settlement of political issues before or after arms control agreements; (4) the administrative structures for negotiating arms control agreements; (5) bilateral versus multilateral arms control agreements; (6) balancing conventional arms control and nuclear arms control; (7) disengagement or arms-free zones; (8) agreements to limit arms sales and military aid to other countries; (9) agreements concerning the banning of certain types of nuclear weapons testing; and (10) the role of the United Nations in achieving arms control.[5]

PROBLEMS WITH AN ECONOMIC EMPHASIS

ECONOMIC REGULATION

The policy field of economic regulation mainly covers the problems involved in governmental efforts to reduce unemployment and inflation and thereby keep the economy prosperous.   Doing so may mean increased governmental spending and/or decreased taxes when private sector activity seems inadequate for full employment. Theoretically, it also means decreasing governmental spending and/or increasing taxes when private sector activity is inflationary due to a relation between demand and supply that is forcing prices up.   For political reasons, however, the anti-inflationary policy may not be as feasible as the pro-employment policy.   For economic reasons, unemployment and inflation may increase simultaneously, thereby further confusing what is the appropriate policy, and possibly generating the issue of whether to institute more direct wage, price, profit, interest, and other controls.

The economic regulation field also deals with (1) regulation of specific industries where natural monopolies tend to exist or competition has been traditionally considered undesirable such as railroads, airlines, communications,

---

[5]For books relevant to defense and arms control policy, see Alexander L. George and Richard Smoke, *Deterrence in American Foreign Policy: Theory and Practice* (New York: Columbia University Press, 1974);   Robert Levine, *The Arms Debate* (Cambridge, Mass.: Harvard University Press, 1963);   and William W. Whitson, *Foreign Policy and U.S. National Security* (New York: Praeger, 1976).

and retail energy; (2) seeking to maintain competition through the use of anti-trust laws directed particularly toward price collusion; (3) consumer protection matters particularly dealing with deceptive business practices; (4) union-management relations, including union recognition elections and the need for bona fide bargaining; and (5) investor protection, particularly regarding truth in securities sales. In recent years there has been an increased concern for deregulation of the pricing of some possibly over-regulated industries (like the airlines) and for increased regulation of the quality and safety of certain products (with the airlines also being an example). In recent years there has also arisen an increased tolerance toward government ownership of industries that seem inherently unprofitable to private business if extensive service is to be provided such as municipal and intercity land passenger transportation.[6]

HOUSING AND LAND USE

Housing and land use policy is especially important from both a consumer's perspective, since shelter is such a basic commodity, and important from an owner's perspective, since the field deals with fundamental property rights. One set of housing issues relates to providing adequate housing for low-income people. Those issues include (1) eligibility criteria and processing procedures for government-aided housing; (2) the use of clustered public housing versus scattered-site public housing; (3) a balance between government-owned housing and government rent or building subsidies in private landlord-tenant relations; (4) government programs to facilitate home ownership for the poor; (5) urban renewal and rehabilitation procedures; (6) governmental policy toward reducing racially segregated public and private housing; and (7) issues dealing with allowable defenses in landlord-tenant disputes over rent or housing conditions. Many of these issues also affect middle-class housing problems.

Land use issues cover government policy toward land that is not necessarily used for housing. These issues involve such matters as (1) zoning ordinances which designate certain areas as qualifying for industrial, commercial, residential, agricultural, or other uses; (2) statutes specifying requirements for new subdivisions; (3) problems concerning the location of highways, airports, parks, and other municipal facilities; (4) the siting of power

---

[6]For books relevant to economic regulation policy, see Marver Bernstein, *Regulating Business by Independent Commission* (Princeton, N.J.: Princeton University Press, 1955); James Anderson (ed.), *Economic Regulatory Policies* (Lexington, Mass.: Lexington-Heath, 1976); and Mark Nadel, *The Politics of Consumer Protection* (Indianapolis, Ind.: Bobbs-Merrill, 1972).

plants, natural acres, mining, and other uses which tend to be state-regulated; and (5) procedures for citizen involvement in land-use policy decisions.[7]

TRANSPORTATION AND COMMUNICATION
    In the broader field of economic regulation, the transportation and communication industries stand out because they are subject to much government policy and regulation.   One could organize those issues in terms of forms of transportation such as railroads, airlines, trucking, shipping, automobiles, and busing, and forms of communication such as radio, television, telephones, and journalistic media.   One could also organize the issues in terms of the geographical units involved such as international, interstate, interurban, or local.   It may, however, be more meaningful to think in terms of issues that cut across these categories.   One such general issue involves the procedures for allowing new firms to enter into the regulated industries of transportation and communication.   On the one hand, one could argue increased competition would benefit the consumer by stimulating lower prices and better products.   On the other hand, one could argue increased competition would often be economically wasteful where it means having duplicate telephone facilities or municipal bus services.   Another issue relates to the regulation of prices to again balance reasonableness from a consumer perspective with the need for maintaining the profit incentives from a managerial perspective, especially in the absence of some forms of competition that might otherwise exist.   There are also issues which relate to (1) the regulation of product quality and safety, (2) the extent to which certain services can be abandoned or must be maintained even though unprofitable, and (3) the regulation of union-management relations where ordinary strikes cannot be so readily tolerated given the essential nature of transportation to the national economy and to local areas.
    There are other transportation and communication issues besides economic regulation ones.   For example, there are free speech problems involved in governmental policy designed to provide more equal access to the mass media, and designed to limit violence and sex in TV and movies.   In the field of transportation, there are also environmental protection problems, particularly with regard to air pollution and noise pollution.   There are also land use problems with regard to the location of airports, highways, and railroad yards, and poverty policy problems with regard to how to bring the cost of transportation more within the reach of low-income people.   At one time an

---

[7]For books relevant to housing and land use, see Henry Aaron, *Shelter and Subsidies* (Washington, D.C.: Brookings Institution, 1972);   Robert Healy, *Land Use and the States* (Washington, D.C.: Resources for the Future, 1976);   Robert Linowes and Don Allensworth, *The Politics of Land Use: Planning, Zoning and the Private Developer* (New York: Praeger, 1973);   and Harold Wolman, *Politics of Federal Housing* (New York: Dodd Mead, 1971).

important policy issue involved the need for government subsidies to develop railroads, airlines, and communication satellites when those activities represented struggling infant industries. New transportation forms may still need substantial government support for research and development and to create a market such as non-internal combustion automobiles, supersonic transports, and innovative municipal rapid transit. The broadest current policy issues in transportation and communication deal with the extent to which those should be unregulated industries, regulated ones or, in some instances, government owned.[8]

TAXING AND SPENDING POLICY

A key issue with regard to taxation policy deals with what kind of taxes should the government levy to pay for government expenditures with the main choices being taxes on income and wealth which tend to be relatively progressive in terms of ability to pay versus taxes on consumption which tend to be relatively regressive. Within each type of taxation there are controversial issues concerning what forms of income or consumption should be taxed and at what levels. Other key taxation issues relate to (1) the extent to which government income should come from borrowing rather than taxation; (2) the extent to which the general level of taxes should be raised or lowered to restrain or stimulate the economy; (3) the use of taxes to discourage various activities as well as raise revenue; (4) how to administer the tax program in order to minimize costs and noncompliance; and (5) how to coordinate the taxing of federal, state, and local governments so as to minimize duplicative and sometimes conflicting programs.

Government spending policy could refer to how the government should spend its money to fight poverty, crime, or pollution, or to support education, health, or defense, or for other government activities. Those issues, however, are more meaningful to discuss as part of each specific policy problem. Spending policy can also refer to the methodology for evaluating the wisdom of expenditures in general. That kind of benefit-cost analysis though is more relevant to the methods of policy analysis. The main spending policy issue, as such, deals with the procedures for developing governmental budgets in order to provide coordination across agencies, application of evaluative methodologies, more effective use of spending to stimulate or restrain the economy, and more efficient and equitable budget-cutting in light of decreased revenues.

---

[8]For books relevant to transportation and communication, see Richard Adler and Douglass Cater (eds.), *Television As a Cultural Force* (New York: Praeger, 1976); Milton Pikarsky and Daphne Christensen, *Urban Transportation Policy and Management* (Lexington, Mass.: Lexington-Heath, 1976); and George Smerk, *Urban Mass Transportation: A Dozen Years of Federal Policy* (Bloomington, Ind.: Indiana University Press, 1975).

Budgeting procedures can be viewed from the perspectives of the central budgeting bureau, the individual line agencies, legislative oversight, or agencies responsible for auditing.[9]

PROBLEMS WITH A SOCIOLOGY-PSYCHOLOGY EMPHASIS

POVERTY AND WELFARE

The policy field of poverty and welfare involves a number of issues. The main issues deal with matters of income maintenance and welfare, or how to provide funds to bring poor people closer to a minimum annual family income. Sub-issues of that general controversy relates to (1) whether welfare programs should be decentralized with different standards and procedures in each state or a more uniform approach throughout the country; (2) how should welfare payments be related to employment incentives, especially where there are one or two parents capable of working; (3) what should be the eligibility criteria, benefit levels, and obligations to repay; and (4) what procedures should be provided for investigations, case workers, and hearings.

Other important poverty issues deal with the problems of poor people in various roles which they have in common with other people, but in which poverty increases the likelihood of one being taken advantage of. These roles include (1) conditions, and nondiscriminatory treatment; (2) being a tenant who may be more subject to housing code violations in private housing and lack of due process in public housing; (3) being a consumer more subject to credit collection abuses, broken warranties, and defective merchandise; (4) being a family member where charges of delinquency, neglect, and abuse may be more prevalent; (5) being a person more lacking in good health and in the funds and facilities to obtain it; and (6) being a child who is provided with relatively poor school facilities and possibly other governmental services. Some of these issues overlap other policy problem fields like economic regulation, housing, race relations, education, and health, but those problems have special features when discussed in the context of low-income people.[10]

---

[9]For books relevant to taxing and spending policy, see Joseph Pechman, *Federal Tax Policy* (Washington, D.C.: Brookings Institution, 1977); Lawrence Pierce, *The Politics of Fiscal Policy Formation* (Pacific Palisades, Calif.: Goodyear, 1971); Ira Sharkansky, *The Politics of Taxing and Spending* (Indianapolis, Ind.: Bobbs-Merrill, 1969); and Aaron Wildavsky, *The Politics of the Budgetary Process* (Boston: Little, Brown, 1974).

[10]For books relevant to poverty and welfare, see Dorothy James (ed.), *Analyzing Poverty Policy* (Lexington, Mass.: Lexington-Heath, 1975); Theodore Marmor, *Poverty Policy* (Chicago: Aldine, 1971); Gilbert Steiner, *Social Inequality: The Politics of Welfare* (Chicago: Rand McNally, 1966); and Clair Wilcox, *Toward Social Welfare: An Analysis of Programs and Proposals Attacking Poverty, Insecurity, and Inequality of Opportunity* (Homewood, Ill.: Irwin, 1969).

BLACKS, WOMEN, AND OTHER MINORITIES

The key issue with regard to public policy toward minorities is how to minimize previous discrimination so as to enable the individuals involved to more fully utilize their skills and talents to the benefit of society and themselves. In the American context, the groups against whom discriminatory barriers have been directed mainly include blacks and other racial minorities, Latinos and other national minorities, women, young people, old people, the handicapped, those with unconventional sexual orientations, and minority religious groups. Court cases and statutes have especially involved blacks, but, increasingly, other groups as well.

The types of discriminatory barriers have mainly related to denials not based on merit with regard to equal access to opportunities relating to political participation, education, equality in criminal procedure, employment, housing, and public accommodations. These barriers have tended to decrease in recent years as (1) minorities have become more vigorous in pressing for changes, (2) as the dominant groups have become more affluent and willing to make concessions, (3) and as both minority and majority persons have become better educated to the harm done by discrimination not based on merit. Such discrimination may now be more clearly seen as detracting from a society's ability to make maximum use of the skills and talents of its members, and also as having a depressing effect on the productivity of the majority. A key problem is how to remove those barriers with a minimum of the friction and alienation which may occur in both directions as a result of realistic or unrealistic rising expectations or perceptions of reverse discrimination.[11]

CRIME AND CRIMINAL JUSTICE

This field basically involves two sets of somewhat conflicting issues. On the one hand are the issues that relate to how to reduce street crime, white-collar crime, and criminal behavior by public officials. On the other hand are issues that relate to how to safeguard the innocent from conviction and harassment by criminal justice decision-makers. Methods for reducing crime tend to relate to three kinds of activities. One kind of activity involves increasing the probabilities of wrongdoing being detected, adjudicated, and negatively sanctioned. Increasing those three probabilities may require greater professionalism on the part of criminal justice decision-makers, although some

---

[11]For books relevant to blacks, women, and other minorities, see Thomas Dye, *The Politics of Equality* (Indianapolis, Ind.: Bobbs-Merrill, 1971); Joe Freeman, *The Politics of Women's Liberation* (New York: McKay, 1975); and Harrell Rodgers, *Racism and Inequality: The Policy Alternatives* (San Francisco: Freeman, 1975).

advocate increasing those probabilities by relaxing the constraints on police surveillance, evidence needed for convictions, and on the imposition of severe penalties like capital punishment. A second kind of activity involves decreasing the benefits that come from illegal behavior. Doing that may require changing the nature of peer group recognition and hardening the targets of criminal wrongdoers. A third kind of activity involves increasing the costs that come from illegal behavior. For many people that means longer prison sentences under harsher conditions, but for other people that might mean increasing the realistic opportunities lost as a result of illegal behavior which may be the main reason middle-class people do not take the risks involved in committing street crimes.

Methods for safeguarding the innocent from conviction and harassment (while at the same time enabling the guilty to be caught) include the right to (1) no retroactive or vague criminal statutes, or statutes declaring named persons to be guilty of wrongdoing, (2) arrest or search only where there is substantial likelihood of guilt, (3) no involuntary confessions or self-incrimination, (4) release pending speedy trial, (5) hired or provided counsel at trial and before, (6) formal notice of charges, (7) unanimous decision by a group of one's peers, (8) questioning adverse witnesses and calling one's own witnesses, (9) no excessive punishment, and (10) no repeated prosecution for the same matter. The right to counsel is probably the most important of those rights, since without an attorney to enforce them the other rights may be meaningless. Providing counsel to the indigent, however, is a costly problem, but one which the Supreme Court has now imposed on all governmental systems in the United States in criminal cases.[12]

EDUCATION

Educational issues can be organized in terms of the level of education involved such as preschool, elementary, college, or adult, or in terms of the government level involved such as local, state, national, or international. Some of the issues overlap other policy problems such as (1) academic freedom for faculty and students relevant to civil liberties, (2) desegregation of students and faculty relevant to minorities, and (3) the allocation of government funds and personnel to schools in low-income areas relevant to poverty. Those are especially important issues since they involve fundamental aspects of the First Amendment and of equal protection under the law.

---

[12]For books relevant to crime and criminal justice, see John Gardiner and Michael Mulkey (eds.), *Crime and Criminal Justice: Issues in Public Policy Analysis* (Lexington, Mass.: Lexington-Heath, 1975); Herbert Jacob (ed.), *The Potential for Reform of Criminal Justice* (Beverly Hills, Calif.: Sage, 1974); and S. Nagel, *Improving the Legal Process: Effects of Alternatives* (Lexington, Mass.: Lexington-Heath, 1975).

Issues more specifically relating to educational policy include: (1) the extent to which the federal government should provide aid to local schools and with strings attached especially regarding desegregation and nondiscrimination; (2) how to provide both citizen involvement and independent professionalism in the administration of the schools; (3) how to provide balance in the curriculum between classical, vocational, life-adjustment, college preparation, and other educational goals; (4) the need for special education programs for the handicapped, non English-speaking, culturally deprived, and other groups; (5) what role the government should play with regard to parochial schools and religious education; (6) government subsidies to private colleges, university research, and college scholarships and loans; (7) the involvement of the courts in suspensions, dismissals, and disciplinary proceedings of students and faculty; and (8) government regulation and mediation relevant to the unionization of educational personnel, collective bargaining, and strikes.[13]

POPULATION POLICY

The key issue with regard to government population policy relates to what role government should play in seeking to control population growth in view of the limited resources of the nation and world. In that regard, there are a variety of relevant government programs and policies including; 1) the subsidizing of birth control purchases through public aid and foreign aid; (2) government programs designed to raise standards of living and thereby stimulate more middle-class values, which include having smaller families partly because educating children is more expensive in middle-class families and they are less of an economic aid; (3) government programs designed to educate the public with regard to the availability of birth control methods; (4) subsidies for birth control research; (5) legalization of abortion which in some countries is a frequent birth control method; and (6) government programs designed to increase and conserve natural resources so as to be able to satisfy the needs of a larger population.

A second key issue concerning government population policy relates to government involvement in population movements. This involvement includes policies relating to: (1) immigration of people to the United States, both legal and illegal; (2) migration from rural areas to cities with resulting congestion problems and the need for government aid in making the transition; (3) migration patterns across nations which sometimes lead to minorities subject

---

[13]For books relevant to education, see Samuel Gove, *Political Science and School Politics* (Lexington, Mass.: Lexington-Heath, 1976); Michael Kirst (ed.), *State, School, and Politics: Research Directions* (Lexington, Mass.: Lexington-Heath, 1972); and Frederick Wirt and Michael Kirst, *The Political Web of American Schools* (Boston: Little, Brown, 1972).

to discrimination, social unrest, and foreign policy problems; and (4) migration patterns within the United States toward the sunbelt, which sometimes leads to competition among the states in offering more lenient industrial regulation laws in order to attract or retain business firms and thus employment opportunities.

A third key population policy area relates to the aging of populations particularly the American population] due to a lowered birthrate and better health care. Having an older population raises problems with regard to: (1) social security coverage; (2) Medicare and special health problems; (3) recreation and leisure activities; (4) housing and nursing homes; and (5) discrimination in employment opportunities against the aged, but also problems in the need for younger workers to move up in the job hierarchy.[14]

PROBLEMS WITH A NATURAL SCIENCE OR ENGINEERING EMPHASIS

SCIENCE AND TECHNOLOGY POLICY

A key issue in science and technology policy is how to determine the social and other effects of new technological developments before they occur so that appropriate governmental policies can be instituted. For example, what are the broad effects likely to be of supersonic transports, electronic calculators, birth control pills, solar energy, new antibiotics, cable television, or other technological developments. Being able to predict the effects of the automobile on suburbanization, depletion of oil resources, and air pollution could conceivably have enabled the government to have more actively subsidized the development of electric and steam transportation when the automobile industry was in the process of deciding among electric, steam, and gasoline combustion engines. Congress now has an Office of Technology Assessment to aid in making such predictions. Requiring environmental impact statements to accompany major governmental decisions is also an important aspect of contemporary technological assessment.

Another key science and technology issue is how governments at various levels can stimulate scientific research and development in order to accelerate socially useful knowledge and inventions. Governments attempt to achieve that goal in various ways including: (1) subsidizing university and non-university research through grants and contracts; (2) having agency staffs of in-house scientists, especially in defense, agriculture, and public health programs; (3)

---

[14]For books relevant to population policy, see Peter Bachrach and Elihu Bergman, *Power and Choice: The Formulation of American Population Policy* (Lexington, Mass.: Lexington-Heath, 1973); Richard Clinton, *Population and Politics: New Directions in Political Science Research* (Lexington, Mass.: Lexington-Heath, 1977); Michael Kraft and Mark Schneider (eds.), *Population Policy Analysis: Issues in American Politics* (Lexington, Mass.: Lexington-Heath, 1977); and A.E. Nash, *Governance and Population* (Washington, D.C.: U.S. Government Printing Office, 1972).

supporting state universities where much research is conducted; (4) providing scholarships and loans to help create new scientists; (5) providing a patent and copyright system to make inventions and ideas profitable; (6) providing a market to purchase new technological developments, especially in transportation, defense, information processing, and teaching devices; and (7) facilitating government utilization of research that may have been developed independent of government policies as mentioned in Chapter 3 on "Utilization of Policy Research."

Another science policy issue concerns government regulation of scientific developments that can be socially detrimental if abused, such as genetic engineering, nuclear experimentation, drug development, experiments with or interviewing humans, and abuses of laboratory animals. A related science policy issue concerns government regulation or subsidization to make useful scientific developments such as life sustaining devices and pollution control devices more widely available where the market forces of supply and demand are such that the developments would not become widespread without government involvement, as in the health policy and environmental policy fields.[15]

HEALTH POLICY

The key issue in governmental health policy is probably what role should the government play in seeking to provide minimum health care for all persons regardless of income. One choice is a laissez-faire policy of allowing the medical profession, the drug industry, and the medical insurance companies to handle the problem by charging in accordance with ability to pay, with some free services to the indigent. At the other extreme would be a form of socialized medicine in which doctors would work mainly for the government and provide service to patients without charge since the taxpayers would be, in effect, paying the medical fees. In the middle are various government programs designed either to subsidize private medical insurance or to incorporate medical insurance into a social insurance system like social security. Sub-issues of the insurance alternative relate to (1) whether all people should be covered or mainly the aged and the poor, (2) whether all medical problems should be covered or mainly medical catastrophes, (3) whether premiums should be paid by employers, employees, or general taxpayers, and at what

---

[15]For books relevant to science and technology policy, see Lynton K. Caldwell, *Science, Technology and Public Policy* (Bloomington, Ind.: Indiana University Press, 1967, with periodic supplements); Daniel Greenberg, *The Politics of Pure Science* (New York: New American Library, 1976); and Joseph Haberer (ed.), *Science and Technology Policy* (Lexington, Mass.: Lexington-Heath, 1977).

levels, and (4) what extent should the government show concern for the quality of the medical services for which it is paying.

Other health policy issues besides health delivery programs include: (1) regulation of the drug industry with regard to prices and quality of products; (2) subsidizing medical education to generate more doctors especially in some geographical areas and some specialties; (3) subsidizing hospital facilities and requiring as part of the subsidy some consideration for the medical problems of the poor; (4) control of contagious diseases, drinking water, and sanitation; (5) industrial health and safety regulation; (6) subsidizing medical research to find cures and preventatives for cancer and other diseases; and (7) special provisions for mental health problems although all of the above issues relate to both mental and physical health.[16]

ENVIRONMENTAL PROTECTION

The policy field of environmental protection involves a number of major issues. The main issue concerns the extent to which the effects of various types of pollution are detrimental enough to warrant large scale regulatory and grant programs. Water pollution, for example, is damaging to public health, recreation, aesthetics, commercial fishing, agriculture, and industrial water supplies. Air pollution is damaging even more so to public health because of the inability to clean the air, as well as damaging plant life, materials, visibility, and climate. On the other hand, massive environmental programs use resources and human effort that could be better devoted to problems of domestic and worldwide poverty. Such programs may also interfere with industrial production and the raising of living standards. Sometimes there may also be too much emphasis in environmental programs on middle-class aesthetics and recreation, as contrasted to the public health problems of pollution, especially in inner-city areas. The concern for developing new energy sources may also sometimes conflict with environmental standards, although energy conservation and environmental protection tend to go together.

Other important environmental protection issues deal with such matters as (1) devising government structures to reduce pollution, which is a public administration matter, (2) devising government procedures to reduce pollution which is largely an administrative law matter, (3) devising pollution reducing incentives, which is where environmental economics can be especially helpful, and (4) such partly philosophical issues as whether and how to compensate

---

[16]For books relevant to health policy, see Theodore Marmor, *The Politics of Medicare* (Chicago: Aldine, 1973); David Mechanic, *Politics, Medicine, and Social Science* (New York: Wiley, 1974); Herman Somers and Ann Somers, *Doctors, Patients, and Health Insurance: The Organization and Financing of Medical Care* (Washington, D.C.: Brookings Institution, 1961); and Robert Alford, *Health Care Politics* (Chicago: University of Chicago Press, 1975).

victims of pollution, provide for displaced workers, and protect consumers from bearing anti-pollution costs. Like all policy problems, environmental policy is a multi-disciplinary matter.[17]

ENERGY POLICY

The field of energy policy is relatively new in importance since until recently the supply of energy has largely been taken for granted, and the demand has not been so large. The need for governmental action has, however, increased as a result of a forthcoming restricted supply of oil and gas and a greatly expanded worldwide demand due to motorized transportation, electrification, industrialization, and increased population. Government energy policy takes a variety of general forms including (1) research and development of new energy sources, (2) stimulation of measures to conserve existing energy sources, and (3) regulation of energy industries with regard to entry, prices, environmental protection, and safety. Other general ways of organizing energy policy issues are in terms of the energy sources of coal, oil, natural gas, nuclear energy and hydroelectric power, or in terms of production, physical distribution, retailing, and consumption problems.

More specific issues deal with (1) the siting of nuclear power plants and the handling of nuclear wastes, (2) the development of coal resources without the adverse effects of air pollution and strip mining, (3) the regulation of energy prices to stimulate energy production, but also to prevent excess profits and to provide an equitable balance between industrial and residential users, (4) the use of taxes to discourage excessive gasoline consumption, (5) the international defense implications of the proliferation of nuclear energy and the shifting balances of power due to the increased importance of oil locations, (6) the need to stimulate oil productivity while simultaneously guarding against oil spills and pipeline accidents, (7) the need to limit the potentially corrupting influence of oil and other energy lobbyists in obtaining governmental favoritism, (8) how far the government should go in seeking to stimulate the development of solar, geothermal, wind, ocean, and other new energy forms, and (9) the balance between domestic production and foreign imports.[18]

---

[17]For books relevant to environmental protection, see Frank Grad, George Rathjens, and Albert Rosenthal, *Environmental Control: Priorities, Policies and the Law* (New York: Columbia University Press, 1971); S. Nagel (ed.), *Environmental Politics* (New York: Praeger, 1975); and Walter Rosenbaum, *The Politics of Environmental Concern* (New York: Praeger, 1973).

[18]For books relevant to energy policy, see Robert Connery and Robert Gilmore, *The National Energy Problem* (Lexington, Mass.: Lexington Books: 1974); David Davis, *Energy Politics* (New York: St. Martin's Press, 1974); David Freeman, *National Energy Policy* (New York: Twentieth Century Fund, 1974); and Richard Mancke, *The Failure of U.S. Energy Policy* (New York: Columbia University Press, 1974).

AGRICULTURAL POLICY

In recent years agricultural policy has undergone a dramatic shift from policies mainly designed to restrict supply and increase demand (in order to provide greater farm income) to a set of policies mainly designed to increase supply and restrict demand (in view of increasing world food shortages), although some overlap exists between the two sets of policies. Former policies that have been cut back include crop restrictions, government purchases, and direct farm income payments. Current policies involve foreign sales, food stamps, and school lunch programs, not just to increase demand but also to aid the needy. Current policies also increasingly emphasize the development of greater farmer autonomy and farm productivity in view of expanded world markets. A government policy that particularly reflects the general shift is the movement from a tariff policy to keep out foreign agricultural competition to talk of an export control policy to limit agricultural sales abroad so as to prevent domestic shortages.

Other less dramatic government policies in the field of agriculture and food deal with such matters as (1) consumer protection concerning the quality of food products, (2) farm labor regulation, (3) environmental protection, particularly with regard to pesticide runoff problems, (4) government crop insurance and farm credit, (5) rural electrification and public utilities, (6) regulation of agricultural marketing both with regard to trading practices and transportation, (7) humane livestock regulation, (8) agricultural research and research utilization, (9) resettlement problems of displaced farm labor, and (10) conservation and irrigation of farm land.[19]

CROSS-CUTTING ASPECTS

An alternative way of conceptualizing policy studies, rather than in terms of specific policy problems, is in terms of general perspectives that cut across all policy problems. One such general perspective is to think in terms of the stages involved in policy studies research. The primary stage is developing basic concepts with regard to such matters as what are the categories of policy causes and policy effects, as well as the even more basic concept of what is public policy. Causes tend to relate to such concepts as social norms, environmental contexts, conflicting interests, policy decision-makers, and evidentiary facts. Effects tend to relate to such concepts as behavioral versus

---

[19]For books relevant to agricultural policy, see Charles Hardin, *The Politics of Agriculture* (Glencoe, Ill.: Free Press, 1952);   Dale Hathaway, *Government and Agriculture* (New York: Macmillan, 1963);   Vernon Ruttan (ed.), *Agricultural Policy in an Affluent Society* (New York: Norton, 1969);   and Ross Talbot and Don Hadwiger, *The Policy Process in American Agriculture* (San Francisco: Chandler, 1968).

attitudinal effects, intended versus unintended effects, short-run versus long-term effects, and effects on policy appliers versus policy recipients. Other stages in policy research besides the conceptualization stage include the methodological development of research designs for testing the validity of various hypothesized causes and effects, and the subsequent utilization of such policy research.

Another general perspective is to think in terms of the stages involved in the development of policies rather than in doing research on them. Those stages include policy formation which relates to how and why statutes get adopted in legislatures, precedents in courts, and administrative decisions among government executives and administrators. Those stages also include policy implementation which deals with the problems of applying policies after they have been adopted, including compliance and impact. Still other general perspectives can emphasize how a variety of policy problems get treated across different nations and cultures, or across different academic disciplines.

With the exception of this chapter, the other chapters in the book tend to emphasize cross-cutting perspectives such as:

1. The establishment of public policy goals, including increased national productivity (Part One).
2. The development of incentives for achieving higher goals, including subsidies, tax breaks, and other government rewards and penalties (Part Two).
3. The improvement of constitutional effectiveness, including basic human rights and government structures (Part Three).
4. Systematic methods for analyzing policy problems (Chapter 10).

10

SYSTEMATIC METHODS FOR ANALYZING POLICIES

The essence of decision-aiding software is that it is designed to process a set of (1) goals to be achieved, (2) alternatives for achieving them, and (3) relations between goals and alternatives, in order to choose the best alternative, combination, or resource allocation in light of the goals, alternatives, and relations.

The main benefits of decision-aiding software are in accurately and quickly handling five key methodological problems in decision-making. They are:

1. Multiple dimensions on multiple goals. This is the apples and oranges problem.
2. Multiple missing information.
3. Multiple alternatives that are too many to be able to determine the effects of each one.
4. Multiple and possibly conflicting constraints.
5. The need for simplicity in drawing and presenting conclusions in spite of all that multiplicity.[1]

ADDING APPLES AND ORANGES

---

[1]For further details on optimizing analysis in terms of goals, policies, relations, and conclusions, see S. Nagel, *Public Policy: Goals, Means, and Methods* (New York: St. Martin's, 1984) and Edward Quade, *Analysis for Public Decisions* (Amsterdam, Holland: North Holland, 1982). These two books could be referred to for any of the eight principles. The first book uses numerous legal examples. Other books that take an optimizing perspective toward law include Richard Posner, *Economic Analysis of Law* (Boston: Little, Brown, 1977); and Gordon Tullock, *The Logic of the Law* (New York: Basic Books, 1971).

Decision-making problems often involve multiple goals measured on a variety of different dimensions, such as miles, hours, dollars, 1-5 attitude scales, yes-no dichotomies, etc.

Some of the ways in which multiple dimensions are handled are:

1. Multiply the apples by two if you like each apple twice as much as each orange. Then everything will be expressed in orange units.
2. Ask whether the gain in apples from choosing one alternative is worth more or less than the gain in oranges from choosing a second alternative.
3. Convert the apple units into percentages by dividing the raw scores on the apple goal by the sum of the apples, and convert the orange units into percentages by dividing the raw scores on the oranges goal by the sum of the oranges.

These methods become clearer with the concrete illustrative example of choosing between two affirmative action programs for a medical school. One program produces a lot of minority students, but treats few patients. The other program produces few minority students, but treats a lot of patients. The example is shown in Table 10-1.[2]

MISSING INFORMATION

We often do not know relation scores of each alternative on each goal, and we often do not know the relative weights of the goals.

The key way in which missing information is handled is to allow the user to quickly and accurately determine the effects of inserting various values for the missing information. More specific techniques include:

1. What-if analysis, whereby the computer shows what would happen if we make changes in the goals, alternatives, and/or relations.
2. Threshold analysis, whereby the computer shows for each relation-score and goal-weight the value which would cause a tie between the second-place alternative and the first place alternative.
3. Convergence analysis, whereby the computer shows for each goal weight

---

[2]On dealing with non-monetary benefits and costs, see Mark Thompson, *Benefit-Cost Analysis for Program Evaluation* (Beverly, Hills, Calif.: Sage, 1980); and Edward Gramlich, *Benefit-Cost Analysis of Government Programs* (Englewood Cliffs, N.J.: Prentice-Hall, 1981), although they may overemphasize monetizing non-monetary variables, rather than working with them in their original form or close to it. Also see S. Nagel, "Nonmonetary Variables in Benefit-Cost Evaluation," 7 *Evaluation Review* 37-64 (1983) and S. Nagel, "Economic Transformations of Nonmonetary Benefits in Program Evaluation" in James Catterall (ed.), *Economic Evaluation of Public Programs* (San Francisco: Jossey-Bass, 1985).

TABLE 10-1. DEALING WITH MULTI-DIMENSIONAL TRADEOFFS

POLICY	RAW SCORE INCREMENTS		PART/WHOLE PERCENTAGING			
	Students Trained (S)	Patients Treated (P)	Students Trained $w=1$	Patients Treated $w=2$	Unweighted Sum	Weighted Sum
Policy A (X_1)	30	10	60%	36%	96%	132%
Policy B (X_2)	20	18	40%	64%	104%	168%
Total (Whole)	50	28	100%	100%	200%	300%
Difference (Increment)	+ 10 S >> - 8P ?					
Threshold			W60 + 36 = W40 + 64 W*= 1.40			

POLICY	PAIRED-COMPARISON MONETIZING			WEIGHTED RAW SCORES		
	Students Trained $Y = (S)^{.92}$	Patients Treated $Y = (P)^{.90}$	SUM	Students (Expressed in Terms of Patients) $W=2$	Patients	Sum
Policy A (X_1)	$22.85	$ 7.94	$30.79	60	10	70
Policy B (X_2)	$15.74	$13.48	$29.22	40	18	58
Total	$38.59	$21.42	$60.01	100	28	128
Threshold				W30 + 10 = W20 + 18 W*= .80		

NOTES:

1. Incremental analysis has the advantage of simplicity, especially when there are only a few policies and goals. It is also applicable to variables that are non-quantitative. It involves minimum transforming of the raw data. It reduces the value judgment to determining whether the incremental gain of one policy is preferred over the incremental gain of a second policy.
2. Percentaging analysis has the advantage of being applicable when there are many policies and goals. It reduces the value judgment to determining the relative weight of the goals.
3. Paired-comparison monetizing tends to consider all the values of the relevant decision makers, although their values are not disaggregated into separate components. Working with monetized variables may also be more comfortable with many people. Paired-comparison monetizing reduces the value judgments to determining at what point a set of non-monetary benefits is equal to a quantity of dollars.
4. Weighted raw scores have the advantage of being relatively easy to apply when all the goals have tangible units like students or patients, rather than intangible units like scores on a 1-9 attitude scale, in which case part/whole percentaging tends to be easier to handle.

at what magnitude the goal tends to dominate the other goals such that nothing is to be gained by increasing the weight further.

4. Best-worst analysis, whereby the computer shows what the conclusion would be using values that most favor a given alternative, and then values that least favor a given alternative. The two conclusions are then averaged.

These methods become clearer with the concrete illustrative example of deciding between nuclear energy and solar energy in light of their long-term value and cost, as is shown in Table 10-2.[3]

ALLOCATING RESOURCES

Decision-aiding software can help in allocating resources, as contrasted to the generally easier problem of just finding a best alternative or combination.

A good way of allocating resources is to convert into percentages the raw merit scores of the objects to which the resources are to be allocated. One can then apply the percentages to the grand total available to be allocated. A good way to convert the raw scores into percentages is by dividing them by their total within the same goal in order to get part/whole percentages. Those percentages can then be summed across the goals, using a weighted sum where the goals have different weights.

Table 10-3A shows how the P/G% software can be used in an allocation problem where the bottom line consists of allocation percentages. The alternative methods shown are trials and plea bargains. Additional alternatives could be added such as diversions or dismissals. The goals shown are to reduce delay and to increase respect for the legal system. Additional goals could be added such as reducing expense and increasing the probability of innocent defendants being acquitted.

The raw data shows that in our hypothetical court system, the average trial takes 120 days, and the average plea bargain takes 30 days from arrest to disposition. The data also shows that the trials alternative receives a respect score of 6 on a 0-10 scale in a rough survey of attorneys, and pleas receives a score of only a 2. It would not be meaningful to add 120 days to a respect score of 6 to get an overall score for trials because (1) delay is measured in days, and respect is measured on a 0-10 scale necessiting a common measure in order to be able to add these scores, (2) delay is a negative goal where

---

[3]On dealing with missing information without having to gather additional information, see Mark Thompson, *Decision Analysis for Program Evaluation* (Cambridge, Mass.: Ballinger, 1982); and Clifford Harris, *The Break-Even Handbook* (Englewood Cliffs, N.J.: Prentice-Hall, 1978). Also see S. Nagel, "Dealing with Unknown Variables in Policy/Program Evaluation" 6 *Evaluation and Program Planning* 7-18 (1983), and S. Nagel, "New Varieties of Sensitivity Analysis," 9 *Evaluation Review* 772-779 (1985).

TABLE 10-2. DEALING WITH MULTIPLE MISSING INFORMATION

GOALS / POLICIES	Long-Term Value (Y_1)	Low Cost (Y_2)	WEIGHTED SUM
Nuclear (X_a)	a_1 +1 4 (3 to ∞)	a_2 +1 3 (2 to ∞)	7
Solar (X_b)	b_1 -1 5 (-∞ to 6)	b_2 -1 1 (-∞ to 2)	6
Weights	W_1 -1 1 (-∞ to 2)	W_2 +2 1 (.5 to ∞)	

NOTES:

1. The symbol in the upper left-hand corner of each cell shows (1) the identifying symbol of each relation, with the letter indicating the goal; (2) the identifying symbol of each weight, with the subscript indicating the goal to which the weight refers.
2. The number in the middle of each cell shows (1) the value of the relation on a 1-5 scale; (2) the value of the weight, with the least important goal having a weight of 1.
3. The number in the upper right-hand corner of each cell shows by how much the gap changes between the two alternatives being compared if the input increases by one unit.
4. The number in parentheses in each cell is the threshold value for each input. At that value, there will be a tie in the weighted sum of the two alternatives being compared.
5. The range in parentheses in each cell is the insensitivity range. That range shows how far down and up each input can go without affecting which alternative is the winner.

TABLE 10-3   ALTERNATIVES IN ALLOCATION PROBLEMS

A.   THE RAW DATA

	Delay (Days)	Respect (0-10 Scale)
Trials	120	6
Pleas	30	2
	150	8

B.   THE TRANSFORMED RAW DATA

	Speed (1/Days)	Respect (-5 to +5)
Trials	1/120 or .00833	+1
Pleas	1/30 or .03333	-3
	5/120 or .04166	-2

C.   THE PART/WHOLE PERCENTAGES

	Speed P/W%	Respect P/W%	Aggregate P/W%	Allocation %
Trials	20%	100%	120%	60%
Pleas	80%	0%	80%	40%
	100%	100%	200%	100%

D.   THE WEIGHTED P/W%'s

	Speed w = 1	Respect w = 2	Aggregate P/W%	Allocation %
Trials	20%	200%	220%	73%
Pleas	80%	0%	80%	27%
	100%	200%	300%	100%

190

1. The raw data are hypothetical but realistic. The object is to decide on the optimum allocation of cases to *trials* versus *pleas* in light of the facts that (1) *trials* receives a score of 120 days on delay and *pleas* 30 days; and (2) *trials* receives a score of 6 on response and *pleas* a score of 2.
2. Transforming the raw data involves (1) calculating the reciprocals for the raw scores of the negative goal of delay; (2) recalculating the raw scores on respect, using a scale that shows absolute zero. If N equals absolute zero, then subtract N from each of the original raw scores. For example, on a 0-10 scale, the number 5 (or below) might be absolute zero.
3. Calculating the correct part/whole percentages involves (1) calculating the part/whole percentages on the inverted negative goal; and, (2) giving zero percent to any alternative that has a negative raw score. Then calculate the part/whole percentages for the other alternatives.
4. Calculating the allocation percentages involves (1) multiplying the part/whole percentages in each column by the relative weight of the goal to which the column pertains; (2) summing the weighted part/whole percentages across each alternative; and (3) dividing those aggregate percentages by the sum of the weights. The results are the allocation percentages for each alternative or budget category.

high scores are undesirable, and (3) a score of 2 on respect may be a negative score such that each additional plea bargain decreases respect for the system.

To deal with those problems, we do the following:

1. The delay scores are converted into part/whole percentages by dividing each score by the sum of the delay column, but after inverting for the negative goal.
2. The inversion is done by working with the reciprocals of the delay scores. That means working with 1/120 and 1/30 rather than 120 and 30. Doing so preserves the fact that trials are four times as bad as pleas on the goal of delay, while making the pleas score higher than the trials score. We are then working with speed rather than delay as a goal. Speed should be given a weight of +1 if delay has previously been given a weight of -1.
3. The respect scores are also converted into part/whole percentages by dividing each score by the sum of the respect column, but after adjusting for the fact that pleas may have a negative score.
4. That means determining the value of a true zero on the 0-10 scale and subtracting that value from the 0-10 scores. Thus, if a 5 is the separation point between positive scores and negative scores, then a 6 is the equivalent of a +1, and a 2 is the equivalent of a -3. Those transformed numbers are shown in Table 10-3B.

Table 10-3C converts the transformed data into part/whole percentages. Pleas is given 0% on respect because one would not want to allocate anything more than the minimum possible if pleas has a negative score and if more respect were the only criterion. We can now add across the percentages and obtain an aggregate percent of 120% for trials and 80% for pleas. We then divide by 2 to bring the sum of those percentages down to 100% because we cannot allocate more than 100%.

Table 10-3D takes into consideration that respect is considered to be twice as important as speed. That means multiplying the percentages in the respect column by 2. The new aggregate percentages are then 220% and 80%. We then divide by 3 or the sum of the weights to obtain the allocation percentages of 73% and 27%. Not all allocation problems involve multiple dimensions, negative goals, or negative scores. If, however, one can follow the allocation analysis of Table 10-3, then one can deal with simpler allocation problems.[4]

ADJUSTING FOR CONSTRAINTS

Decision-aiding software can help in dealing with constraints that require minimums or maximums on the alternatives or the goals or other conditions that must be met, regardless how high the scores are of an alternative on the goals.

The main ways in which constraints are handled are:

1. The constraints can be met before one allocates scarce resources or determines the relation scores. Doing so tends to result in giving an alternative more than it is entitled where it only deserves the minimum. That result cannot occur if adjustments are made after allocating so as to bring alternatives up to their minimums.
2. The best way of resolving conflicting constraints is to expand the total benefits available or reduce the total costs to be imposed so that all the constraints can be satisfied simultaneously. If that is not possible, then resolve conflicting constraints by developing compromises that satisfy each constraint in proportion to its importance. Other less desirable alternatives

---

[4]On diverse methods for dealing with the multiplicity of alternatives in allocation problems, see Philip Kotler, *Marketing Decision Making: A Model Building Approach* (New York: Holt, 1971) (calculus and statistical analysis); Claude McMillan, *Mathematical Programming: An Introduction to the Design and Application of Optimal Decision Machines* (New York: Wiley, 1970) (reiterative guessing and operations research); and S. Nagel, *Policy Evaluation: Making Optimum Decisions* (New York: Praeger, 1982) (variations on part/whole percentaging in chapters 10-13). Also see S. Nagel, "Optimally Allocating Federal Money to Cities," 5 *Public Budgeting and Finance* 39-50 (1985).

involve partially satisfying all constraints equally, or fully satisfying certain constraints in the order of their priority.

Adjusting for constraints is illustrated by allocating a budget to the police and the courts in light of crime reduction and fair procedure as is shown in Table 10-4. The constraints specify minimum amounts to the police and the courts, but those minimums may add to more than the total budget available.

A good way to adjust to satisfy the equity constraints with two, three, and four budget categories is as follows:

1. With two budget categories, suppose category A is below its minimum and category B is above its minimum. After allocating in proportion to their aggregate scores, then give category A its minimum. Give the rest of the total budget to category B.
2. With three budget categories, suppose A is below its minimum and B and C are above their minimums. Then give A its minimum. Divide the rest of the total budget between B and C in proportion to their aggregate scores.
3. With four or more budget categories, one can reason by analogy to the three category situation. No matter how many budget categories are below their minimum in the initial optimizing, give them their minimums and then remove them from further allocating. The remainder of the total budget then gets divided proportionately among the other budget categories.[5]

SIMPLICITY OF ANALYSIS

Decision-aiding software that is based on multi-criteria decision-making can greatly simplify the analysis of a variety of decision-aiding problems that have traditionally used more complicated and often less valid methods, such as arrow diagrams, payoff matrices, decision trees, optimum level curves, indifference curves, functional curves, and multi-objective programming. The essence of MCDM software is that it works with a table, matrix, or spreadsheet with alternatives on the rows, evaluative criteria on the columns, relation scores in the cells, and a summation column at the right showing the overall score or allocation percent of each alternative.

---

[5]On dealing with constraints in public policy analysis in general, see S. Nagel, *Public Policy: Goals, Means, and Methods* (New York; St. Martin's, 1984), especially the chapters on equity, effectiveness, human rights, discretion, economic structure, government structure, political feasibility, and ethical constraints. On quantitative constraints in allocation problems, see "Allocation Logic" in S. Nagel, *Policy Evaluation: Making Optimum Decisions* (New York: Praeger, 1982) where the problem of allocating to police, courts, and corrections is also discussed.

TABLE 10-4. DEALING WITH EQUITY CONSTRAINTS

BUDGET CATEGORIES	RAW SCORES		TRANSFORMED SCORES			ALLOCATION RESULTS				
ALLOCATION CRITERIA	Crime Reduction (1)	Fair Procedure (2)	Aggregate Scores (3)	Allocation Percentages		Optimum Allocations		Minimums (6)	Adjusted Allocations	
				2-way (4a)	3-way (4b)	2-way (5a)	3-way (5b)		2-way (7a)	3-way (7b)
POLICE	2.00	1.00	3.00	43%	39%	$214	$195	$240	$240 (Min.)	$240 (Min.)
COURTS	1.00	3.00	4.00 / 7.00	57%	51%	$286	$255	$ 80	$260 (100% of $260)	$218 (84% of $260)
CORRECTIONS	.50	.25	.75	N/A	10%	N/A	$ 50	$ 40	N/A	$ 42 (16% of $260)
Totals	—	—	7.75	100%	100%	$500	$500	$360	$500	$500

Notes:

1. In Table 2 optimizing is done first, and then adjustments are made to satisfy the constraints if they have not been satisfied already. In other words, if we optimally allocate without considering the minimums, we obtain what is shown in column 5a (for two budget categories) and column 5b (for three budget categories). If we consider the minimums, we obtain what is shown in columns 7a and 7b.

NOTES TO TABLE 10-4 Continued:

2. There is $500 available to be allocated this year. There was $450 available to be allocated last year (N/A = not applicable).
3. The minimums in column 6 are equal to 80 percent of last year's budget. Last year, the police received $300. The courts received $100, and corrections received $50.
4. The numbers in columns 1 and 2 are based on a rough survey of a small sample of some people who are knowledgeable about the criminal justice system.
5. The formulas for the numbers in the other columns are:

$(3) = (1) + (2)$
$(4a) = (3)/7.00$
$(4b) = (3)/7.75$
$(5a) = (4a) (\$500)$
$(5b) = (4b) (\$500)$
$(6) = 80\%$ of last year's allocation
$(7a) = (5a) \pm \$26$
$(7b) = (5b) \pm X$, where X is clarified in the text

6. The best way of making the adjusted allocations is to give any budget category its minimum (from column 6). If its optimum (from column 5a or 5b) falls below its minimum, then divide the residue among the other budget categories in proportion to their aggregate scores (from column 3).

A good illustration of the simplicity of MCDM and P/G% software is the decision whether to take away or leave an abused child with the child's family. Table 10-5 shows the problem analyzed with a traditional payoff matrix, and Table 10-5B shows the problem analyzed with a P/G% spreadsheet table. Both approaches show the alternatives on the rows. The payoff matrix shows contingent events and possibly their probabilities on the columns, whereas the P/G% approach shows goals and their relative weights on the columns. The payoff matrix shows relative payoffs in the cells, whereas the P/G% approach shows relation scores on a 1-5 scale in the cells between the alternatives and the goals. The payoff matrix shows benefits minus costs on the right side with each element discounted by the probability of its occurring, whereas the P/G% approach shows the weighted summation scores for each alternative at the right side.

Both approaches are applied to the same empirical situation in Table 10-5. The payoff matrix tends to lead to a decision to take the child away because the probability of severe abuse is likely to be greater than the threshold probability. The P/G% approach leads to a closer decision because it emphasizes multiple criteria of avoiding abuse, preserving family love, and saving the taxpayer cost. One could argue that those three criteria are taken into consideration in the relative payoffs in the cells of the payoff matrix. However, by lumping all three criteria together, their separate existences and sensitivity values get overwhelmed by the criterion of avoiding abuse. The payoff matrix may thus lead to results that are less valid in terms of the decision-maker's goals than the P/G% approach.

The advantages of the P/G% approach over a payoff matrix include:

1. P/G% can explicitly consider any number of criteria such as the three shown above.
2. P/G% can explicitly consider any number of alternatives such as, take away to an institution, take away to a foster home, take away to a relative's home, leave with counselling, or leave without counselling.
3. Being able to consider multiple criteria and multiple alternatives makes the P/G% approach more validly in conformity with reality, and not just a simplistic abstraction.
4. P/G% is also simpler with its 1-5 scales, weighted criteria, computerized threshold analysis, and logical way of analyzing a problem in terms of alternatives, criteria, and relations.[6]

SOME CONCLUSIONS

As mentioned at the beginning of this chapter, the main benefits of the decision-aiding software are its accuracy and speed in handling the five key methodological problems in evaluation analysis. To fully appreciate the relevance of the software, it is necessary to actually use it. We can, however, briefly describe how the software applies to each problem.

On the matter of multiple dimensions on multiple goals:

1. In comparing any two alternatives, one can show for each goal the incremental gain of the better alternative over the other alternative. This can be more easily done by putting the goals on the rows and the two alternatives on the columns since the software subtracts across the rows. One can then pick the alternative that has the more desired set of increments.
2. One can specify the importance of each goal relative to the least important goal. Those weights can consider both importance and the nature of the measurement units where raw scores are used.
3. The software is capable of working with the relations either as raw scores or part/whole percentages by exercising an option on the data management menu.

On the matter of missing information:

---

[6]On the matter of simplicity in drawing and presenting conclusions in evaluation analysis, see S. Nagel, "Comparing Multi-Criteria Decision Making and P/G% with Traditional Optimizing," in Yoshikazu Sawaragi (ed.), *Multiple-Criteria Decision Making* (Berlin, Germany: Springer-Verlag, 1987) and "Simplifying Basic Methods" in S. Nagel, *Public Policy: Goals, Means, and Methods* (New York: St. Martin's, 1984). On the subject of taking away abused children, see "Neglect" in George Cooper et al., *Law and Poverty: Cases and Materials* (St. Paul, Minn.: West, 1973).

TABLE 10-5. THE NEED FOR SIMPLICITY IN COMPLEX SITUATIONS

A. THE PAYOFF MATRIX

SEVERE SUBSEQUENT ABUSE

	Would Not Occur	Would Occur	
TAKE AWAY	a −50	b +100	Benefits − Costs
LEAVE	c +50	d −100	$(P)(100) -$ $(1-P)(50)$

B. THE P/G% APPROACH

	Avoid Abuse (w=2)	Preserve Family Love (w=1)	Save Taxpayer Cost (w=1)	Weighted Sum
TAKE AWAY	4	2	2	12
LEAVE	2	4	4	12

NOTES FOR THE PAYOFF MATRIX IN TABLE 10-5A:

1. The cell entries are arrived at by asking the decision makers the following questions:
   (1) Of the four possible occurrences, which ones are desirable (marked plus), and which ones are undesirable (marked minus)?
   (2) Of the undesirable occurrences, which one is the most undesirable (marked -100)?
   (3) How much more undesirable is the most undesirable occurrence (marked -100) in comparison to the least undesirable occurrence (marked -50) to show Cell d is twice as bad as Cell a)?
2. With that information, one can determine the threshold probability as follows:
   (1) At the threshold, the discounted benefits equal the discounted costs (i.e., $100P = 50 - 50P$).
   (2) The solution for P in that equation is $P* = d/(a+d)$ or $P* = 100/50 = .33$.
   (3) That means, if the probability is greater than .33, that there will be severe subsequent abuse and the child should be taken away.

NOTES FOR THE P/G% APPROACH IN TABLE 10-5A:

1. The scoring of each alternative on each criterion is on a 1-5 scale, where 5 = highly conducive to the goal, 4 = mildly conducive, 3 = neither conducive nor adverse, 2 = mildly adverse to the goal, and 1 = highly adverse. Decimal scores can be given between these numbers, where appropriate.
2. Avoiding abuse is considered to be twice as important as preserving whatever family love might exist or saving taxpayer cost.
3. By considering multiple criteria rather than emphasizing the probability of severe subsequent abuse, the decision is a much closer decision, and more dependent on the specific facts or scores on the first two criteria than on a general threshold probability.
4. If the criteria are given equal weight and a threshold analysis is performed, then leaving the child wins 10 points to 8 points. The threshold or tie-causing values of the weights are then 2,0, and 0. The threshold values of the relation scores are then 6,4,4,0,2, and 2, reading across the matrix.

1. The software can do what-if analysis by allowing the user to change any of the inputs and quickly see how those changes affect the bottom-line conclusion.
2. The main menu gives the user an option to do a threshold analysis or a convergence analysis to determine the critical values for relation scores or goal weights, above which one alternative would be better and below which another alternative would be better.
3. In specifying the criteria, one can divide each criterion into a best version and a worst version, such as the best possible cost on each alternative and the worst possible cost. The computer can then show the overall best score, the overall worst score, and the midpoint for each alternative.
4. The software can also draw indifference curves or threshold curves showing the combination of scores on two or more variables which would lead to a tie between any two alternatives.

On the matter of allocating resources:

1. The user can specify the grand total available to be allocated. The program will multiply that grand total by the allocation percentages for each alternative or budget category.
2. The allocation percentages are calculated by obtaining an overall score for each alternative and then dividing each overall score by the sum of the scores in order to obtain part/whole allocation percentages.
3. The program can transform the raw scores by determining their reciprocals where negative goals are involved, or by subtracting the value of absolute

zero from each raw score where negative scores are involved. Those transformations may, however, be easier to do with a calculator and then just enter the results into the data matrix.

On the matter of adjusting for constraints:

1. The user can enter minimum constraints for each alternative, and the program can guarantee they will be met in whatever allocation is done. A better approach though would be to optimize ignoring the constraints. and then make adjustments for any alternative or criterion that violates its minimum or maximum.
2. The ease of doing what-if analysis facilitates resolving conflicting constraints and conflicting decision-makers by enabling both sides or a mediator to try different alternatives, criteria, weights, constraints, relations, and other inputs until a mutually satisfying solution is found.

On the matter of simplicity:

1. The essence of the software is the idea of putting alternatives on the rows of a spreadsheet matrix, criteria and weights on the columns, relations in the cells, and overall scores for the alternatives in the right-hand column.
2. That system is in conformity with a great deal of systematic decision making, as indicated by the popularity of spreadsheet software, payoff matrices, decision trees, and other formats that can be reduced to a decision matrix.

This kind of evaluation analysis could be done with pencil and paper or even implicitly in one's mind. The analysis is, however, substantially facilitated by the availability of the software and microcomputers. The software encourages thinking more explicitly about evaluation problems without confining the user to quantitatively measured variables. It facilitates creativity by allowing changes to be so easily made. We may be at the advent of new ways of thinking about program evaluation, policy analysis, and decision-making to the benefit of the decision-makers and those who are affected by their decisions.[7]

---

[7] On Policy/Goal Percentaging and the P/G% software, see Benjamin Radcliff, "Multi-Criteria Decision Making: A Survey of Software" 4 *Social Science Microcomputer Review* 38-55 (1986); S. Nagel, "P/G% Analysis: An Evaluating Aiding Program," 9 *Evaluation Review* 209-214 (1985); and S. Nagel, "A Microcomputer Program for Evaluation Analysis," 10 *Evaluation and Program Planning* 159-168 (1987). On the applicability of P/G% to all five analytic problems, see S. Nagel, *Evaluation Analysis with Microcomputers* (Greenwich, Conn.: JAI Press, 1987).

PART SIX:

PROJECTING TRENDS

IN PUBLIC POLICY

11

TRENDS IN CROSS-CUTTING ISSUES

Chapters 11 and 12 are concerned with projecting trends in public policy. Chapter 11 is concerned with trends in the cross-cutting issues of incentives for encouraging socially desired behavior, government structures for more effective goal achievement, the coordination of public-private relations, and systematic methods of public policy evaluation.

INCENTIVES

Table 11-1 summarizes some of the trends regarding incentives for encouraging socially desired behavior. One overall trend is an increasing reliance on rewarding the rightdoer, as contrasted to punishing the wrongdoer. The emphasis on right doing manifests itself more in decreasing the costs of rightdoing (such as tax deductions), rather than in increasing the benefits of rightdoing (such as reward subsidies) since tax deductions are more politically feasible. Within the concern for wrong-doers, there is an increasing emphasis on penalties other than traditional jail and fines, such as confiscating profits-property, reimbursement of victims, and penalties by way of missed opportunities that might otherwise be meaningfully available.

The administration of incentives programs may be improving toward a higher probability of the benefits and costs occurring. On the other hand, the role of socialization to make various kinds of wrongdoing unthinkable has lessened with the decreased impact of the family and the school. There is a trend toward more physical structuring to make wrongdoing difficult, such as better street lighting to discourage mugging and rapes, more areas within the

TABLE 11-1. TRENDS IN INCENTIVES FOR ENCOURAGING SOCIALLY DESIRED BEHAVIOR

INCENTIVES	EXAMPLES	TRENDS	ADVANTAGES
Increase benefits of rightdoing	Reward subsidies	Increase	Can buy cooperation but expensive & politically unpopular.
Decrease costs of rightdoing	Tax deductions	Bigger increase	Buys less cooperation but politically more feasible.
Decrease benefits of wrongdoing	Confiscate profits	Increase but only in criminal activities	Could change behavior but difficult to apply.
Increase costs of wrongdoing	Big penalties	Increase	Penalties tend to be absorbed as an expense & hemmed in by due process.
Increase probability of benefits & costs occurring	Better monitoring & bounties	Increase through improved personnel	Essential for benefits & costs to be meaningful, but worthless if benefits are not substantial.
Socialization to make wrongdoing unthinkable	Street crimes among middle class people	Decrease in the importance of conscience	May require special upbringing.
Physical structuring to make wrongdoing difficult	Gun prohibition or control	Mild increase	Effective but may not be politically feasible.

control and responsibility of individual apartments, and more gun control to reduce the availability of lethal weapons. The biggest overall trend is the combining of an increased variety of approaches for dealing with wrongdoing across all policy problems, including pollution, discrimination, not just traditional criminal behavior.[1]

GOVERNMENT STRUCTURES

Table 11-2 summarizes some of the trends in the roles of different levels and branches of government regarding the formation and implementation of public policy.

The overall trend is toward increasing activity at all levels and branches of government for reasons mentioned in discussing the general public-private controversy. Within that overall trend the national government has especially increased its role largely as a result of the increased geographical broadness, complexity, and expensiveness of public policy problems. Also within the overall trend, the executive branch of government has especially increased, largely as a result of the need for speed, technical specialization, and a broader constituency.

Saying there has been an increase at the national level and in the executive branch may tend to over-simplify since the policy-making role of states, cities, legislatures, and courts has also increased. It is also an oversimplification because it does not adequately recognize that some public policy fields are very much in the domain of (1) the states, such as policies that relate to contracts, property, torts, and family law, (2) the cities or other local governments, such as zoning, sanitation, police, and schools, (3) the legislatures, such as taxing-spending policy, and (4) the courts, such as free speech, criminal justice, and equal protection under the law.[2]

PUBLIC-PRIVATE RELATIONS

---

[1]For further details on trends regarding incentives to encourage socially-desired behavior, see Barry Mitnick, *The Political Economy of Regulation: Creating, Designing, and Removing Regulatory Forms* (New York: Columbia University Press, 1980); William Hamilton, Larry Ledebur, and Deborah Matz, *Industrial Incentives: Public Promotion of Private Enterprise* (Washington, D.C.: Aslan Press, 1984); and Alfred Blumstein (ed.), *Deterrence and Incapacitation* (Washington, D.C.: National Academy of Sciences, 1978).

[2]For further details on trends in the division of labor among levels and branches of government, see James Sundquist, *Constitutional Reform and Effective Government* (Washington, D.C.: Brookings Institution, 1985); David Walker, *Toward a Functioning Federalism* (Boston, Mass.: Winthrop, 1981); and Michael Reagan and John Sanzone, *The New Federalism* (New York: Oxford University Press, 1981).

TABLE 11-2

TRENDS IN THE ROLES OF LEVELS AND BRANCHES OF GOVERNMENT

LEVELS OR BRANCHES	TRENDS	ADVANTAGES
LEVEL		
National	Increasing, especially on unemployment-inflation, foreign-defense policy, & civil liberties.	Coordination & uniformity across states.
States	Increasing, but not as much with an emphasis on criminal justice, property rights, & family relations.	Coordinated across cities & counties, plus being closer to where programs are implemented.
Cities	Increasing, especially on zoning, sanitation, police, fire, & schools.	Closer to where programs are implemented.
BRANCHES		
Executive	Increasing, especially on foreign-defense policy & unemployment-inflation.	Speed, unity, & possibly decisiveness.
Legislative	Increasing, but not as much, with an emphasis on taxing-spending policy.	Debate & diversity of viewpoints.
Judicial	Plateauing after previous increases especially in civil liberties & liability.	Relative immunity from the pressures of re-election.

Table 11-3 summarizes some of the trends concerning various public-private sector activities. The overall idea is that we are moving away from the more extreme activities toward more pragmatic intermediate approaches. That can be seen at both ends of the five-point continuum. The pure marketplace as an approach for dealing with public policy matters has greatly lessened. If one looks at the list of policy fields in Chapter 1, none of them are being handled from a pure marketplace perspective, even though the marketplace was substantially more important a generation or two ago. Thus there is more government regulation, litigation, and use of subsidies and tax breaks in all 11 fields.

For example, the top row concerning labor was almost completely a marketplace matter until the 1930's. The Supreme Court had held that minimum wage laws were unconstitutional and also maximum hour laws and child labor laws. There were no laws yet for the Supreme Court to hold unconstitutional regarding race or sex discrimination. The year 1938 brought the Fair Labor Standards Act governing wages, hours, and child labor. The year 1964 brought the Civil Rights Act which contained prohibitions against race and sex discrimination. The year 1980 brought the Reagan administration with its Enterprise Zones designed to provide subsidies and tax breaks for business firms that reduce unemployment in the inner city.

At the opposite end of the continuum, one should note the reduced advocacy of government ownership even by those associated with socialist politics. The Socialist Party of Eugene Debs in the early 1900's and of Norman Thomas in the 1930's received many votes when advocating government ownership and operation of the basic means of production and distribution in America. Many people say that the Democratic Party destroyed the Socialist Party by adopting socialist ideas concerning social security and labor legislation, but the Democratic Party never pushed the idea of government ownership with the possible exception of the Tennessee Valley Authority. That lessening of advocacy of government ownership is not peculiar to the United States. The idea has substantially decreased in the program of the British Labor Party, the German Social Democrats, and the French Socialists. It has lessened in various aspects of agriculture and retail sales within eastern Europe and China. Even traditional government functions are now sometimes being contracted out to private enterprise, such as the operating of some prisons, although the government retains control and responsibility.[3]

---

[3]For further details on trends in the division of labor between the public and private sectors, see Martin Rein and Lee Rainwater (eds.), *Public/Private Interplay in Social Protection: Comparative Study* (Armonk, N.Y.: M. E. Sharpe, 1986); David Linowes (ed.), *Privatization: Toward More Effective Government* (Washington, D.C.: Government Printing Office, 1988); and Dennis Thompson (ed.), *The Private Exercise of Public Functions* (Port Washington, N.Y.: Associated Faculty Press, 1985).

TABLE 11-3. TRENDS IN PUBLIC-PRIVATE SECTOR ACTIVITIES

ACTIVITIES	TRENDS	ADVANTAGES
Pure marketplace	Decreasing except where competition benefits consumers or where government contracts out government functions.	Good for prices, quality, & safety where competition present.
Subsidies & tax breaks	Increasing to encourage socially desired behavior.	Good where politically feasible & where discretion is allowable.
Litigation	Increasing as injured persons acquire more rights & relations become more anonymous.	Good for compensating injured persons, especially if on a no-fault basis.
Government regulation	Plateauing after previous increases.	
Government ownership	Decreasing in advocacy.	Good for activities that private enterprise does not want to conduct.

METHODS OF POLICY EVALUATION

Table 11-4 summarizes some of the trends regarding methods of public policy evaluation. The key overall trend is toward new ideas that combine both simplicity and validity. There is a trend toward the use of microcomputer software which facilitates systematic trial-and-error experimentation. There is also a trend toward an expert systems perspective which seeks to develop methods by analyzing how good decision makers implicitly decide, rather than trying to deduce how they should decide in light of unrealistic and/or unfeasible premises that relate to calculus optimization or mathematical programming.

More specific trends relate to how to deal with each of the six major obstacles to systematic evaluation mentioned in the methods column of Table 11-4. Those separate trends involve moving toward (1) multi-criteria decision-making, rather than single objective functions, (2) variations on breakeven analysis to determine critical values of missing information, rather than trying to devise expensive ways of not having missing information, (3) the use of percentaging methods to deal with allocation problems, (4) an expansionist philosophy to deal with conflicting constraints, (5) variations on if-then analysis for multiple prediction, and (6) spreadsheet analysis as the most popular decision-aiding software.[4]

---

[4]For further details on trends regarding methods of public policy evaluation, one can compare relevant books from the 50's, 60's, 70's and so on, such as Daniel Lerner and Harold Lasswell (eds.), *The Policy Sciences* (Palo Alto, Calif.: Stanford University Press, 1951); Raymond Bauer and Kenneth Gergen (eds.), *The Study of Policy Formation* (New York: Free Press, 1968); Irving Horowitz and James Katz, *Social Science and Public Policy in the United States* (New York: Praeger, 1975); Nick Smith (ed.), *New Techniques for Evaluation* (Beverly Hills, Calif.: Sage, 1981); and S. Nagel, *Evaluation Analysis with Microcomputers* (Greenwich, Conn.: JAI Press, 1988).

TABLE 11-4. TRENDS IN METHODS OF PUBLIC POLICY EVALUATION

METHODS	EXAMPLES	TRENDS	ADVANTAGES
Multiple dimensions on multiple goals.	Multi-criteria decision-making	Increase	Can deal with non-monetary benefits & monetary costs, & multiple goals.
Missing information	Breakeven analysis, best-worst scenarios, & graphics.	Increase	Can deal with missing info without having to gather the info.
Allocation analysis	Part/whole percentaging	Increase	Avoids assumptions & measurement needs of OR/MS
Multiple & conflicting constraints	Prioritizing, compromising, or expanding the constraints.	Increase	The expanding approach encourages growth where everyone comes out ahead.
Multiple prediction	If-then analysis	Increase	Fits what good decision-makers actually do.
Simplicity	Spreadsheet analysis	Increase	Easy to manipulate including what-if analysis.

210

12

TRENDS IN SPECIFIC POLICIES AND GOALS

This chapter is concerned with describing some of the major changes which have occurred in the main fields of public policy since 1900. Those changes have generally occurred during three time periods. The first period was the era of Woodrow Wilson, partly continuing the public policy program of Theodore Roosevelt. The second period was the era of Franklin Delano Roosevelt, partly continued by Harry Truman. The third time period was the 1960's during the presidencies of John F. Kennedy and Lyndon Johnson. The intermediate time periods tended to legitimize the policy changes which had occurred during the 1910's, 1930's, and 1960's. Thus, the subsequent non-repeal of (1) the Wilson legislation later in the 1920's, (2) the FDR legislation later in the 1950's, and (3) the Kennedy-Johnson legislation later in the 1980's has served to make those changes less controversial and more accepted.

Another way of thinking in terms of cycles in policy change is by periods that promote greater equality or sharing of productivity advances, as contrasted to periods that concentrate on technological improvements for increasing national productivity. Thus the 1910's, 1930's, and 1960's were periods emphasizing more rights to consumers, workers, minorities, and other non-dominant groups. The 1920's, 1950's, and 1980's were periods with a relative emphasis on economic growth, rather than equalizing of previous gains.

In discussing each specific policy field, one can ask what happened in that field in the 1910's, 1930's, and 1960's in order to see better how things have changed, although important changes may have also occurred in the intermediate periods. Some subject matters have been undergoing substantial change as early as the 1910's or 1930's, such as consumer and labor matters. Others have not shown much activity until the 1960's or later, such as poverty-discrimination and environment-energy.[1]

ECONOMIC ISSUES

On unemployment, inflation, and regulating the business cycle, the big contribution of the 1910's was the establishment of the Federal Reserve System. That system allows for stimulating the economy to reduce unemployment by lowering interest rates and by lowering the cash requirements banks need to keep on reserve. The opposite is to be done in time of inflation to dampen the economy. It is interesting to note that this kind of monetary policy which had been a radical proposal in the Wilson administration is now conservative economics, especially associated with Milton Friedman.

The contribution of the 1930's was the explicit establishment of Keynesian economic policy. It involves stimulating the economy to reduce unemployment by decreasing taxes and increasing government spending. The opposite is to be done in times of inflation to dampen the economy. Keynesian economics largely replaced Federal Reserve monetary policy for dealing with the depression because no matter how low the interest rates are and how much lending money is available, business firms are unwilling to borrow to expand their plants if they are currently operating at substantially less than 100% of capacity.

The contribution of the 1960's and later to the handling of unemployment and inflation is the increasing adoption of a more focused incentives approach. Keynesian policy did not work well for dealing with inflation of the 1960's or later because it is politically unfeasible to sufficiently increase taxes and decrease government spending. Worse is the fact that in the 1970's, we were faced with increased unemployment and increased inflation simultaneously due to the ability of businesses and unions to keep prices and wages high even though demand had fallen off. Monetary and Keynesian approaches advocate stimulating the economy to deal with unemployment and dampening the economy to deal with inflation, but both cannot be done simultaneously.

The more contemporary Reagan and Carter administrations increasingly looked toward using a system of incentives to stimulate potential employers to

---

[1]For further details on the recent history of developments in the fields of public policy, see Theodore J. Lowi and Alan Stone (eds.), *Nationalizing Government: Public Policies in America* (Beverly Hills, Calif.: Sage, 1978); John Schwarz, *America's Hidden Success: A Reassessment of Public Policy from Kennedy to Reagan* (New York: Norton, 1988); Robert Bremmer et al., (eds.), *American Choices: Social Dilemmas and Public policy since 1960* (Columbus, Ohio: Ohio State University Press, 1986); and David Rothman and Stanton Wheeler (eds.), *Social History and Social Policy* (New York: Academic Press, 1981).

hire the unemployed and aid to stimulate unemployed people to obtain jobs and training. The incentives system can also help stimulate new technology and increased income, thereby expanding the need to hire people. The incentives system can also be used to reduce inflation. In that regard, tax breaks can be given to business firms and labor unions for not raising prices or wages. This has been discussed in the economic policy literature, but not yet implemented. The inflation of the early 1980's was mainly dealt with by raising interest rates, but that may be too costly an approach in terms of hurting economic growth.

Prior to about 1910, consumer-business relations in the United States were controlled almost completely by the marketplace and a pro-business legal system. As of the Woodrow Wilson years, the Clayton Anti-Trust Act was passed. It was slightly more consumer-oriented than the previous Sherman Anti-Trust Act, which emphasized protecting business firms from monopolies, although business firms are important consumers from other businesses. More important was the establishment of the Federal Trade Commission and the Pure Food and Drug Administration which had a definite consumer orientation. In the field of common law, Justice Cardozo of the New York Court of Appeals established the principle that consumers could sue manufacturers for defective products even if the consumer had not dealt directly with the manufacturer and even if the consumer could not prove the manufacturer was negligently responsible for the defect except by circumstantial evidence. That was the beginning of effective products liability litigation. Consumer rights were strengthened in the 1960's as a result of Congressional legislation establishing the Products Safety Commission. The common law courts also established the idea that a consumer contract could be too unconscionable to be enforced and that consumers must be given minimum due process before they can be subjected to product repossession or a lien on their wages or property.

Prior to about 1910, labor-management relations in the United States were controlled almost completely by the marketplace and a pro-management legal system. Some gains were made during World War I in essential industries like railway labor where strikes could be highly effective. The really important legislation, though, did not come until the 1930's partly because the Supreme Court found wage, hour, and child labor legislation to be unconstitutional. The key 1930's legislation was the National Labor Relations Act. It allowed workers to petition for a secret ballot election to determine whether they wanted to be represented by a union, and it prohibited management from firing workers simply because they wanted to join a union. Also highly important was the Fair Labor Standards Act which provided for minimum wages, overtime pay, and a prohibition on child labor. There have been amendments to the NLRA in subsequent years, but the extremely emotional and sometimes lethal battles between labor and management in the 1930's are now relatively noncontroversial.

SOCIAL ISSUES

In the development of public policy, the have-not groups who have relatively greater power are more likely to achieve their policy goals first. Thus, the consumers succeeded in obtaining important legislation and judicial precedents in the 1910's. Most people considered themselves consumers. Labor succeeded in obtaining important policy changes in the 1930's. Labor has less political influence than consumers collectively do. It was not until the 1960's, however, that poor people and race-sex minorities succeeded in obtaining important policy changes since they have the least power of those three sets of interest groups.

The war on poverty was an important policy activity of the 1960's. Perhaps its greatest gains were in the form of judicial precedents which held (1) welfare recipients were entitled to at least minimum due process and non-arbitrary classification before they could be terminated, (2) indigent defendants were entitled to court-appointed counsel in felony and misdemeanor cases, (3) delinquents, illegitimate children, and neglected children were entitled to hearings with at least minimum due process and no arbitrary denial of equal protection, and (4) tenants could withhold rent if landlords failed to satisfy minimum implied warranties of habitability. Also important was the beginning of work incentive programs which provided for (1) being allowed to keep a portion of one's earning without losing welfare benefits, (2) being provided with day-care facilities so that mothers of pre-school children could work, and (3) being provided with meaningful training. Also important was legislation for rent supplements to rent economic housing in the marketplace, and for food stamps to buy food in the marketplace rather than rely on federal commodities or food handouts. The Reagan administration has added an increased emphasis on the importance of economic prosperity and growth for dealing with poverty, as contrasted to specific anti-poverty programs, and also the importance of incentives to business to provide on-the-job training and to hire welfare recipients.

In the realm of race discrimination, the gains have been mainly at the Supreme Court and congressional levels during the 1960's in such areas as (1) voting right by abolishing the poll tax and racial malapportionment, (2) criminal justice by abolishing discrimination in becoming a juror, lawyer, or a judge, (3) education, by prohibiting legally required segregation and providing federal aid to education which stimulates compliance with desegregation guidelines, (4) housing, by prohibiting race and sex, discrimination in job activities. Any judicial precedent or legislation which benefits the poor is likely to benefit blacks, and vice versa, given the correlation between those two policy fields.

On the matter of criminal justice, the early 1900's first saw the Supreme Court say that something in the Bill of Rights was applicable to the states starting with the principle against double jeopardy.   In the 1930's, right to counsel was established but only for capital and serious felony cases.   The 1960's saw the important right to counsel extended to misdemeanor cases, pre-trial interrogation, and post-trial appeal.   The 60's also saw the establishment of the rule excluding illegally seized evidence on a nationwide basis.   That was also a time for bail reform which involved more releasing of defendants prior to trial accompanied by screening, periodic reporting, notification, and prosecution for skipping out.   There were also increased experiments and concern for reducing delay in the criminal and civil justice process.   The Supreme Court established minimum rights for people on parole, probation, or in prison.

SCIENCE POLICY ISSUES

The end of the 60's saw an increased concern for two sets of policy problems which had not previously been salient.   The first was environmental protection.   Prior to about 1970, people tended to think of air, water, and landfills as virtually unlimited goods, unless they lived in an area where there was a water shortage.   As of about 1970, people became much more concerned with the public health aspects of air pollution, water pollution, and solid waste disposal.   Federal legislation was passed providing for standard setting, permits, inspections, hearing procedures, and other rules designed to protect the environment.   Along related lines, prior to 1970, energy was also thought of as an almost unlimited inexpensive product.   Since 1975, however, there has been increased legislation designed to stimulate energy conservation and regulate new forms of energy production such as nuclear energy.

Prior to the 1960's, health policy was largely left to the marketplace and private charity.   Probably the first big breakthrough with regard to government responsibility was the establishment of Medicare for the aged and Medicaid for the poor.   Such programs might have been established sooner, but they required mustering sufficient public support to overcome the power of the American Medical Association.   As the elderly have increased in absolute and percentage terms, increased pressure has been placed on Medicare funds.   The idea of federal funding is now well-accepted, and even the Reagan Administration is proposing federally funded catastrophic health insurance.   Some day there may be government salaried doctors for Medicaid and Medicare patients, as there are government salaried lawyers under the Legal Services Corporation.   Doing so is substantially less expensive to the taxpayer than reimbursing the private health care providers.

POLITICAL POLICY ISSUES

The previous issues tend to have a chronological relation in the order of consumer, labor, poverty-discrimination, and environment-elderly. The political issues tend to be a more constant concern like the economic issue of unemployment-inflation. One can argue that free speech is the most important public policy issue because all the other policy problems would be poorly handled if there were no free speech to communicate the existence and possible remedies for the other problems. Free speech, however, was not recognized as a national right in the sense of being applicable to the states by way of the first and the fourteenth amendment until the 1930's. At that time, the Supreme Court first declared the states had an obligation to respect first amendment free speech. The early cases though involved blatant forms of government censorship and suppression of ideas, including criticism of mayors of Minneapolis and Jersey City. In the 1960's, the Supreme Court declared unconstitutional less severe non-political activities such as (1) restrictions on most pornography, (2) allowing ordinary libel suites by public figures instead of requiring intentional libel or gross negligence, and (3) restrictions on commercial speech such as lawyer advertising.

On the matter of world peace, the same time periods of expansion in public policy were also time periods when the United States became involved in World War I in the 1910's, World War II in the late 1930's, and the Vietnam War in the 1960's. Part of the explanation might be that the liberal Democrats of the 1910's and the 1930's were more prone to go to war with the reactionary governments of Kaiser Wilhelm, Adolf Hitler, and Hideki Tojo. In the 1960's, the liberal Democrats may have been trying to avoid appearing to be soft on communism more than the Republicans would have to be, which could have been a factor leading to the Vietnam War. More important in terms of current trends is the fact that there has been no international war comparable to World War I or II in the second half of the twentieth century, and the likelihood of such a war may be decreasing as a result of recent changes in the Soviet Union and agreements between the USSR and the USA. That trend could be very desirable in terms of making funds available for economic growth which would otherwise be wasted on armament.

The third subfield under political policy is government reform. It can be subdivided into legislative, judicial, and administrative reform. Government reform refers to changes in the structures and procedures of those institutions so as to make them more effective in achieving their purposes and more efficient in doing so with less time and expense. Effective and efficient functioning of government structures affects all public policies. During the twentieth century in the United States, there have been significant challenges in all three sets of institutions.

At the congressional and state legislative level, the reforms include (1) redrawing legislative districts so as to provide for equal population per district, (2) the lessening of the filibuster whereby a minority bloc of the U.S. Senate could prevent a bill from coming to a vote, (3) an overemphasis on the power of seniority in choosing committee chairs as contrasted to merit or a vote by the committee members, (4) less power to the House speaker and committee chairs to make binding agenda decisions, (5) more voting rights for women, blacks, poor people, and young people, (6) more technical competence available through legislative staffs, and (7) more open disclosure of activities of interest groups and income of legislators. An especially important reform for the future that relates to legislative representation is the idea of expanding representation and participation to provide for voter registration by way of being on the census, and vote-casting at any polling place in the country on election day.

At the judicial level or branch, the reforms include (1) free counsel for the poor in criminal and civil cases, (2) encouraging out-of-court settlements through pre-trial procedures, (3) shifting cases away from the courts to administrative agencies, (4) the computerizing of court records for increased efficiency, (5) encouraging alternative dispute resolution through ad hoc arbitration, (6) clearer guidelines for more objective sentencing and the determination of damages, and (7) higher standards for admission to the bar and the bench with more emphasis on professional responsibility. An important reform for the future that relates to the judicial process is the idea of selecting judges on the basis of having been specially trained and tested for the bench in law school like high-level civil servants, rather than through a system of political appointment or election.

At the administrative level or branch, the reforms include (1) more emphasis on hiring on the basis of merit rather than political considerations, (2) more performance measurement and evaluation of government programs, (3) more professional training, especially in schools of public affairs and administration, (4) a lessening of elected department heads in state government, so as to have better coordinated control in the hands of state governors, (5) more use of professional city managers to supplement mayors at the municipal level, (6) improved grievance procedures, collective bargaining, and working conditions, (7) the development of the field of administrative law for clarifying due process in administrative adjudication, rule making, and judicial review, (8) better coordination of administrative agencies across different levels of government, and (9) more freedom of information for the public to be able to obtain access to administrative records.

MUTUALLY BENEFICIAL RESULTS

Table 12-1 summarizes some of the trends in specific policy fields. The overall idea is that there have been increased benefits for people who had few rights as of the base years of 1910, 1930, or 1950. These people have been the immediate beneficiary of the policy changes. It is, however, unduly narrow to limit the analysis to those immediate effects. The longer-term and broader effects have generally been to benefit the dominant groups as well or the total society.

This is shown, for example, on the top row. Labor has benefitted from better wages, shorter hours, better working conditions, the ending of child labor, and the lessening of race and sex discrimination. Also highly important is the stimulus those labor policies have had on encouraging the development and adoption of labor-saving technology. The United States as of 1980 might still be using slave labor or cheap immigrant labor and be a backward low-technology country if it had not been for the successful efforts of labor unions and working class people to increase the cost of their labor. A third-level result is that the labor-saving technology has made labor more productive and more skilled. This has the effect of increasing wages still further, thereby stimulating greater consumption and the creation of new jobs, especially in service fields.

Likewise, one can go through each of the 11 policy fields and see that the initial policy changes have tended in a direction of increasing the rights of the have-not's. Those increases have in turn stimulated benefits for the total society, regardless whether one is talking about consumer rights, free speech, criminal justice, equal treatment, government reform, world peace, trade, poverty, education, environment, or health.

PREDICTING AND PRESCRIBING FUTURE PUBLIC POLICY

Table 1-1, back in Chapter 1, summarizes the ideas presented with regard to doing better than the optimum. It shows how that kind of thinking can apply to all policy problems including (1) economic problems like unemployment, inflation, and consumer rights, (2) political problems like world peace, free speech, and government reform, (3) social problems like crime, poverty, discrimination, and education, and (4) science policy problems like health policy and environmental policy.

Table 1-1 does not indicate what the trend is in defining goals for each policy problem. The implication, however, is that if one goal is better than another, there would eventually be a trend toward the better goal. "Better" in this sense brings us to a high level of generality such as the standard of the greatest happiness for the greatest number. There is a trend toward higher goals, although that varies depending on the policy field. Goals in civil liberties, education, and health are frequently being raised. Other fields may involve some reduction in goals in order to accommodate problems that have become more severe, such as the problems of pollution and drug-related crime.

Table 1-1 fits this section "Projecting Trends in Public Policy", not so much

TABLE 12-1. SOME TRENDS IN SPECIFIC POLICY FIELDS

POLICY FIELDS	BENEFITS FOR THE HAVE NOTS	BENEFITS FOR THE HAVES OR ALL
ECONOMIC POLICY		
Labor	Better wages, hours, working conditions. No child labor. Less discrimination.	Stimulus to labor-saving technology. Happier and more productive workers.
Consumer	More rights concerning product liability.	Stimulus to providing better products & greater sales.
POLITICAL-LEGAL POLICY		
Free Speech	More rights in politics, art, and commerce	Stimulus to creativity.
Due process & criminal justice	More rights to counsel, notice, hearings.	More respect for the law.
Equal treatment	More rights to blacks, women, & the poor on voting, criminal justice, schools, employment, housing, & consumer.	More equality of opportunity and allocation on the basis of merit.
Government reform	Less corruption, intimidation, & incompetence.	More effectiveness & efficiency.
World peace & trade	Increased standards of living for developing countries.	Uplifted countries become good trading partners.
SOCIAL POLICY		
Poverty	More rights as employees, consumers, tenants, welfare recipients, & family members.	The same rights apply to middle-class employees, consumers, tenants, & family members.
Education	More access to more education.	More efficient economy from better training. Less welfare.
SCIENCE POLICY		
Environment	More rights to cleaner air, water, solid waste, noise, radiation, and conservation.	The same rights are important to all people.
Health	More access to medical help.	That includes catastrophic help from which even the rich benefit.

because the table tells what will be, but because it implies what ought to be. One can make a case for saying that the world is getting better on many important dimensions. That is a key idea of Table 11-1 on some trends in specific policy fields. One can make a case even easier for the idea that the world should be getting better. Both optimists and pessimists are likely to agree that there is room for improvement. Optimists believe that the improvement can occur more readily than pessimists do. Table 1-1 could be interpreted from an optimistic perspective as at least a partial projection of future trends in public policy. Table 1-1 can be more easily interpreted from either perspective as a worthy agenda for the future of public policy.

It is hoped that this book will stimulate further ideas about what will be and why. It is even more hoped that this book will stimulate further ideas about what should be and how. On that matter, perhaps there has traditionally been too much emphasis on the idea of being satisfied with less than the best. It has now become almost commonplace to talk about having a positive attitude that emphasizes, "Why not the best?" What may be needed (as is emphasized in the first chapter and other parts of this book) is a realistic desire to do better than what has traditionally been considered the best, along with realistic ideas for achieving those higher goals.[2]

---

[2]For further details on trends regarding the development of higher goals for America and elsewhere, one can compare relevant books from the 60's, 70's, and 80's, such as Henry Wriston, (ed.), *Goals for Americans: The Report of the President's Commission on National Goals* (Englewood Cliffs, N.J.: American Assembly and Prentice-Hall, 1960); Kermit Gordon (ed.), *Agenda for the Nation* (Garden City, N.Y.: Brookings and Doubleday, 1968); Henry Owen and Charles Schultze (eds.), Setting National Priorities: The Next Ten Years (Washington, D.C.: Brookings, 1976); and Isabel Sawhill (ed.), *Challenge to Leadership: Economic and Social Issues for the Next Decade* (Washington, D.C.: Urban Institute, 1988).

BIBLIOGRAPHY

Alberts, David, *A Plan for Measuring the Performance of Social Programs* (New York: Praeger, 1970).

Aaron, Henry, *Shelter and Subsidies* (Washington, D.C.: Brookings Institution, 1972).

Adler, Richard and Douglass Cater (eds.), *Television As a Cultural Force* (New York: Praeger, 1976).

Alford, Robert, *Health Care Politics* (Chicago: University of Chicago Press, 1975).

Allison, Graham, Essence of Decision: Explaining the Cuban Missile Crisis (Boston: Little, Brown, 1971).

Anderson, James (ed.), *Economic Regulatory Policies* (Lexington, Mass.: Lexington-Heath, 1976).

Aranson, Peter, *American Government: Strategy and Choice* (Cambridge, Mass.: Winthrop, 1981).

Ares, Charles et al., "The Manhattan Bail Project: An Interim Report on the Use of Pretrial Parole," 38 *New York University Law Review* 67-95 (1963).

Bachrach, Peter and Elihu Bergman, *Power and Choice: The Formulation of American Population Policy* (Lexington, Mass.: Lexington-Heath, 1973).

Bailey, Stephen, *Congress Makes a Law: The Story Behind the Employment Act of 1946* (New York: Columbia University Press, 1950).

Ball, Howard, *Constitutional Powers Cases on the Separation of Powers and Federalism* (St. Paul, Minn.: West, 1980).

Baumer, D. and Carl Van Horn, *The Politics of Unemployment* (Washington, D.C.: Congressional Quarterly, 1985).

Baumol, William and Wallace Oates, *The Theory of Environmental Policy* (Englewood Cliffs, N.J.: Prentice-Hall, 1975).

Bayley, David, Constitutional Law in Charles Szladits, *A Bibliography on Foreign and Comparative Law Books and Articles in English* (Dobbs Ferry, N.Y.: Oceana Publishers, 1955 to present).

_____, *Public Liberties in the United States* (Chicago: Rand McNally, 1964).

Becker, Theodore, *The Impact of Supreme Court Decisions: Empirical Studies* (New York: Oxford, 1969).

Becker, Gary and William Landes (eds.), *Essays in the Economics of Crime and Punishment* (New York: Columbia University Press, 1974).

Bedau, Hugo, *The Death Penalty in America* (New York: Anchor, 1967).

Berger, Monroe, *Equality by Statute* (New York: Doubleday, 1967)

Bernstein, Marvey, *Regulating Business by Independent Commission* (Princeton, N.J.: Princeton University Press, 1955).

Bickel, Alexander, *The Supreme Court and the Idea of Progress* (New York: Harper & Row, 1970).

Bloom, G. and H. Northrup, *Economics of Labor Relations* (Homewood, Ill.: Irwin, 1954).

Blumstein, Alfred (ed.), *Deterrence and Incapacitation: Estimating the Effects of Criminal Sanctions on Crime Rates* (Washington, D.C.: National Academy of Sciences, 1978).

Bremmer, Robert et al., (eds.), *American Choices: Social Dilemmas and Public policy since 1960* (Columbus, Ohio: Ohio State University Press, 1986).

Burns, Edwards, *Ideas in Conflict: The Political Theories of the Contemporary World* (New York: Norton, 1960).

Caldwell, Lynton K., *Science, Technology and Public Policy* (Bloomington, Ind.: Indiana University Press, 1967, with periodic supplements).

Canto, Victor, D. Joines, and A. Laffer, *Foundations of Supply-Side Economics* (New York: Academic Press, 1983).

Carley, Michael, *Social Measurement and Social Indicators: Issues of Policy and Theory* (Boston: Allen and Unwin, 1981).

Carlson, Richard (ed.), *Issues on Electoral Reform* (New York: National Municipal League, 1974).

Casper, Jonathan, *The Politics of Civil Liberties* (New York: Harper and Row, 1972).

Chambers, William and Walter Burnham (eds.), *The American Party Systems* (New York: Oxford University Press, 1975)

Charlesworth, James (ed.), *Contemporary Political Analysis* (New York: Free Press, 1967), 72-107.

Clinton, Richard, *Population and Politics: New Directions in Political Science Research* (Lexington, Mass.: Lexington-Heath, 1977).

Cochran, Clarke et al., *American Public Policy* (New York: St. Martin's, 1986).

Coleman, James et al., *Equality of Education Opportunity* (Washington, D.C.: Office of Education, 1966) (Also known as the Coleman Report).

Connery, Robert and Robert Gilmore, *The National Energy Problem* (Lexington, Mass.: Lexington Books: 1974).

Cook, T. (ed.), *Performance Measurement in Public Agencies*, (Westport, Conn.: Greenwood Press, 1986).

Cooper, George et al., "Neglect," *Law and Poverty: Cases and Materials* (St. Paul, Minn.: West, 1973).

Crotty, William J., *Political Reform and the American Experiment* (New York: Crowell, 1977).

Davis, David, *Energy Politics* (New York: St. Martin's Press, 1974).

Dogramaci, A., *Productivity Analysis: A Range of Perspectives* (Amsterdam, Netherlands: Martinus Nijhoff, 1981).

Dorfman, Robert, *Measuring Benefits in Government Investments* (Washington, D.C.: Brookings, 1964).

Duggan, Paula, The *New American Unemployment* (Washington, D.C.: Center for Regional Policy, 1985).

Dunn, Charles, *American Democracy Debated* (Glenview, Ill.: Scott, Foresman, 1982).

Dye, Thomas, *The Politics of Equality* (Indianapolis, Ind.: Bobbs-Merrill, 1971).

Eckstein, Otto, *Inflation: Prospects and Remedies* (Washington, D.C.: Center for National Policy, 1983).

Elazar, Daniel, *American Federalism* (New York: Crowell, 1972).

Emerson, Thomas et al., *Political and Civil Rights in the United States 1-28* (Boston: Little, Brown, 1967), and the 1969 Supplement.

Etzioni, *Amitai, An Immodest Agenda: Rebuilding America Before the Twenty-First Century* (New York: McGraw Hill, 1983).

Feierband, Ivo and R. Feierband, "The Relationship of Systematic Frustration, Political Coercion, International Tension, Political Instability: A Cross-National Study" (Paper presented at the annual meeting of the American Psychological Association, 1966).

Fellman, David, *The Defendants Rights* (New York: Rinehart, 1958)

Ferguson, John and Dean McHenry, *The American System of Government* (New York: McGraw-Hill, 1977).

Frances, Wayne, *American Politics: Analysis of Choice* (New York.Goodyear, 1976).

Freeman, David, *National Energy Policy* (New York: Twentieth Century Fund, 1974).

Freeman, Howard, Peter Rossi, and Sonia Wright, *Evaluating Social Projects in Developing Countries* (Paris, France: Organization for Economic Cooperation and Development, 1980).

Freeman, Joe, *The Politics of Women's Liberation* (New York: McKay, 1975).

Friedman, Milton, *Capitalism and Freedom* (Chicago: University of Chicago Press, 1963).

Funston, Richard, *A Vital National Seminar: The Supreme Court in American Political Life* (Palo Alto, Calif.: Mayfield, 1978).

Gardiner, John and Michael Mulkey (eds.), *Crime and Criminal Justice: Issues in Public Policy Analysis* (Lexington, Mass.: Lexington-Heath, 1975).

Gardiner, John (ed.), *Public Law and Public Policy* (New York: Praeger, 1977).

George, Alexander L., and Richard Smoke, *Deterrence in American Foreign Policy: Theory and Practice* (New York: Columbia University Press, 1974).

Gibbs, Jack, *Crime, Punishment, and Deterrence* (New York: Elsevier, 1975).

Gilmartin, K. et al., *Social Indicators: An Annotated Bibliography of Current Literature* (New York: Garland, 1979).

Ginzberg, Eli, *The Unemployed* (New York: Harper, 1963).

Gordon, Kermit (ed.), *Agenda for the Nation* (Garden City, N.Y.: Brookings and Doubleday, 1968).

Gove, Samuel, *Political Science and School Politics* (Lexington, Mass.: Lexington-Heath, 1976).

Grad, Frank, George Rathjens, and Albert Rosenthal, *Environmental Control: Priorities, Policies and the Law* (New York: Columbia University Press, 1971).

Gramlich, Edward, *Benefit-Cost Analysis of Government Programs* (Englewood Cliffs, N.J.: Prentice-Hall, 1981).

Green, Edward, "Race, Social Status, and Criminal Arrest," 35 *American Sociological Review* 476-490 (1970).

Greenberg, Daniel, *The Politics of Pure Science* (New York: New American Library, 1976).

Greenberg, Edward, *The American Political System: A Radical Approach* (Cambridge, Mass.: Winthrop, 1977).

Greiner, John et al., *Productivity and Motivation: A Review of State and Local Government Initiatives* (Washington, D.C.: Urban Institute, 1981).

Grier, G. and E. Grier, *Equality and Beyond* (New York: Quadrangle, 1966).

Haberer, Joseph (ed.), *Science and Technology Policy* (Lexington, Mass.: Lexington-Heath, 1977).

Hackett, Judith et al., *Contracting for the Operation of Prisons and Jails* (Washington, D.C.: National Institute of Justice, 1987).

Hackett, Judith, "Privatization of Prisons," 40 *Vanderbilt Law Review* 813-902 (1987).

Hamilton, Alexander, James Madison, and John Jay, *The Federalist Papers* (New York: New American Library, 1961), Chapter 13.

Hamilton, William, Larry Ledebur, and Deborah Matz, *Industrial Incentives: Public Promotion of Private Enterprise* (Washington, D.C.: Aslan Press, 1984).

Hardin, Charles, *The Politics of Agriculture* (Glencoe, Ill.: Free Press, 1952).

Harrington, Michael, *Why We Need Socialism in America* (New York: Dissent, 1971).

Harris, Clifford, *The Break-Even Handbook* (Englewood Cliffs, N.J.: Prentice-Hall, 1978).

Hathaway, Dale, *Government and Agriculture* (New York: Macmillan, 1963).

Healy, Robert, *Land Use and the States* (Washington, D.C.: Resources for the Future, 1976).

Heidenheimer, Arnold, Hugh Heclo, and Carolyn Adams, *Comparative Public Policy: The Politics of Social Choice in Europe and America* (New York: St. Martin's, 1983).

Heilbroner, Robert, *Marxism: For and Against* (New York: Norton, 1980).

Herzberg, Donald and Alan Rosenthal (eds.), *Strengthening the States: Essays on Legislative Reform* (New York: Doubleday, 1972).

Horowitz, Donald, *The Courts and Social Policy* (Washington, D.C.: Brookings, 1977).

Jacob, Herbert (ed.), *The Potential for Reform of Criminal Justice* (Beverly Hills, Calif.: Sage, 1974).

James, Dorothy (ed.), *Analyzing Poverty Policy* (Lexington, Mass.: Lexington-Heath, 1975).

Jeffrey, C. Ray, *Crime Prevention Through Environmental Design* (Beverly Hills, Calif.: Sage, 1977).

Johnson, Chalmers (ed.), *The Industrial Policy Debate* (San Francisco: Institute for Contemporary Studies, 1984).

Johnson, Richard, *The Dynamics of Compliance: Supreme Court Decision-Making From a New Perspective* (Evanston, Ill.: Northwestern University Press, 1967).

Kalven, Harry and Hans Zeisel, *The American Jury* (Boston: Little, Brown, 1966), p.56.

Kariel, Henry, *Frontiers of Democratic Theory* (New York: Random House, 1970).

Kirst, Michael (ed.), *State, School, and Politics: Research Directions* (Lexington, Mass.: Lexington-Heath, 1972).

Koontz, H., and R. Gable, *Public Control of Economic Enterprise* (New York: McGraw-Hill, 1956), 487-590, 758-794.

Kotler, Philip, *Marketing Decision Making: A Model Building Approach* (New York: Holt, 1971).

Kraft, Michael and Mark Schneider (eds.), *Population Policy Analysis: Issues in American Politics* (Lexington, Mass.: Lexington-Heath, 1977).

Krislov, Samuel and Malcolm Feeley, *Compliance and the Law* (Beverly Hills, Calif.: Sage, 1970).

Kristol, Irving, *Two Cheers for Capitalism* (New York: Basic Books, 1978).

Ladd, Everett and Charles Hadley, *Transformations of the American Party System* (New York: Norton, 1978).

LeBouef, Michael, *The Productivity Challenge: How to Make it Work for America and You* (New York: McGraw-Hill, 1982).

Lee, M., *Economic Fluctuations* (Homewood, Ill.: Irwin, 1955) 421-538.

Lefstein, Nathan and Vaughn Stapleton, *Counsel in Juvenile Courts* (Washington, D.C.: National Council of Juvenile Court Judges, 1967).

Levine, Herbert, *Political Issues Debated: An Introduction to Politics* (Englewood Cliffs, N.J.: Prentice-Hall, 1982).

Levine, James, "The Bookseller and the Law of Obscenity: Toward an Empirical Theory of Free Expression" (Northwestern University Ph.D. Dissertation, 1967).

_____, "Methodological Concerns in Studying Supreme Court Efficacy," 4 *Law and Society Review* 583-611 (1970).

Levine, Robert, *The Arms Debate* (Cambridge, Mass.: Harvard University Press, 1963).

Linowes, David (ed.), *Privatization: Toward More Effective Government* (Washington, D.C.: Government Printing Office, 1988).

Linowes, Robert and Don Allensworth, *The Politics of Land Use: Planning, Zoning and the Private Developer* (New York: Praeger, 1973).

Lipson, *Leslie, The Great Issues of Politics* (Englewood Cliffs, N.J.: Prentice-Hall, 1981).

Little, I. and J. Mirries, *Project Appraisal and Planning for Developing Countries* (New York: Basic Books, 1974).

Lockard, Duane, *The Perverted Priorities of American Politics* (New York: Macmillan, 1971).

Lockhart, William, Yale Kamisar, and Jesse Choper, *Constitutional Rights and Liberties* (St. Paul, Minn.: West, 1970).

Lowi, Theodore J. and Alan Stone (eds.), *Nationalizing Government: Public Policies in America* (Beverly Hills, Calif.: Sage, 1978).

MacRae, Duncan, *Policy Indicators: Links Between Social Science and Public Debate* (Chapel Hill, N.C.: Duke University, 1986).

Magaziner, Ira and Robert Reich, *Minding America's Business: The Decline and Rise of the American Economy* (New York: Harcourt, Brace, 1982).

Mancke, Richard, *The Failure of U.S. Energy Policy* (New York: Columbia University Press, 1974).

Marmor, Theodore, *Poverty Policy* (Chicago: Aldine, 1971).

_____, *The Politics of Medicare* (Chicago: Aldine, 1973).

Martindale, Don (ed.), *Functionalism in the Social Sciences: The Strength and Limits of Functionalism in Anthropology, Economics, Political Science, and Sociology* (Philadelphia: American Academy of Political and Social Science, 1965).

Mayhew, Leon, *Law and Equal Opportunity* (Cambridge, Mass.: Harvard University Press, 1967).

Mayo, Henry, *An Introduction to Democratic Theory* (New York: Oxford, 1960).

McMillan, Claude, *Mathematical Programming: An Introduction to the Design and Application of Optimal Decision Machines* (New York: Wiley, 1970).

Mechanic, David, *Politics, Medicine, and Social Science* (New York: Wiley, 1974).

Medalie, Richard et al., "Custodial Police Interrogation in our Nation's Capital: The Attempt to Implement Miranda," 66 *Michigan Law Review* 1347-1422 (1968).

Merritt, Richard (ed.), *Foreign Policy Analysis* (Lexington, Mass.: Lexington-Heath, 1975).

Michalos, A. C., What Makes People Happy? (unpublished paper presented at the Conference on Quality of Life in Oslo, Norway, 1986).

_____, Multiple Discrepancies Theory (MDT), 16 *Social Indicators Research* 347-414 (1985).

Mitnick, Barry, *The Political Economy of Regulation: Creating, Designing, and Removing Regulatory Forms* (New York: Columbia University Press, 1980).

Morris, Robert, *Rethinking Social Welfare: Why Care for the Stranger?* (New York: Longman, 1986).

Muir, William, *Prayer in the Public Schools: Law and Attitude Change* (Chicago: University of Chicago Press, 1967)

Nadel, Mark, *The Politics of Consumer Protection* (Indianapolis, Ind.: Bobbs-Merrill, 1972).

Nagel, S., "Testing the Effects of Excluding Illegally Seized Evidence," *Wisconsin Law Review* 283-310 (1965).

_____, *Improving the Legal Process: Effects of Alternatives* (Lexington, Mass.: Lexington-Heath, 1975).

_____, *Public Productivity Review* (National Center for Public Productivity, since 1976).

_____, *Policy Evaluation: Making Optimum Decisions* (New York: Praeger, 1982).

_____, "Dealing with Unknown Variables in Policy/Program Evaluation" 6 *Evaluation and Program Planning* 7-18 (1983).

_____, "Nonmonetary Variables in Benefit-Cost Evaluation," 7 *Evaluation Review* 37-64 (1983).

_____, *Public Policy: Goals, Means, and Methods* (New York: St. Martin's, 1984).

_____, "Economic Transformations of Nonmonetary Benefits in Program Evaluation" in James Catterall (ed.), *Economic Evaluation of Public Programs* (San Francisco: Jossey-Bass, 1985).

_____, "New Varieties of Sensitivity Analysis," 9 *Evaluation Review* 772-779 (1985).

_____, "Optimally Allocating Federal Money to Cities," 5 *Public Budgeting and Finance* 39-50 (1985).

_____, "P/G% Analysis: An Evaluating Aiding Program," 9 *Evaluation Review* 209-214 (1985).

_____, "A Microcomputer Program for Evaluation Analysis," 10 *Evaluation and Program Planning* 159-169 (1987).

_____, "Comparing Multi-Criteria Decision Making and P/G% with Traditional Optimizing," in Yoshikazu Sawaragi (ed.), *Multiple-Criteria Decision Making* (Berlin, Germany: Springer-Verlag, 1987)

_____, *Evaluation Analysis with Microcomputers* (Greenwich, Conn.: JAI Press, 1988).

Nagel, S. (ed.), *Environmental Politics* (New York: Praeger, 1975).

_____ (ed.), *Encyclopedia of Policy Studies* (New York: Marcel Dekker, 1983).

Nagel, S. and M. Neef, *Decision Theory and the Legal Process* (Lexington, Mass.: Lexington-Heath, 1979).

_____, "Using Decision Deterrence Theory to Encourage Socially Desired Behavior" in *Decision Theory and the Legal Process* (Lexington, Mass.: Lexington-Heath, 1979).

Nash, A. E., *Governance and Population* (Washington, D.C.: U.S. Government Printing Office, 1972).

Navarro, J., and J. Taylor, *Data Analysis and Simulation of a Court System for the Processing of Criminal Cases* (Washington, D.C.: Institute for Defense Analysis, 1967).

Odegard, Peter and Victor Rosenblum (eds.), *The Power to Govern: An Examination of the Separation of Powers in the American System of Government* (White Plains, N.Y.: Fund for Adult Education, 1957).

Owen, Henry and Charles Schultze (eds.), Setting National Priorities: The Next Ten Years (Washington, D.C.: Brookings, 1976).

Pechman, Joseph, *Federal Tax Policy* (Washington, D.C.: Brookings Institution, 1977).

Pennock, Roland, *Liberal Democracy: Its Merits and Prospects* (New York: Rinehart, 1950).

Peretz, Paul, *The Political Economy of Inflation in the United States* (Chicago: University of Chicago Press, 1983).

Pierce, Lawrence, *The Politics of Fiscal Policy Formation* (Pacific Palisades, Calif.: Goodyear, 1971).

Pikarsky, Milton and Daphne Christensen, *Urban Transportation Policy and Management* (Lexington, Mass.: Lexington-Heath, 1976).

Posner, Richard, *Economic Analysis of Law* (Boston: Little, Brown, 1977).

Prentice, Paula, *Inflation* (Washington, D.C.: U.S.D.A. Economics and Statistics Section, 1981).

President's Commission on Law Enforcement and Administration of Justice: 1967, *The Challenge of Crime in a Free Society* (Washington, D.C.: U.S. Government Printing Office, 1967),

Quade, Edward, *Analysis for Public Decisions* (Amsterdam, Holland: North Holland, 1982).

Radcliff, Benjamin, "Multi-Criteria Decision Making: A Survey of Software" 4 *Social Science Microcomputer Review* 38-55 (1986).

Rankin, Anne, "The Effect of Pretrial Detention," 39 *New York University Law Review* 641-55 (1964).

Reagan, Michael and John Sanzone, *The New Federalism* (New York: Oxford University Press, 1981).

Rein, Martin and Lee Rainwater (eds.), *Public/Private Interplay in Social Protection: Comparative Study* (Armonk, N.Y.: M. E. Sharpe, 1986).

Riker, William, *Federalism: Origin, Operation, Significance* (Boston: Little, Brown, 1964).

Riemer, Neal (ed.), *Problems of American Government* (New York: McGraw-Hill, 1952).

Rieselbach, Leroy, (ed.), *Legislative Reform* (Lexington, Mass.: Lexington-Heath Books, 1977).

Roberts, Paul, *The Supply Side Revolution* (Cambridge, Mass.: Harvard University Press, 1984).

Rodgers, Harrell, *Racism and Inequality: The Policy Alternatives* (San Francisco: Freeman, 1975).

Rodgers, Harrell and Charles Bullock, *Law and Social Change: Civil Rights Laws and Their Consequences* (New York: McGraw-Hill, 1972).

Rosenau, James, *The Scientific Study of Foreign Policy* (New York: Free Press, 1971).

Rosenbaum, Walter, *The Politics of Environmental Concern* (New York: Praeger, 1973).

Rothman, David and Stanton Wheeler (eds.), *Social History and Social Policy* (New York: Academic Press, 1981).

Roucek, Joseph (ed.), *Social Control for the 1980's: A Handbook for Order in a Democratic Society* (Westport, Conn.: Greenwood, 1978).

Russo, Francis and George Willis, *Human Services in America* (Englewood Cliffs, N.J.: Prentice-Hall, 1986).

Ruttan, Vernon (ed.), *Agricultural Policy in an Affluent Society* (New York: Norton, 1969).

Saeger, Richard, *American Government and Politics: A Neoconservative Approach* (Glenview, Ill.: Scott Foresman, 1982).

Sawhill, Isabel (ed.), *Challenge to Leadership: Economic and Social Issues for the Next Decade* (Washington, D.C.: Urban Institute, 1988).

Schwartz, Gail and Pat Choate, *Being Number One: Rebuilding the U.S. Economy* (Lexington, Mass.: Lexington-Heath, 1980).

Schwartz, Hugh and Richard Berney (eds.), *Social and Economic Dimensions of Project Evaluation* (Washington, D.C.: Inter-American Development Bank, 1977).

Schwarz, John, *America's Hidden Success: A Reassessment of Public Policy from Kennedy to Reagan* (New York: Norton, 1988).

Sharkansky, Ira, *The Politics of Taxing and Spending* (Indianapolis, Ind.: Bobbs-Merrill, 1969).

Sheley, Joseph, *America's Crime Problem: An Introduction to Criminology* (Belmont, Calif.: Wadsworth, 1985).

Siegel, Richard and Leonard Weinberg, *Comparing Public Policies: United States, Soviet Union, and Europe* (Homewood, Ill.: Dorsey, 1977).

Sigler, Jay, *American Rights Policies* (Homewood, Ill.: Dorsey Press, 1975).

Silverstein, Leon, *Defense of the Poor* (Boston: Little, Brown, 1966).

Slawson, David, *The New Inflation* (Princeton, N.J.: Princeton University Press, 1981).

Smerk, George, *Urban Mass Transportation: A Dozen Years of Federal Policy* (Bloomington, Ind.: Indiana University Press, 1975)

Somers, Herman and Ann Somers, *Doctors, Patients, and Health Insurance: The Organization and Financing of Medical Care* (Washington, D.C.: Brookings Institution, 1961).

Steiner, Gilbert, *Social Inesecurity: The Politics of Welfare* (Chicago: Rand McNally, 1966).

Sternlieb, George and David Listokin (eds.), *New Tools for Economic Development: The Enterprise Zone, Development Bank, and RFC* (New Brunswick, N.J.: Rutgers University, 1981).

Stouffer, Samuel, *Communism, Conformity, and Civil Liberties* (New York: Doubleday, 1955).

Straayer, John and Robert Wrinkle, *Introduction to American Government and Policy* (Columbus, Ohio: Charles Merrill, 1975).

Student Note, "The Effects of Segregation and the Consequences of Desegregation," 37 *Minnesota Law Review* 427 (1953).

Sundquist, James, *Dynamics of the Party System: Alignment and Realignment of Political Parties in the United States* (Washington, D.C.: Brookings, 1973).

_____, *Constitutional Reform and Effective Government* (Washington, D.C.: Brookings Institution, 1985).

Sweezy, Paul, *Socialism* (New York: McGraw-Hill, 1949).

Talbot, Ross and Don Hadwiger, *The Policy Process in American Agriculture* (San Francisco: Chandler, 1968).

Tapp, June and Felice Levine (eds.), *Law, Justice, and the Individual in Society: Psychological and Legal Issues* (New York: Holt, Rinehart & Winston, 1977).

Thompson, Dennis (ed.), *The Private Exercise of Public Functions* (Port Washington, N.Y.: Associated Faculty Press, 1985).

Thompson, Mark, *Benefit-Cost Analysis for Program Evaluation* (Beverly, Hills, Calif.: Sage, 1980).

_____, *Decision Analysis for Program Evaluation* (Cambridge, Mass.: Ballinger, 1982).

Thurow, Lester, *The Zero-Sum Society: Distribution and the Possibilities for Economic Change* (Baltimore, Md.: Penguin, 1980).

Tornatzky, Louis et al., *Innovation and Social Processes: National Experiment in Implementing Social Technology* (Elmsford, N.Y.: Pergamon, 1980).

Tufte, Edward (ed.), *Electoral Reform* (Symposium issue of the *Policy Studies Journal*, 1974).

Tullock, Gordon, *The Logic of the Law* (New York: Basic Books, 1971).

Walker, David, *Toward a Functioning Federalism* (Boston, Mass.: Winthrop, 1981).

Walker, Samuel, *Sense and Nonsense About Crime: A Policy Guide* (Monterrey, Calif.: Brooks/Cole, 1985).

Wasby, Stephen, *The Impact of the United States Supreme Court: Some Perspectives* (Homewood, Ill.: Dorsey Press, 1970).

_____, (ed.), *Civil Liberties: Policy and Policy-Making* (Lexington, Mass.: Lexington-Heath Books, 1976).

Welch, Susan and John Peters, (eds.), *The Impact of Legislative Reform* (New York: Praeger, 1977).

Wenger, D. and C. Fletche, "The Effect of Legal Counsel on Admissions to a State Mental Hospital: A Confrontation of Professions" (Paper Presented at the annual meeting of the American Sociological Association, 1967).

Wheare, Kenneth, *Federal Government* (New York.Oxford University Press, 1963).

White, Michael et al., *Managing Public Systems: Analytic Techniques for Public Administration* (Scituate, Mass: Duxbury, 1980).

Whitson, William W., *Foreign Policy and U.S. National Security* (New York: Praeger, 1976).

Wilcox, Clair, *Toward Social Welfare: An Analysis of Programs and Proposals Attacking Poverty, Insecurity, and Inequality of Opportunity* (Homewood, Ill.: Irwin, 1969).

Wildavsky, Aaron, *The Politics of the Budgetary Process* (Boston: Little, Brown, 1974).

Wilkerson, Albert (ed.), *The Rights of Children: Emergent Concepts in Law and Society* (Philadelphia: Temple University Press, 1973).

Wilner, Daniel, *Human Relations in Interracial Housing* (Minneapolis: University of Minnesota Press, 1955).

Wirt, Frederick and Michael Kirst, *The Political Web of American Schools* (Boston: Little, Brown, 1972).

Wolman, Harold, *Politics of Federal Housing* (New York: Dodd Mead, 1971).

Wriston, Henry (ed.), Goals for Americans: The Report of the President's Commission on National Goals (Englewood Cliffs, N.J.: American Assembly and Prentice-Hall, 1960).

Zeisel, Hans et al., *Delay in the Court* (Boston: Little, Brown, 1959).

Zimring, Franklin and Gordon Hawkins, *Deterrence: The Legal Threat in Crime Control* (Chicago: University of Chicago Press, 1973).

NAMES INDEX

SUBJECT INDEX

About the Author

STUART S. NAGEL is a professor of political science at the University of Illinois and a member of the Illinois bar. He is the secretary-treasurer and publications coordinator of the Policy Studies Organization. He has been an attorney to the U.S. Senate Judiciary Committee, the National Labor Relations Board, the Legal Services Corporation, and the Lawyer's Constitutional Defense Committee. His recent authored books include *Policy Studies: Integration and Evaluation* (Greenwood-Praeger, 1988), *Law, Policy, and Optimizing Analysis* (Greenwood-Quorum, 1987), and *Public Policy: Goals, Means, and Methods* (St. Martin's, 1984). His recent edited books include *Public Policy Analysis and Management* (JAI Press Research Annuals, since 1986), *Public Policy Studies: A Multi-Volume Treatise* (JAI Press, 1985-1988), and *Encyclopedia of Policy Studies* (Marcel Dekker, 1984). He has received research grants from such federal departments as Agriculture, Commerce, Education, Energy, Health and Human Services, Housing and Urban Development, Interior, Justice, Labor, and Transportation.